T0339848

NOISE WARS

NOISE WARS

COMPULSORY MEDIA
AND
OUR LOSS OF AUTONOMY

Robert Freedman

Algora Publishing
New York

Library of Congress Cataloging-in-Publication Data —

Freedman, Robert, 1960-
    Noise Wars: Compulsory Media and Our Loss of Autonomy / Robert Freedman.
       p. cm.
    Includes bibliographical references.
    ISBN 978-0-87586-714-4 (soft cover: alk. paper) — ISBN 978-0-87586-715-1 (hard
cover: alk. paper) — ISBN 978-0-87586-716-8 (ebook) 1. Mass media—Social aspects. 2.
Mass media—Technological innovations. 3. Advertising—Social aspects. 4. Advertising—
Psychological aspects. I. Title.

    HM1206.F74 2009
    302.23—dc22
                            2009011275

Front Cover, clockwise:
Figure With Megaphone © Images.com/Corbis by Campbell Laird
Two young women © S. Hammid/Corbis
Audio Equipment © Images.com/Corbis by Teofilo Olivieri

Printed in the United States

TABLE OF CONTENTS

PREFACE

In 1953, Ray Bradbury published a short story called "The Murderer" about a man in a futuristic setting who's driven to the edge of insanity by an inescapable barrage of electronic media: in his home, on the street, in offices, in stores, on trains. No matter where he goes, the environment has been commandeered by some form of digital entertainment or communication. To preserve his sanity he turns to "murder" and destroys each and every media device in his path until he's arrested and locked away in a cell.

His world wasn't always this way. People acquiesced to the gradual spread of media because, like the frog who finds the warm bath relaxing only to realize too late he's about to be cooked, it provided a welcomed distraction from the business of living: "If a little music and 'keeping in touch' was charming, they figured a lot would be ten times as charming."

It's probably not a coincidence that Bradbury's story came out a year after the U.S. Supreme Court decided a case in favor of a public transit agency that was piping in commercial radio on a commuter train, turning the commuters into a captive audience.

Clearly, there's a big gap between the environment Bradbury foresaw in his story and the issue of audience captivity that the Supreme Court looked at. But as a result of the explosive growth of digital media, the gap between the two environments has been narrowing rapidly and today we're on the cusp of seeing Bradbury's world realized. At an accelerating pace, audio and video media are becoming ubiquitous on planes, trains, buses, cabs, street corners, building lobbies, elevators, offices, stores, bars, restaurants, hospitals, doctors' offices, banks, gyms, coin laundries, even restrooms — in short, every setting in which we conduct the business of our lives.

On the one hand, the spread of digital media represents little more than an extension of our already print-saturated world, and thus hardly a cause for alarm. Whether it's digital media or print, it's all content and on what grounds can we privilege one medium over another?

But as supporters of captive-audience media are quite frank about, the two types of media are hardly the same. Digital media are far more invasive than print, and it's indeed the quest to leverage this invasiveness that media companies are driving the introduction of digital media to every setting in which people gather. As one media executive has said, "We're looking for places we can be intrusive," where "you can't turn us off."

In the pages ahead, we'll be looking at what makes digital media so different from print media, why the former media is invasive in a way that the latter isn't, and the extent to which captive-audience media has grown in recent years. We'll also look at where captive-audience media is heading, what's driving its growth, what people exposed to audience captivity say about it, and how people are resisting it.

Our look into these issues is based on interviews with some leaders in the effort to curb media intrusion, and it also dips into the blogosphere to get a raw taste of people's anger at being made captive to invasive media. Surveying the online environment in this way provides a good counterview to the feel-good press releases that media companies offer up to position their programming as something for which people are clamoring.

To be sure, as the Supreme Court has ruled, audience captivity has a place in our world. But when you consider the level of animosity it generates, at least among a sizable minority of the people it touches, and when you consider the degree to which captive-audience platforms are migrating to places where previously audience captivity was unheard of, it's hard not to wonder whether some form of backlash won't be the inevitable result.

To help survey the issues, I've included in the back of the book appendices that contain some of the source material I've used, including a dissent by Associate Justice William O. Douglas in the U.S. Supreme Court case that looked at audience captivity on the commuter train as well as the text of another case, *Kovacs v. Cooper*, that was decided just a couple of years before the commuter train case and that rules against a type of captive-audience media. Thus the legal terrain for captive-audience media remains complicated and unclear. I've also included extensive endnotes. They're organized in the back of the book in the same way as the text. To check a reference, flip to the section in the notes that corresponds to the text in which you're interested and scan until you find what you're looking for.

Chapter 1. Silence at 99¢ a Pop

One who tunes in on an offensive program at home can turn it off or tune in another station, as he wishes ... But the man on the streetcar has no choice but to sit and listen, or perhaps to sit and to try not to listen — Justice William O. Douglas, dissenting in Public Utilities Comm'n v. Pollak [343 U.S. 451 (1952)]

I live in a large metropolitan area, and each weekday as I walk to the train station to go to work I pass by a restricted area closed off by a high chain-linked fence. I had walked by that fence hundreds of times without giving any thought to what was behind it until an acquaintance of mine commented on how neglected the area was. And of course the person was right. It was a magnet for litter and yet it took someone's comment for me to notice it; before it had just blended into the background, outside my awareness. Today, I can't walk by without wondering why no one who has access to the area cleans it up.

It's my intent with this book to play a similar role as my acquaintance and put on your radar screen an issue that for most people goes by unnoticed but every day is there for all of us to see and hear if we can just notice it for that first time. This is the rising use of media in ways in which our freedom to choose whether or not we consume that media is taken away from us.

Imagine for a moment that every time you ran the water in your kitchen faucet a built-in device played a recorded message that said, "Thank you for using your local water utility. Each day the hundreds of dedicated professionals at your local water utility work hard to bring you this necessary resource."

Clearly such an ad is a far-fetched idea and I don't expect any water utility to ever do anything like this, but that kind of messaging is becoming increasingly commonplace, at least outside the sanctuary of our home. What makes the message intrusive isn't its commercial nature — the built-in device might just as well be playing a movement from Beethoven's Fifth Symphony as an ad for the water utility. The intrusiveness, rather, flows from the type of media that's being used. As audio, the message is proactive. It comes to us whether we want it to or not, and our only option is to accept it or try to tune it out. Whether we like the message or not is beside the point because matters of taste are accidental. Sure, I like Beethoven, so I guess I'm okay hearing one of his pieces every time I run the water in my kitchen sink. But what if every time I run the water I get a message from Kim Jong-il on the superiority of collective agriculture over private farms? Suddenly the mode of messaging is no longer okay?

Unwanted messaging has always been and will certainly always be a characteristic of our world and as a person who's done a fair share of pushing out unsolicited messages to other people (I've been in one form of communications or another for more than 25 years) I can certainly say I'm comfortable with the practice. What's different today is the changing nature of our media. On my desk is a magazine that's full of messaging that has nothing to do with the reason I subscribe to it. There's an advertisement for a brand of toothpaste that's entirely unsolicited by me, yet as a print ad it's unobtrusive because I determine whether or not I consume it. I can occupy an environment that's saturated with unwanted print messaging because I'm in control of my relationship with the content. Is there a message from Kim Jong-il on the superiority of collective agriculture over private farms in one of the dozens of magazines and newspapers scattered around me? That's nice. I won't be consuming that message today, thank you.

With the rise of electronic media, the dynamic that characterizes our relationship with unsolicited messages is flipped on its head. The content on the large TV screens at the busy downtown street corner or on the gas station pump isn't passive messaging that I can consume or ignore at will. Like the water utility's audio message, that content comes to me whether I want to consume it or not, and my only option if I don't want to consume it is to make an effort to tune it out. Or go somewhere else.

Certainly no one would find it tolerable if that same advertisement for toothpaste that's in the magazine on my desk were in the form of an audio message that repeats every two minutes. The message can be exactly the same: buy this toothpaste because it makes your teeth whiter. Yet those same words that are unobtrusive in a print ad become an intolerable invasion of our private space if they are in the form of an audio ad. No one would permit such noise pollution in their home, and when looked at in this light no one can contend that audio and video media are simply an extension of print media. Our relationships to the different types of media are not at all the same.

It's because of its invasive nature that industry insiders refer to audiences of strategically located digital media as "captives." This notion of consumer captivity is fueling the growth of the captive-audience media platforms that we're seeing on street corners, in hotel and office elevators, gyms, taxi cabs, subways and buses, at gas station pumps, school cafeterias, doctors' offices, and in stores with point-of-sale monitors — any place where people go for reasons other than consuming media. The massive investment in captive-audience platforms isn't being made on the hope that audiences will consume this unsolicited messaging; it's being made with the understanding that the audiences are held hostage to it, and are thus going to consume the messaging whether they want to or not.

As George Schweitzer, marketing chief for CBS, a big captive-audience player, has said, "We're looking for places we can be intrusive," where "you can't turn us off."

For all but a minority of people, the spread of captive-audience media is arguably an unremarkable extension of our content-saturated world. In a newspaper article published shortly after a major television network cut a deal with a New York City taxi company to air its content on backseat televisions, a passenger was quoted as saying she was too busy talking on her cell phone to notice what content had been playing on the TV screen.

But our obliviousness to audience captivity will recede as the practice continues its inexorable spread, because for each and every one of us there's a limit to how much intrusion into our lives we're willing to accept. I know that today there remain few bars without TVs, so if I want to have a beer at a bar I know I must accept the TV, because to get the one thing, I know I must accept the other.

That seems like an acceptable trade-off to me because I don't have to patronize bars and in any case the amount of time I spend in bars is limited. I feel the same way about gyms. I know to work out in a gym today is to accept TV, because the two have become linked together inextricably.

But will I feel the same way when TVs are ubiquitous on street corners, at bus stops, and in restaurants, office lobbies, doctors' waiting rooms, coin laundries, grocery stores, clothing stores, gas stations, subways, buses, taxis, airport gates, elevators, public restrooms, movie theaters — essentially every place where people gather outside the few environments that I personally control?

As Jean Lotus, founder of a responsible-TV advocacy group called White Dot, says, "Perhaps soon the only location where we will have a choice not to watch television is in our own home. Video screens chase us out of the house and down the streets, invading the very places we eat and the stores we enter."

To be sure, if I enjoy watching TV then having TV in most of the environments in which I spend my time is surely a good thing. But even I will reach my limit when the intrusion of TV and other forms of digital media becomes so oppressive that I feel I must go somewhere just to have uninterrupted quiet time. It's at that point that I become aware of how much of my mindscape is being consumed by messaging that I haven't asked for and over whose consumption I exercise only negative control — that is, the decision to tune it out, something at which I might or might not be successful.

For most of us, our relationship with captive-audience media platforms isn't at such a tipping point today. We still exercise control over our mindscape in our own homes, and the vast majority of our environments outside the home remain free of digital media.

But, like the polar ice caps, these areas are dwindling, in both their number and their variety, and it's not hard to see the direction in which things are heading. With people tuning out traditional broadcast media and looking at newspapers as a medium from a passing era, all of the economic pressure is on the growth side of captive-audience media, and as we know from hundreds of years of economic history in this country, woe to anyone or anything that tries to stand in the way of economic growth. The hand of the marketplace might be invisible but the carnage it leaves behind is very visible indeed.

Broadcasting business writer Allison Romano captures the sense of inexorable rise in audience captivity in an article for *Broadcasting & Cable* a few years ago when she says, "The last vestiges of TV-free space are vanishing as marketers recognize the value of the consumer's inability to turn away or tune out."

Concern over captive-audience media certainly isn't new. The issue has been around for just about as long as popular electronic mass media has been around, which says something about the universality of the desire of media companies to get their content in front of a captive audience. For the types of audience captivity we'll be talking about here, the issue first received widespread attention in 1952, when the U.S. Supreme Court heard a case involving piped-in commercial radio on a publicly funded commuter train in Washington, D.C.

The issue was very much like today's controversial issue over commercial radio on school buses, a business model championed by a company called Bus-Radio and opposed by education and parenting groups around the country, including the national branch of the PTA. The difference between the two issues is the constituency involved. BusRadio involves children on school buses and the Supreme Court issue involved the general population on a commuter train.

In the commuter-train case, the Court said the radio programming didn't constitute an infringement of people's liberty because the riders boarded the train voluntarily, thereby providing their tacit acceptance to consuming the messaging. But its decision didn't end the controversy. Associate Justice Felix Frankfurter abstained from voting because he found audience captivity so personally distasteful that he couldn't trust himself to vote rationally on the issue. As he says, "My feelings are so strongly engaged as a victim of the practice in controversy that I had better not participate in judicial judgment upon it."

And Associate Justice William O. Douglas issued a blistering dissent on the grounds that the constitutionality of captive-audience media must rely on a narrowly construed definition of liberty rather than the definition of liberty that we broadly recognize outside the courtroom.

"The present case involves a form of coercion to make people listen," he says. "The listeners are of course in a public place; they are on streetcars traveling to and from home. In one sense it can be said that those who ride the streetcars do so voluntarily. Yet in a practical sense they are forced to ride, since this mode of transportation is today essential for many thousands. Compulsion which comes from circumstances can be as real as compulsion which comes from a command."

Justice Douglas' dissent is reproduced in its entirety in Appendix II.

Importantly, in a less-visible case just a few years prior to this one, the Supreme Court ruled against a different type of captive-audience media: the use of a sound truck to spread "loud and raucous" audio content. In the case, the court affirmed the constitutionality of a city ordinance against such media because, unlike print media, it made it impossible for people to choose whether or not they consumed it. In other words, unlike the passengers on the commuter train, the recipients of the audio content weren't even given the opportunity to provide their tacit consent.

"The unwilling listener is not like the passer-by who may be offered a pamphlet in the street but cannot be made to take it," the Court said in its decision. "In his home or on the street, he is practically helpless to escape this interference with his privacy by loudspeakers except through the protection of the municipality."

Nor, said the Court, is such a restriction an infringement on free speech, because the restriction wasn't on content but rather the mode of transmission. "We cannot believe that rights of free speech compel a municipality to allow such mechanical voice amplification on any of its streets. . . . It is an extravagant extension of due process to say that, because of it, a city cannot forbid talking on the streets through a loudspeaker in a loud and raucous tone. . . . Opportunity to gain the public's ears by objectionably amplified sound on the streets is no more assured by the right of free speech than is the unlimited opportunity to address gatherings on the streets. The preferred position of freedom of speech in a society that cherishes liberty for all does not require legislators to be insensible to claims by citizens to comfort and convenience. To enforce freedom of speech in disregard of the rights of others would be harsh and arbitrary in itself." The text of this decision, which looks at a whole range of captive-audience issues, is reproduced in its entirety in the appendices.

Notwithstanding these judicial concerns, the writing is clearly on the wall. The environments today in which we're captives to someone else's media choices comprise just the beginning of a long march to a far different world than what we're used to. Jack Powers of the Pervasive.TV Project, a digital communications research organization, sums up our future vividly. "Video is moving out of the standalone TV set into the everyday world, pervading our visual environment and changing how we consume . . . moving images."

WHEN ENOUGH IS ENOUGH

For some people, the point at which intrusive media becomes too much is just a few years away; for most others, though, that point won't be reached for a much longer time, I suspect, because TV and other digital media at their core remain fun diversions that people generally welcome into their lives. But like the 10-year-old boy who goes through a stage of wanting to eat only peanut butter and jelly sandwiches for lunch, at some point even the most avid media consumers are going to wake up one morning and realize they've reached a limit to the amount of unsolicited audio and video messaging they can consume without it starting to feel oppressive. And when they reach that point, they'll wonder where all the unfettered room in their mindscape has gone and how they can get it back. But by then it might very well be too late. As we'll see, our commercial environment isn't just being infiltrated by captive-audience environments; it's being reorganized *around* it. A decade from now, excising this spread will surely require a surgery that would kill the patient.

Fortunately, at least for critics of captive-audience platforms, people aren't waiting for invasive media to spread everywhere before they take action. Already there are signs of consumer restiveness:

• More than a dozen organizations whose missions are all or in part devoted to the fight against unwanted media intrusion have been launched in the past 15 years.

• In virtually every case in which a local or regional transportation authority has announced plans to put TVs on commuter rails or other public transit, commuters have expressed opposition, in some cases organizing into formal opposition, with some success.

• A coalition of more than 50 education, parenting, civics, youth, and religious organizations succeeded in financially crippling the highly controversial in-school compulsory TV network, Channel One, forcing it into near bankruptcy in 2006 and onto the sale block, at a steep discount, in 2007.

• The medical profession has come out staunchly against the spread of TVs to environments in which children spend time outside the home, including day care facilities and school cafeterias, among others.

• One of the hottest selling "underground" products of the decade has been the "universal remote" called TV-B-Gone, manufactured by Cornfield Electronics in San Francisco, that can turn off virtually any TV anywhere. The device's inventor, Mitch Altman, has become something of a folk hero throughout North America and Europe. But what's equally notable is that some 400,000 applications have been submitted to the U.S. Patent and Trademark Office in each of the last couple of years for gadgets whose sole purpose is to turn off unwanted electronic media and other types of intrusion into people's lives. Techies categorize these gadgets as "annoyancetech," a market niche that, to say the least, has been exploding in popularity among both inventors and consumers in the past few years.

- Dozens of laws have been enacted locally in the last decade to control the intrusion of "boom cars" and other loud electronic noises, including backyard speakers, that inadvertently make people captives to others' personal media use.

But my favorite development in recent years is the popularity of "silence" as a download on iTunes (there are at least nine different versions for sale). The roots of its introduction go back to a joke about the infamous John Cage composition, 4´33˝, which contains four minutes and 33 seconds of silence. ("I have nothing to say, and I am saying it," is his explanation.) But when you consider how consumers use personal stereos like iPods and white noise machines defensively — that is, to block out unwanted noise — it's at least worth considering whether there isn't something else underwriting the popularity of the novelty. After all, at 99¢ a pop, you can't say "silence" is a laugh you can get for free.

To be sure, this developing backlash is mostly noticeable for its obvious inadequacy in the face of rising captive-audience media. But it shows the battle lines being drawn around the increasingly scarce resource of what we might call the ambient peacefulness of our common spaces. As *New York Times* reporter Louise Story says in a piece on media she wrote in 2007, "[captive-audience environments] may lead to more showdowns."

Make no mistake, we in the west gave up on the ideal of ambient peacefulness when we embraced the broad-shouldered world of industrialization a century ago; forging steel is not a peaceful activity and neither is the construction of the bridges that come from that steel.

But for the thousands of people who are joining these anti-captive-audience media organizations, the issue at its core isn't about noise; it's about autonomy. It's about who will be the active agent in our relationship to the content we consume. In a print culture, autonomy is centered in the reader, because it's the reader who engages the text and dictates the terms at which the text is consumed. That's why I can be reading a magazine at a newsstand and be surrounded by literally thousands of print messages without feeling overwhelmed by the content. But in a digital media culture, it's the content that engages the recipient and the recipient is left with only a negative, reactive choice: either accept the media or try to ignore it. Nobody in the print culture talks about capturing an audience; in the digital culture, that's all they talk about.

I like to think of the differences between the two types of media on the basis of their mode of delivery: does it push out or does it pull in? Audio-video media pushes out to us, so it doesn't really matter whether we find the content compelling or not; we don't have a say in our consumption of it. It washes over us just by virtue of our being in proximity to it, so for obvious reasons anyone who has content they want to deliver would like the opportunity to push it out. Print media, by contrast, is "pull" media because it must pull us into its content. We're the ones who decide whether or not we consume it. For that reason, print content faces a far higher bar. It must be good enough to compel; the bar for "push" content is considerably lower. It only must avoid offending. To the extent we're moving from a culture of "pull" media to a culture of "push" media, we can expect to exercise less and less control over the media we consume, because the driver's seat, the autonomy, is shifting from us as the ones being communicated to, to those doing the communicating.

It has to be said that in today's world of exploding social media platforms and "long tail" marketing, all of the talk by new-media gurus is in the other direction, that consumers are in control, information has been "democratized," and everyone manages one's own media operation thanks to the tools that enable us to be producers of our own content. So, for me to say that digitalization is pointing to a loss of autonomy goes against the grain of the new-media story.

But the issue here isn't about the democratization of content, which is one of the inarguable goods to come out of the digitalization of media. Sitting in our home or in our office, we want nothing more than to be free of the bonds of the traditional hegemony that characterized our mediascape over the last century. The issue here is about controlling when and where we consume our media, regardless of its content. Having access to everything by everyone thanks to the likes of YouTube, Facebook, and Amazon is a good thing because such access expands our world; having content streamed to us without asking for it while we're in an environment explicitly to do something other than consume media (in a restaurant to eat, in an elevator to go to the eighth floor) is a bad thing because it narrows our world.

Children's health advocates today are beating the drum against immersive media consumption by our children because their formative years are increasingly characterized by virtual rather than real experiences, forcing us to deal with all the negative fallout from that. Think of declining attendance at our national parks and the rise in obesity and adult-onset diabetes in preteens. At the same time, educational specialists continue to wring their hands over the downward spiral in basic academic skills like reading and mathematics in children even while teachers acknowledge inflating grades above what was acceptable a generation ago.

These are familiar complaints and, like the debate over climate change, there are plenty of experts on the opposite side of the issue who point to research showing that things are just fine or at least no worse than they ever were, and say all the worrying is for nothing.

These debates are among the many in our world that will never be resolved to everyone's satisfaction, but the one point on which all people can agree is that digital media must change the way our children will expect to engage content going forward. If I grow up watching TV in the backseat of my parents' minivan or in my bedroom or on my iPod Touch when I'm out walking, then it follows that I'm not looking out the window of my car, I'm not sitting in my room reading a book, and I'm not listening to the ambient sounds around me while I'm walking to school.

What else could be expected, then, if I'm not reading or doing math at the level my parents would like me to? When my primary access to content involves images and sounds rather than letters and numbers, what other outcome can there be?

In the concluding words of a study by the Center on Media and Child Health on TV-viewing patterns, "Children in heavy-TV households spend less time reading and are more likely to be unable to read."

So be it. That's life as a "long tail" consumer in today's world. One can argue the pluses and minuses of having the mindscape of children, the most impressionable among us, so circumscribed. But the facts are what they are.

Yet we mustn't let this cultural shift obscure the issue with audience captivity. When we move away from media consumption in the environments we control — my car, my bedroom, my iPod — to environments we don't control, and for which our reason for being in the environments has nothing to do with the consumption of media, the distinction becomes clear. In the former case we're making choices, and each of us will take a different approach to those choices; in the latter we're having our choices taken away from us. The result is a new scarcity of space that's neutral of electronic content, and we all know what happens when a precious resource becomes scarce.

Audience captivity of the kind I've been talking about is primarily commercial in character. It's organized around the same logic that underwrites network TV (and indeed is fueled significantly by network TV trying to recapture its increasingly fragmented and disengaged audience). But not all audience captivity is of this nature. The same innovation behind the rise of captive-audience platforms — wireless communications, ultra lightweight and weather-tight materials and coatings for hardware, and the miniaturization of computing components — is fueling the rise of *personal technology* that is contributing to the growing scarcity of content-free space in a non-commercial context as well. That's certainly an unintentional outcome but one that's equally inexorable.

Boom cars, outdoor rooms, PDAs, and desktop audio and video conferencing are among the personal technology trends that are making each of us — inadvertently, to be sure — captives to the communication whims of others. When you put together these two parallel trends — the rise in platforms intended specifically to leverage audience captivity for commercial purposes and the explosion in personal technology whose consumption doesn't respect personal boundaries — then the stage is set for a new scarcity: a scarcity of space we share in common with others that's free of the invasive noise and images of digital communication.

For our task here, not only will we be looking at the rise of captive-audience media — what's driving the trend, how far it's reaching into our lives, how it's changing our relationship to our environments, and what people are doing about it. We'll also be looking at the rise of several consumer trends, including boom cars and outdoor rooms, which are contributing to the growing scarcity of content-free space. We'll close our look at digital media by spending a little time talking about the relationship between autonomy and noise — audio noise and visual noise — because that relationship is at the heart of the notion of captivity, both intentional and unintentional. And it will help us understand why captivity is a concept that applies in today's digital age in a way that it doesn't apply in yesterday's print age.

Chapter 2. The New World of Captivity

When Western Development Corp. in 2007 installed three giant TV screens at a high-traffic street corner in the Chinatown neighborhood of Washington, D.C., the company effectively commandeered a shared resource (the soundscape and viewscape of a public intersection) for a private end. As a result, anybody walking or driving down the public street is made captive to the messaging.

The messaging itself is innocuous, the usual lowest-common denominator fare we see in every TV monitor in every airport gate and at every hotel bar. Its main purpose is to sell advertising time, reportedly at around $45,000 a slot, so deep-pocketed companies can get their message out to the 29,000 pedestrians and 71,000 drivers estimated to pass through the intersection each day.

Residents in the area complained about the TVs immediately after their introduction, because without warning they had the noise and light from three monstrous screens intruding into their homes. "I can't even sleep in my own bed at night," one resident said in a *Washington Post* piece. "All day and all night?" another resident complained. "Is this a joke?"

Herb Miller, head of Western Development, protested that the TVs were part of a larger effort to revitalize the Chinatown section of D.C. and were integral to attracting economic investment in the area, and in any case there's plenty of precedent for what he was doing. Just look at Times Square. Yet in response to residents' concerns the company turned down the volume. But otherwise the company has emerged the undisputed winner in this conflict because its TVs continue to operate and the advertising revenue continues to flow.

There's little remarkable about this incident and it's precisely because of that that it makes a good entry point into a discussion about the rise of captive-audience media. Because we generally welcome TV into our lives as a fun diversion from the business of living, the rise of TVs in our common areas — both public and private — will in all likelihood proceed without interruption into the foreseeable future. Indeed, in another 10 or 15 years we might become so used to having TV wherever we gather that in its absence we could find the silence unsettling, just as Judith Shulevitz, writing in *Slate*, suggests she already does: "Television is like air conditioning," she says. "You can't imagine how we ever survived without it."

LIKE POLAR ICE CAPS, BUT FASTER MELTING

No doubt, for the medium's fans, that fun and fantastic future of TV everywhere can't get here quickly enough. Look around and, unless you're in a restaurant or coin laundry or new office building, there's unlikely to be a TV in sight. So, what are critics complaining about? Clearly, it's a leap to say we're heading into a world of all-TV all the time.

But thanks to the collapse in the traditional network TV model, the future is here. It just needs a few more years to unfold.

Since 2003, growth in advertising revenue flowing into network television annually has averaged about 3 percent — just about the rate of inflation — while Internet advertising has skyrocketed, growing at about 17 percent a year, according to TNS Media Intelligence. The network TV figures would be even lower if not for the bump they received in 2004 because of the Olympic games and the presidential race, two quadrennial events that continue to attract a lot of network ad spending. If you remove those events from the equation, network ad spending would have dropped below the level of inflation and thus registered as a decline in real terms during the five-year period to the close of 2007.

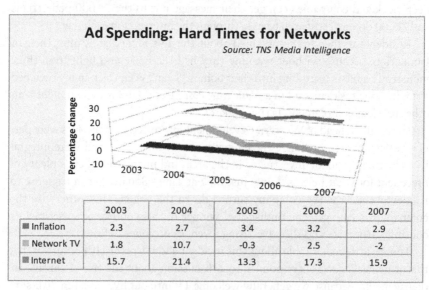

Ad Spending: Hard Times for Networks

Source: TNS Media Intelligence

	2003	2004	2005	2006	2007
Inflation	2.3	2.7	3.4	3.2	2.9
Network TV	1.8	10.7	-0.3	2.5	-2
Internet	15.7	21.4	13.3	17.3	15.9

In 2008 the networks enjoyed another bump in revenue because of the Olympics in Beijing and the big ad-spending presidential race between Barack Obama and John McCain, but even those events couldn't help the networks.

In a *Wired* piece called "Add another reason the TV networks are screwed," Betsy Schiffman talks about the negative impact of the global economic crisis on broadcast TV ad spending in 2008 and 2009.

"Ratings stink; piracy is rampant as viewers migrate to the Web; and now, thanks to this little credit crisis, advertisers are expected to cut ad spending or cancel buys," says Schiffman. "Network television is underperforming GDP the most it has in nearly five decades." She then quotes an industry executive who forecasts network advertising revenue to tailspin, falling by 8 percent in 2009.

The drop in ad spending mirrors the drop in traditional TV audiences, which have shrunk by a third since 2005, according to industry data.

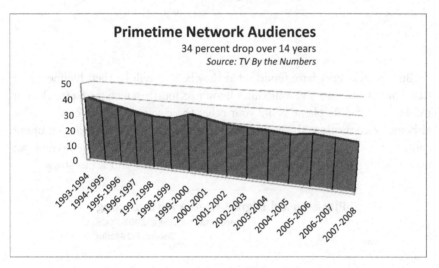

The idea that the Internet might be categorically destroying the business model of network TV is old news. Television programming and the ability to stream video on the Web is making the traditional TV model, with its time-slotted shows, seem quaint. Online TV viewing has doubled since 2006, and in 2008 at least one fifth of U.S. households were using the Internet to watch television broadcasts at home, according to TNS Media Intelligence data. And that figure doesn't count the far greater number of people who watch non-broadcast programming online.

"For years and years people were thinking about money migrating out of traditional television, and now it's really starting to happen," Mark Mitchell, executive vice president of sales for Premiere Retail Networks, a place-based media company, says in a *MediaPost* article.

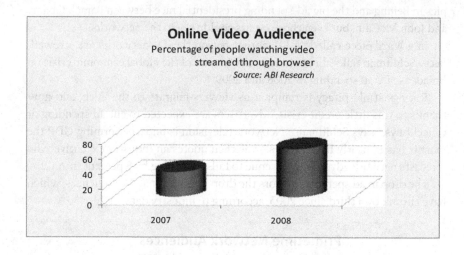

Online Video Audience
Percentage of people watching video
streamed through browser
Source: ABI Research

But the networks have found what they believe will be their lifeline: place-based or out-of-home TV, sometimes known as fourth-screen media (with your TV, PC, and mobile phone being your other three screens). Place-based or out-of-home video media is the industry-wide effort to take TV viewing out of our control by moving it out of the house and into the places where we live out our lives: in stores, offices, trains, gas stations, grocery stores, and at bus stops.

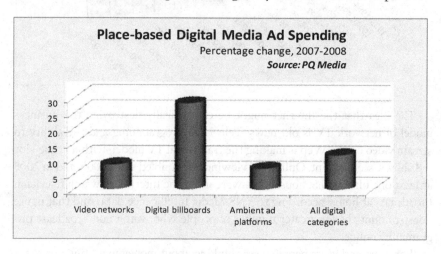

Place-based Digital Media Ad Spending
Percentage change, 2007-2008
Source: PQ Media

In just one measurement of the growth of this new media, networks and other media companies poured $1.7 billion into place-based video media in 2006, an increase of almost 30 percent year-over year, according to data from media econo-metrics company PQ Media in Stamford, Conn. Meanwhile, it generates about $7.5 billion in annual ad revenue, or about 16 percent of the total outdoor ad market, says the Outdoor Advertising Association of America.

For 2008, despite the severe economic downturn, place-based digital media ad spending was on track to grow 11.2 percent, to a total spend of $2.43 billion, according to PQ Media. In the five-year span between 2002 and 2007, the sector grew an eye-popping 23.1 percent on an average annual basis, and was projected to grow at a 11.9 percent annual average clip — despite the global economic slow-down — between 2007 and 2012, PQ Media data show.

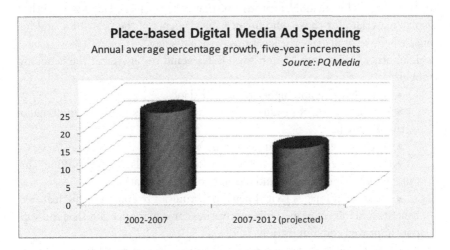

Place-based Digital Media Ad Spending
Annual average percentage growth, five-year increments
Source: PQ Media

"Alternative-out-of-home media is being electrified by what could be dubbed a perfect storm," says PQ Media chief Patrick Quinn. "Ironically, the trends im-peding traditional media — consumer fragmentation and control, advertising ac-countability, and the emergence of digital technology — are the very catalysts stimulating the tremendous growth in alternative out-of-home advertising. Un-like its mass media peers, alternative out-of-home advertising is impervious to channel or Web surfing and is immune to audience fragmentation."

"We are the unzappable medium," says Francois de Gaspe Beaubien, chairman of Montreal-based Zoom Media, an out-of-home media company. "Advertisers will increase their out-of-home budget."

The Pervasive.TV Project, the private research group, estimates that the num-ber of place-based TVs will grow to five times the number of household TVs. That's a huge number when you consider that in 2008 U.S. households had an estimated 105 million TV sets. The universe of off-site TV is thus poised to reach more than half a *billion* units in as little as two years, according to the group. That's two TVs for every man, woman, and child in the United States.

In an influential white paper written in 2004 called "Electronic signage networks: next 'killer app,'" the author, Lyle Bunn, a digital media consultant, compares electronic signage networks, or ESNs (fourth-screen video technology), with other game-changing innovations like word processing, e-mail, and electronic product codes and predicts such networks will become pervasive in our environment because of their economic potential.

"ESNs are emerging as the next generation of broadcasting, narrowcasting, and stand-alone signage," Bunn says, because they "satisfy a commercial imperative: They make money. Revenues and profit are generated for the organizations that choose to display on the devices, for all parties in hardware, telecom, and software supply for the ESN, for the firms that create, sell or place ads and other display materials, for those who finance the elements of the networks, and for those who own or manage the locations of each display."

Like other "killer apps," Bunn says, ESNs stand to "energize" the economy through:

- New, different and higher value-added jobs
- Increased scale of production [through] the commoditization of manufactured elements
- Software-related revenue and profit growth
- [Emergence of] service-related organizations related to installing, sustaining, providing, training and usability of the application
- Creation of images [with] new opportunities to communicate features, benefits and information, while motivating consumer selection that can support improved communications, and
- Local economic development and service supply to others [as] image creation and display revenues grow after an initial capital outlay for installation of the signage network.

What's not old news, though, are what the scale of this shift from traditional TV to place-based TV means to our freedom to choose when and where we consume our media.

Let's look at just a few facts.

ELEVATOR TV

In the late 1990s, "elevator TV" was an idea on the back of someone's napkin; in 2008 it was a reality in more than 7,000 commercial buildings operated by dozens of the largest commercial property owners across North America and reaching more than two million people a day. And those figures apply to just one elevator TV company, Captivate Network, owned by media giant Gannett.

Other companies are jumping into the space, including *The Wall Street Journal*, now owned by media mogul Rupert Murdoch, which in 2007 took its Wall Street Journal Office Network into elevators to compete against Captivate. "The expansion into elevators is the next logical step," Jim Harris, the company's CEO, says in a *MediaPost* piece.

More companies are sure to join the space, although a lawsuit by Captivate Network against the Wall Street Journal Office Network in early 2008 might discourage other competitors while patent issues involved in the lawsuit are worked out. Captivate alleges that the model used by the Wall Street Journal Office Network to display programming in elevators is too much like its model.

Michael DiFranzia, Captivate's founder, says he inaugurated the concept of elevator TV after he observed the discomfort of his fellow passengers on an elevator one day. "Elevator behavior is dysfunctional," he says in an interview he gave for the book *Mass Affluence* (2004: Harvard Business Press) by Paul Nunes and Brian Johnson. "People head for the corners and try to avoid eye contact. They are hungry for distraction."

DiFranzia says 90 percent of tenants in a field test of elevator TV in a Boston office building that his company conducted early on gave a thumb's up to the programming.

But, as one tech writer has wondered aloud, is "one person's advertising another person's insufferable video pollution?"

Leo Kivijarv, a researcher for PQ Media, says most people accept video programming in captive-audience situations such as elevators as long as they perceive it as entertainment. "Right now the consumers are not complaining much since many times there is an entertainment part to the content," he says in an interview for *Live Science*.

But for some people even entertaining content isn't welcome because the intrusion isn't invited. "It has come to this," says Sally Kalson, who wrote about her experience with elevator TV for the Pittsburgh *Post Gazette*. "I actually miss Muzak. Another sensory frontier is breached. This business of bombarding captive audiences with electronic input is way out of hand."

"Is there any harm from one elevator with a TV screen?" says Les Blomberg, executive director of the Noise Pollution Clearinghouse in Montpelier, Vt. "No. But when you combine the cell phones and beeping laptops and TVs in public places and boom cars on the streets, then yeah. It's cumulative." Kalson quoted Blomberg in her piece.

TAXI TV

Around the same time that DiFranzia was launching elevator TV, other entrepreneurs were launching "taxi TV" and by 2008 it was a reality in almost 15,000 taxis in just one metropolitan area: New York City. That's just the tip of the iceberg, with taxi TV networks already growing quickly in major markets across the country, including Chicago and Boston.

As one of the industry's biggest players, NY10 Taxi Entertainment Network, puts it, the goal is to make "taxi rides more fun, entertaining and informative" for

"10.2 million captive passengers a month." The company's numbers refer just to New York City riders.

That's surely a view shared by many riders but a quick dip into the blogosphere shows a very different picture, one that's at least as trustworthy as all the positive quotes in taxi TV companies' press releases.

"Taxi TV is another grotesque intrusion, for tourists only, to further monetize the process for [New York City]," one person says in a comment to *New York* magazine, which ran an article on the issue in April 2008 and invited people to give their opinion.

"This is a horrible development," John Del Signore says in the New York City-based *Gothamist* blog.

"Taxi TV is OK if you don't mind a living hell," technology blogger Brian Morrissey writes.

Some New York celebrities interviewed by the magazine seemed to care as little for the concept as the bloggers:

Jerry Stiller: "I don't find it something that I want to be listening to while I'm riding in a cab and trying to get to a destination where I'm thinking of something in my life. Suddenly I'm getting weather and other things. At the same time, everybody has to make a living, and I hope the cab drivers are getting a piece of the action."

Debbie Harry (of Blondie): ". . . New York is very entertaining. We don't need TV in the car."

Estelle Parsons (Best Supporting Actress in Bonnie and Clyde (1967)): ". . . I want to do other things in the cab like make calls and read my scripts. . . ."

Riders in the cabs are supposed to be able to turn the TVs off, but the system doesn't have a history of being that dependable. For a period, the off button in the New York system was inoperable, and riders flooded the city's Taxi and Limousine Commission (TLC) with letters like this one, from big-band leader Gregory Moore (Gary Moore and his Cosmopolitan Orchestra), which was reproduced in the *Gothamist* blog:

> [For riders] the new forced advertising inside of taxis is no less than being held hostage and made to listen to unwanted noise. Now that the TLC has determined that most thinking riders choose to turn off these backseat televisions, they have made it so that one is forced to watch and listen, with no access to the on-off or volume button.... [T]his is no less than a violation of my privacy and ability to choose. I made a list of all the advertisers that participate in this 'innovation' and I am going to actively boycott their products, starting with WNBC. Absolutely the worst invasion of privacy I've been subjected to. I plan to ask the driver if there is an on-off button before entering a cab and will refuse to ride in a cab that does not have one. This is absolutely shameful, in light of rising taxi fares. You should all be ashamed of yourselves for thinking this was acceptable.

Meanwhile, a company called TVinMOTION has launched taxi TV in Boston and a company called Creative Mobile Technologies has launched it in Chicago, streaming NBC and Clear Channel content into TVs in that city's taxis.

POINT-OF-SALE *TV*

The growth of "point-of-sale" TV in retailers, a concept scarcely heard of before the early 1990s, is following its own stunning upward trajectory. Although it got off to a rocky start in the 1990s, when network TVs were still in command of audiences and point-of-sale content still had a lot of evolving to do, the industry is now in the midst of explosive growth.

By 2006, point-of-sale TV networks had already reached a penetration rate of 700 million viewers a month (a figure that's based on repeat viewership) through the 220,000-screen network of just one company, Premiere Retail Networks.

The in-store TV network of just Wal-Mart already reaches as many people on a weekly basis as all the broadcast networks combined, according to Nigel Hollis, a media analyst.

That's not something everyone who shops at Wal-Mart is happy about. As two people say in an electronics trade publication:

> "Does anyone else find this whole 'Wal-Mart TV' thing kind of creepy? Of all of the annoying things that Wal-Mart does, this is one of the worst. I am tired of being pitched to. I want to shop and not have this 'Big Brother' screen up there telling me what I need."

> "Those damn TVs are one of the biggest reasons I avoid going in there. The whole damn store is loud and makes me very irritable. I'll pay a couple extra cents for peace."

By 2011, ninety percent of all stores will have TVs playing content from an in-store network, according to market research firm Frost & Sullivan. Already networks dedicated to just about every retail and service category you can think of — drug stores, grocery stores, pet shops, wine stores, medical offices, daycare facilities, gyms — are either in place or on the drawing board.

Indeed, Nielsen, the company that measures the viewership of TV shows, has just launched a division that will focus exclusively on measuring out-of-home network audiences. "We're seeing a new birth," says Ceril Shagrin, a senior vice president of Nielsen.

By all accounts, then, point-of-sale TV faces a lucrative future. "Every year, hundreds of advertisers turn to [us] to reach over 650 million shoppers every month," the company mentioned above, Premier Retail Networks, says in its sales pitch to potential advertisers. "These shoppers spend $360 billion a year in more than 6,500 stores nationwide, and every one of them shops in a store served by a retail media solution from PRN."

But the picture you get about point-of-sale TV isn't bright when consumers have a chance to talk about the concept. Within just hours after the *Washington*

Post ran a short, first-person essay from a reporter on her experience with point-of-sale TV in the checkout line of her local grocery store, almost 50 readers blasted the concept as invasive and dismissed a comment in the piece from a Premier Retail Networks spokesperson, who said company polls show people like the TVs. Not a single comment spoke in favor of the TVs.

"Where on earth do these marketing people get their information?" one person wrote. "Who do they poll about these things? Is there actually one normal person who enjoys these TVs? They take the survey results and manage to translate it into whatever they want."

"I'd much prefer to zone out or scan the tabloids than have some obnoxious advertising blaring at me," another person said. "Can't we go anywhere and have it be QUIET? Sometime I like to hear my own thoughts, amazingly enough."

"I'm either going to bring ear plugs to the grocery store or just shoot myself in the head when I see one of those TVs," another commenter said. "Maybe that'll get them to stop."

"Online shopping and delivery are looking better all the time," another person said.

I provide excerpts from a handful of the comments in the back of this book in Appendix VI.

GAS STATION TV

Several big players, including ABC, are making a go at gas station TV. The network broadcaster has a deal to provide content to a company called PumpTop TV that operates some 7,500 screens in 750 gas stations across the country. The TVs are mounted exactly at eye level at the pump so consumers fueling their cars cannot avoid them.

Another company in the space, Gas Station TV, operates several thousand screens in about 1,000 stations across the country.

"It's clear that alternative media like PumpTop TV have proven to be successful reaching and engaging consumers during the natural dwell times of their daily routines," says Roy Reeves, vice president of sales and marketing for the company.

Reeves is surely correct that many people enjoy the TV programming while they pump their gas, but it's equally clear many people don't share his company's enthusiasm for TVs on gas pumps. In comments directed at gas station TVs in general, not PumpTop TV specifically, commuters who took the time to respond to an article in an electronics industry trade publication — usually a tech-happy bunch — found the TVs intrusive and an impetus to find another gas station to buy their gas.

"I avoid using Esso stations whenever possible due to the incredibly insipid and annoying top-of-the-pump television advertising. I'd rather pump my gas in peace. There should at least be an 'opt-out' button provided, so that a customer has the option of disabling the feed."

"I find those things so annoying I will not go to stations that have them. So, as a result, I have not been to a Shell station in months. (I live in the Chicago area and they are the only stations with them so far.) I can only hope other people are doing the same thing. If not, this sort of irritating constant sales bombardment will start going on everywhere."

"Here's the question: will the screens turn off enough users (who will then cease visiting the stations) that the increased sales of driving other customers into the store for a purchase don't cover (or more accurately, exceed) that loss?"

"People don't need nor want to be assaulted by noise and advertisements every moment of the day. Basically, to get gas at a Shell, I am forced to listen to this. I don't want to, so I go elsewhere. Personally, I don't find them annoying only at gas stations, but I find them annoying everywhere and will not go to places that have them. I hope people do have enough balls to stop going to these places."

Restroom TV

Probably the winner in the unfortunate-but-necessary-to-talk-about category is restroom TV, a platform that's growing along with other types of restroom, or "indoor," advertising, a space not considered worthy of serious attention by marketers until fairly recently. Today, the amount spent on restroom advertising is about $50 million annually, according to the Indoor Billboard Advertising Association.

That's a drop in the bucket compared to the tens of billions of dollars marketers spend annually across all advertising platforms. But restroom ad spending is growing at about 12-13 percent a year, IBAA says. And that spending will grow even more once restroom TV catches on with the big advertising firms, as signs suggest it will.

Starting in 2006, restroom TV got what's probably its biggest publicity boost when Charmin, the familiar bathroom tissue brand, sponsored 20 luxury public restrooms in New York City. Each restroom is manned by a white-gloved attendant, outfitted with the best in bathroom components, and features high-end flat-screen TVs to make bringing your own reading material into the stalls unnecessary.

The publicity stunt is a lot of fun but it's not representative of what's really happening in the space. More characteristic is what a company called In Ad TV, based in the Kansas City, Mo., metro area, is doing.

The company, launched in 2005, mounts flat-screen TVs above urinals in men's rooms and in the vanity in women's restrooms in restaurants, bars, and stores to stream in content that includes a mix of ads and information supplied by the host business.

"When I was at Best Buy one afternoon, I was observing all the TVs on display when something hit me," the company's founder, Michael Quijas, said in an interview he gave in 2008 to the Kansas City *Star*. "The screens all had the same thing playing. This piqued my curiosity. So I asked the clerk how something like this is made possible. The clerk took me to the video switch and showed me how it all worked. That was the afternoon that my wheels started turning."

Restroom TV is already a fixture in some high-profile public places, including some major airports and in big sports arenas. What will be different going forward is the scale. The cost-structure of streaming in video is dropping enough that it won't be out of the question for even a neighborhood bar to push TV commercials to their customers.

"In a bar or a nightclub, the average patron uses a restroom almost three times per stay," a past IBAA president, David Turner, says in an *Advertising Age* interview. That's a target that advertisers will find hard to ignore once the cost of reaching them at the urinal or in the toilet stall becomes so low that nothing beyond good taste and a respect for people's privacy will be standing in their way.

New flat-screen and rear-projection technology is also helping to heighten interest in the space, because marketers are sensitive to the need for restroom TV to be clever, otherwise it poses a risk to companies, which likely don't want their products or services associated with a place whose *raison d'etre* involves bodily functions.

"You really have to work with the humor of the fact that you are in the bathroom," Gina Broderick, a marketing executive, says in the same *Advertising Age* interview. "The link between the message, the media, and the target has to be at play."

The flat-screen technology fits into this cleverness goal nicely by enabling marketers to coat the TV experience with a veneer of novelty by doing things like having the image appear in the vanity mirror while patrons are looking at themselves.

"Patrons will be amazed by this display," says promotional copy from a company representing a manufacturer of this mirror-TV platform.

Amazing or not, it's still TV, and therefore invasive, say critics.

"Is nothing sacred anymore?" says Brian Fuller, a writer for the electrical engineering trade magazine *EE Times*. "I was in the bathroom at a rental car center recently, and there was a TV there. What's next, church, synagogue, and mosque TV? At some point, someone's got to get a grip. Electronics, semiconductors, and software have become so ingrained in our culture that we take them for granted. The problem is, electronics companies have all this technology and sometimes just dump it out there because, well, they need the volume. Now almost every public facility in America has a TV. They started in bars (can we really be that bored with our drinking pals?), moved to restaurants, and quickly surged into airports (which weren't loud and uncomfortable enough, I guess), and doctors' waiting rooms. Now they're infiltrating gift stores in airports and local grocery stores (in the checkout lines). You'd think it would stop there, but no.

"If you're involved in proliferating the boob tube, stop it before I find you. If I do, I'm going to duct-tape you in front of an endlessly looping video of Britney Spears trying to formulate a thought on a talk show, or a CNN correspondent trying to explain something he doesn't understand. If you're a silicon vendor, have an honest heart-to-heart with your TV customer. I know it's tricky to explain to them how [TV everywhere] is sucking the culture out of America. But try, at least. You'll die happier."

DOCTOR'S OFFICE TV

One category of place-based TV that has met with more than just the occasional disapproval among constituents is medical facility networks, both for hospitals and doctors' offices, which have seen significant growth. In 2006, just one company, Healthy Advice Networks, provided programming to almost 100,000 screens in medical facility waiting rooms across the country. Media companies say their intent is to provide relevant information to a targeted audience at a point in time when that audience is highly engaged, which is a point that anyone would be hard-pressed to dispute.

But the media companies are also aware that such engaged audiences are highly receptive to the drug advertisements that underwrite the TV programming. On its Web site, Healthy Advice Networks says drug companies that buy time on its network will see an increase in new prescription (NRx) orders by 8–12 percent.

"Give your brand the power to influence patients just before seeing their physicians," the company says in a message directed at pharmaceutical company ad buyers on its Web site. "Award-winning editorial content and Flash animation health segments about disease-state awareness, prevention and management are displayed in high-traffic physicians' waiting rooms. With networks in primary care, cardiology, obstetrics-gynecology, arthritis, and dermatology and an average NRx lift of +8 – 12%, Healthy Advice Networks digital screens Waiting Room Network gives your brand the impact and reach required in today's competitive marketplace."

Adriane Fugh-Berman, an associate professor in the Department of Physiology and Biophysics at Georgetown University School of Medicine, has taken issue with the idea of using the TVs to inflate drug demand by patients. In a piece for *Bioethics Forum*, she calls the TVs part of a "multimedia assault" whose aim is to direct patients to doctors' Web sites that have been provided by the drug companies to collect the patients' information. "Are these programs successful?" Fugh-Berman says in her piece. "Of course; pharmaceutical companies wouldn't pay for them if they didn't increase prescriptions for targeted drugs."

The TV programming on the media network highlighted by Fugh-Berman is silent, making the content far less intrusive than other types of TV programming. But not all TVs in health facility settings are that way, and for some patients, their inability to command quiet time when they want it seems to go against the medical profession's Hippocratic oath to first do no harm.

"Some years ago, when I was lying in hospital bed after some surgery, with tubes running in and out of me, I was treated to nearly a week of television pounding away in my room day and night," says Lawrence Wittner, a history professor at State University of New York. "I began complaining to the nurse that I had had a serious operation and was supposed to be recuperating, rather than distracted from my own thoughts and reading during the day and kept awake at night by constant television commercials, quiz shows, and idiotic howling. But she seemed mystified as to how I could I possibly object to this treatment. Wasn't television the American Way?

"Ultimately, near the end of the week, after complaints to numerous hospital officials, I was transferred to a double room where it turned out I was the only patient. It was an enormous relief — at least until I discovered that, even in this setting, a television set was churning out the usual loud and hysterical drivel. Slowly and painfully, I crawled out of bed, wheeled my various carts over to the howling monster on the wall, and turned it off! I immediately felt much better. And I was becoming personally acquainted with the phenomenon of compulsory television."

In something you might find in a Franz Kafka novel, the TVs in patients' rooms a few years ago in about 30 public hospitals in Britain *couldn't* be turned off by the patients under any circumstances.

The BBC brought out the drama of the situation in its coverage:

"Patientline, the company which supplies the sets, said they can be pushed against the wall when not in use, but patients say the TV screens continue to flicker, with some saying it hurts their eyes.... The sets are switched on by the hospital at 7 a.m. and can stay on until 10 p.m.... If [patients] choose not to use the sets, trailers advertising the service run constantly. Matt Durcan, an IT specialist, said he complained to staff at North Hampshire Hospital after he was unable to turn off the TV set beside his son's bed. His son had been admitted with suspected meningitis. Mr. Durcan said the glare from the TV made his son's headache worse. 'The glare of the light from the screen hurt his eyes and exacerbated his headache,' he said in a letter of complaint to the hospital. 'I tried to turn it off but this proved to be impossible even with help from nursing staff.'"

Patientline has since replaced the sets with a second-generation model of TVs that come with an on-off switch. "The majority of terminals now being installed in the NHS [National Health Service] are type 2 terminals which do, indeed, have an off switch," an NHS spokesperson was quoted in the BBC piece.

STREET-FURNITURE TV

One of the newer trends in fourth-screen programming is street-furniture TV, in which media companies install TV screens in "street furniture" like bus stops, kiosks, benches, and the other structures that make up the familiar urban landscape. "People can actually watch movie trailers at bus stops," says Jean-Luc Decaux of J.C. Decaux North America, a French marketing group with U.S. operations based in Chicago.

A test by the big handset maker Nokia provides a glimpse of what street-furniture TV will look like in the future. In a one-time demonstration it conducted in the airport in Lisbon in 2006, the company hosted an interactive display in a kiosk that swivels around when a person walks by, snaps the person's picture, and displays the photo on a screen on the kiosk. Then, with the photo having attracted the person's attention, the display peddles the company's wares in a video that incorporates the photo.

In the beginning of a likely trend, Cemusa, a Spanish company, was granted a long-term license to build TV-based street furniture and bus shelters in New York, according to an issue of *Jack Myers Media Business Report*. That's a deal worth almost $1.5 billion.

"Times Square led the way," says Jack Powers of the Pervasive.TV Project. "But now video images that sell, demonstrate, entertain, brand, and snag audience attention are popping up on Main Street, on the freeway, in shopping malls, and on store shelves. Here's a form of television that's all commercials all the time."

GYM TV

Probably the one type of place-based video programming that's most popular with viewers — or at least the most tolerated — is gym TV, and for a reason that's not hard to understand; gym members rely on the TV to keep their focus away from the stress and pain of exercising.

Vicky Hallet, in a piece she wrote for the *Washington Post* in 2008, says she's gotten into the habit of letting the TV occupy her brain while her legs strain on the treadmill — and she thinks the diversion provided by the TVs is why others like to have them there, too.

"Habits like mine are why health clubs have gotten into showbiz in the past 15 years," she says.

But as with other captive-audience platforms, the TVs are typically loathed as much as they're loved.

"Where I do cardio there's six TVs up front," one club member says in a discussion forum on gym etiquette. "One guy will come in and turn on *four* of them, or someone will come in and turn one up loud, then someone else will turn their TV up louder. I'm thinking of bringing my universal remote next time and muting them all with one click."

The incessant sound of TVs is one of the recurring complaints of gym members whenever the topic of top gym annoyances comes up, as in this comment from another online forum on gym pet-peeves:

"I can add one more annoying thing... those people who just HAVE to watch TV while exercising, turning the volume out loud!"

For gyms as well as media companies, though, there's no ambiguity about whether their business plans should include an integral role for TV. IdeaCast, a multi-platform out-of-home media company, with TVs in at least 1,000 gyms, said in 2008 it was on track to generate 500 million annual viewer impressions for the year, which would represent a 100-percent increase over three years. And Gold's Gym, one of the largest get-in-shape chains in the country, is pushing heavily into TV, launching what it calls its "Cardio Cinema," a darkened room set up like a theater with bikes, treadmills, and elliptical machines for seats.

Because of its role in providing user distraction, the video programming is very much part of the gym offering the same way in which TVs are part of the offering at bars and lounges. People today go to gyms knowing TVs are part of the mix, and although a certain percentage of gym-goers find them annoying, enough either like them or are willing to tolerate them to give the media companies a reason to keep upping the ante. As one gym member says, "If it wasn't for gym, I wouldn't even know about shows like 'Flavor of Love,' and all those other cheesy 'Best of' shows. It's like reading *People* magazine at the dentist's office."

But there remain two issues that ought to give the companies pause. First, the TVs might provide so much distraction that it actually takes way from the impact of the workout. "Watching TV while you exercise is such a distraction that it diminishes the quality of exercise," says Costas Karageorghis, a sports psychologist at Brunel University in London. "When you combine video with audio, it requires more from your brain." Karageorghis was quoted in Hallet's piece in the *Washington Post*.

One facility manager said club members are shooting themselves in the foot because of the extent to which the TVs are impacting the rigor of their workout. "I can write an entire article on this and I probably will," the manager said on a health and fitness Web site, Fitness.com. After "managing a YMCA fitness center for the last two years, I have found ... people pick the cross trainer or treadmill in front of a TV, plug in their headphones, put on their favorite show, and walk at a 2.5 pace. After a half hour, they haven't broken a sweat and their cardio session is complete. They feel content because [their workout met American College of Sports Medicine (ACSM) fitness guidelines]. But to pay attention to the show, they need to walk at a reasonable pace [otherwise] they'll have to focus on maintaining balance, endurance, and effort — the very things needed to generate power output."

Second, and more importantly from our standpoint, is the number of club members the gyms are losing because of the TVs. Although many club-goers clearly like, or are at least not put off by, the TVs, those who don't go to the gyms because of the TVs are never counted, and yet based on the high annoyance level people attribute to the TVs, it would be hard to discount that sizable number of people don't become members for just that reason.

"I was on an elliptical machine watching an episode of MTV Cribs when it dawned on me," says a former gym patron on a forum hosted by a health and fitness Web site, Cranky Fitness. "This is totally lame. What the hell was I doing sweating in a dingy gym full of boneheads and bad techno? Why was I mindlessly watching bad TV? And worst of all, why was I paying for the privilege? That day, I ended my workout early and cancelled my gym membership."

PLACE-BASED TV IN GENERAL

The video programming in elevators, taxis, stores, doctors' offices, gyms, and on street furniture is just a portion of the total. When looked at in its entirety, the world of place-based or out-of-home TV is a many-headed hydra whose growth is limited only by the imagination of the people who seek to leverage new ways to stream video content to people as they go about their business. The list of place-based TV categories include networks for all types of retail stores, bowling alleys, coin laundries, street corners, restaurants, bars, even commercial and public restrooms, not to mention arenas, convention centers, cinemas, and concert halls.

Since 2002, 700 place-based or out-of-home TV networks have been launched, and that figure is probably low.

"It's a lot like when all the dot.coms were coming out," says Stephen Diorio, a partner at Profitable Channels, a marketing consulting firm. "Anyone with a venue and a good audience is launching something and calling it media." Diorio was quoted in a *Publishing 2.0* piece.

Diorio's firm issued a report a couple of years ago that estimated the growth of all place-based TV networks at 10 a month.

"With all of that capacity and investment money you can be sure of a substantial push to put 'glass' everywhere," Mike Spindler, head of retail marketing consultancy Panther Mountain Companies, says in his blog, *The Branded Pantry*.

Just one company, NBC Everywhere, is on track to generate three *billion* viewer impressions in one year, a goal it's seeking to reach because those viewer impressions are captive, unlike the viewer impressions of its parent company's broadcast TV programming. "You've got to make people want to watch the screen," Mark French, head of NBC Everywhere, says in an early 2008 Reuters dispatch.

NBC Everywhere's goal is to put NBC content everywhere it can go on a practical basis: universities, taxis, schools, gas stations, supermarkets, ballparks, maternity rooms, and gyms. Its goal in 2008 was to generate that three billion viewer impressions for the year. Based on an early 2008 report in *TV Week*, it was well on its way to reaching that goal, having generated the following results:

- Taxis: 5.88 million impressions a month in New York City
- Gas stations: 8.64 million impressions a month in Los Angeles, San Diego, Chicago, Washington, D.C., and Miami
- Supermarkets: 50 million impressions a month in 1,000 stores across the country
- Ballparks: 138 million impressions a year in a variety of facilities
- Maternity rooms: 3.4 million impressions a month in a variety of facilities
- Schools: 6 million students a day throughout the country
- Gyms: 13 million members a month throughout the country

George Schweitzer, who in 2006 headed up marketing for CBS, another player in the placed-based media business, said at that time that his company's specific intention was also to put its content in environments where people are made captive to it. "We're looking for places we can be intrusive," he says, where "you can't turn us off."

The CBS effort, called CBS Outernet, is taking an approach not unlike NBC Everywhere to bring the broadcast network's content to people where they are. One of its pushes is into grocery stores, and in pursuit of that market it acquired a company called SignStorey to get into a network of 1,400 stores across the U.S., including Shaw's, Albertsons, and Pathmark. In early 2008, the company announced plans to expand into other types of stores, including coffee shops and bookstores. The company is also in car dealerships.

The number of players who've joined this push into "place-based" media is too broad and ever-changing to make any kind listing here meaningful, but it's worth nothing that in addition to every major broadcaster, hundreds of smaller media companies, as we've seen, are pushing heavily into this space. Together, this industry is trying to expand on what Arbitron says is an 88-million strong audience on out-of-home TV viewers in the U.S.

Where are all of those 88 million viewers watching all of those TVs? According to the Arbitron data, from late 2007, 30 percent are in restaurants and bars and 13 percent are in hotels. And 33 percent are in uncategorized locations, which are where we would likely find the TVs at gas station pumps, coin laundries, buses, and other captive-audience environments.

The remaining 24 percent include people watching TV in other people's homes, a category which doesn't concern us here.

"This out-of-home audience, says Arbitron executive George Brady, is "not just men in bars."

Out-of-home media associations, which represent the interests of these place-based networks, are now growing alongside the industry. In the U.S., the Out-of-Home Video Advertising Bureau, launched just in 2007, was already at more than 30 members by mid-2008, a 400 percent growth rate in just one year. And its counterpart in Canada, the Canadian Out-of-Home Video Association, had grown to 30 members in a relatively short history as well.

As of mid-2008, the members of the Out-of-Home Video Advertising Bureau by themselves accounted for more than 400,000 video screens in 34,500 locations, according to a piece in *Digital Signage Today*.

You'll find a list of the two organizations' members, along with a summary of their media focus, as of early 2009, in Appendix VIII.

LIFE-PATTERN MARKETING

What these trend lines tell us is that, if left to its own devices, the invisible hand of the marketplace will fill as many types of common space as it efficiently can with TV, because the market forces are being driven by an intersection of technological advancement, marketing, and profit motive. The only limitation that stands in the way of this advancement is time, which is why I say the future is here but needs more time to unfold.

Without a doubt, as private businesses operating in a free-market economy, the companies that own the places in which captive-audience platforms are taking root — the taxis, gas stations, restaurants, bars, coin laundries, grocery stores, drug stores, retail centers, offices, theaters, gyms, hotels, hospitals, and other places — are merely acting on their entitlement to use their space as they see fit.

But we mustn't confuse this free-market entitlement with the broader issue of scarcity. If we live in a world where only privately owned grocery stores are the practical alternative for us to get food, and only privately owned gas stations are the practical alternative for us to fuel our cars, and only privately owned elevators in privately owned office buildings are the only practical alternative for us to see our doctor, then we live in a world where private owners manage much of the environment in which we do our living. It's immaterial if 80 percent of our world outside our personal space is TV-free if the 20 percent of the world in which we do the bulk of our living is where those half a billion TV sets that the Pervasive.TV Project says is coming will be located.

"Perhaps soon the only location where we will have a choice not to watch television is in our own home," says Jean Lotus, founder of White Dot, a responsible-TV advocacy group. "Video screens chase us out of the house and down the streets, invading the very places we eat and the stores we enter."

"Television sets now broadcast programs constantly in airports, train stations, bars, fast food areas and cafeterias on college and university campuses, elevators, and many restaurants," says Wittner, the history professor whose encounter with TV in during his hospital stay we quoted earlier. "Have you noticed their blaring presence in waiting rooms while your car is being serviced, while you are seeing a doctor, or while you are visiting a hospital?"

One place-based media executive has a term for the ubiquity of TV outside the home: life-pattern marketing. The term is meant to describe the practice of placing companies' brand messages on digital screens and billboards at every intersection point in which people live out their lives, "while they pump gasoline in the morning, shop for groceries in the afternoon, and withdraw money from an ATM in the evening," says Monte Zweben, chairman and co-founder of See-Saw Networks, a digital media consulting company. "The key is context. The psychological impact on a consumer getting the brand message in many different contextual settings permeates the 'noise' and builds awareness and retention."

Information on the Web site of SeeSaw Networks opens up the concept of life-pattern marketing further:

"Not only is 'media consumption' changing, but where people consume media is changing. People are increasingly out-of-home, spending a large majority of their waking hours in places where traditional media simply does not reach them. [Life-pattern marketing] blends into a person's experiences, creating a sense of ubiquity for a brand and the impact for a brand message unparalleled by any other media."

Jean Lotus' responsible-TV group, White Dot, not long ago created a database on its Web site to compile comments on captive-audience environments and the core theme throughout the comments is a kind of despair over the shrinking range of places we have for doing the things we like to do without having to do them against the backdrop of television:

"The management team has videos screaming at each checkout, and even larger screens in the produce and seafood areas," one person writes. "Don't they realize it makes people want to leave and not linger over their purchases?"

"This [hideaway] used to be a great, quiet little traditional pizza diner, but the last time we went, not only did they have the speakers blasting pop music, they had two large flat screens to make sure we didn't miss that evening's Wheel of Fortune and Jeopardy — so annoying."

"All of the [hospital] waiting rooms — scratch that, just about every single room [in the hospital] — has a television. Some have sound, some don't; either way, it's annoying being constantly bombarded with TV, particularly when you're sick."

"The top deck [of the restaurant] is uninhabitable; the giant screens are left on all day."

But the one comment in the database that seems to capture the essence of them all is this one, suggestive of a plaintive cry:

"We are turning people into complete TV slaves with no escape from it."

INVASIVE V. NON-INVASIVE MEDIA

We would all agree to the absurdity of being turned into "complete slaves" if the idea referred to our being surrounded by books, magazines, and newspapers;

people with little interest in reading can live without harassment in a world of print media because it's the individual who decides when, where, and what to read. Even a person who's no fan of reading can sit in a library surrounded by thousands of books without having cause to complain of being made a slave to the content in those books, because in the relationship between the reader and the book, there's no question who's in the driver's seat. The reader is.

But complaining about enslavement is a refrain increasingly heard, without the air of absurdity, about TV and other digital media, because the invasive na-ture of the media flips the relationship between content and consumer on its head. For that reason, our transition from a print to a digital media culture can't be seen as merely an evolution in the way we deliver content to people; it must instead be seen as a revolution in the relationship between people and content. This changing relationship is the essence of what 1960s media guru Marshall McLuhan tried to capture when he crafted his sound bite heard around the world about the medium being the message.

We see this in our response to junk messages in our home. We've endured for years, and will continue to endure, mailboxes full of junk solicitations because although this content is an annoyance, we largely put up with it because once it's in our home we control it and can dump it in the trash can as we see fit. Our re-sponse to sales calls has been very different, though, because our sense of control is much weaker; we can't control the number or frequency of calls we receive at the dinner table, so we take action to keep such calls out: through caller ID and even through acts of Congress, with passage of federal do-not-call legislation half a dozen years ago. Would anyone ever think to press for a do-not-mail law?

As a general matter, it's the intrusive nature of certain types of media that set them apart from other types of media. No editor of a print publication talks about having a captive audience of readers, even if the publication has a devoted readership. That's because it's the nature of print that it's the reader, not the print medium, that's in control of the consumption of the messaging in the medium.

No matter how profound my thoughts are in a book I've written, if no one chooses to open up the book and read my words then my thoughts don't get com-municated. I am the author of the book but I'm wholly at the mercy of the reader to engage what I have to say by choosing to open the book and read it, and not only to read it but understand it.

It's because it's the reader and not the author that's in control of the con-sumption side of this relationship that print is a non-intrusive medium.

That readers are the active agent in a print-media context has long vexed not only authors but marketers. If I'm a marketing executive, I'm playing a game of chance when I spend $40,000 to place a car ad in a magazine. I first have to hope someone opens up the magazine then I have to hope the reader sees the ad, and not only see it but attend to it rather than simply skip by it. Of course, as a marketing professional, I can draw on generations of best practices by those who've come before me in my industry to improve my odds in attracting an audience. I can choose a magazine that I know has a strong readership and whose readers would be expected to like my car, and I can design the ad to attract the reader's attention. I'll keep it simple and I'll design it around an eye-catching image.

So while I've done a lot to improve my odds, the fact remains that my effort is held hostage to the reader. Once I've placed the ad, there's little else I can do except wring my hands and hope the reader comes through for me. Will the reader pick up the magazine? Will the reader open it? Will the reader flip to the page on which the ad is placed? Will the reader notice and then attend to the ad?

Our relationship with electronic media is entirely different. Messaging in a video or audio context doesn't wait for its audience to come to it; it goes to the audience. While as a reader I can keep a magazine unopened on my lap, and thereby keep its content sealed up until I choose to attend to it, as a recipient of electronic media I don't have that control. A TV or a radio playing overhead delivers its content to me without regard to my choices, and as long as I'm in an environment in which a program is playing, I have to consume that content unless I exercise the ability to tune it out. In this case, the active agent is the media and the recipient is passive. That's the exact opposite relationship that we have with print media.

When considered in this way, it's clear that there are implications for us in the growth of digital media in all the environments in which we spend time — restaurants, bars, grocery stores, gyms, and so on. The rise of digital media in all of these environments can't be considered an extension of or an evolution in the print media we're already surrounded by. Installing TVs in a subway car is not simply an extension of the print ads that are already there. Although they both are vehicles for delivering content to people, the nature of the media is so different that to compare one to the other is disingenuous, because the lexis of control is different in the two types of media.

Clearly, it's left to each individual to decide his or her preference for receiving content — either actively through reading or passively through TV watching or consumption of other digital content — and what we're talking about here has little to say about that. Our concern, rather, is with TV and other digital media commandeering the space we share in common with others to create environments in which all of us are made captive to content we haven't asked for, and by which consumption of our own preferred content is impeded.

You'll find additional thoughts on the differences between invasive and non-invasive media in Appendix I: Channel inefficiencies: a theory of communication.

Chapter 3. TV in Public Spaces

When you consider this new dynamic of content delivery, the notion of scarcity becomes apparent. Suddenly, common space becomes content space, so each time I consider occupying a space I must weigh whether what I'm seeking in that space is worth the intrusion that comes with it. Like when I weigh whether I want a beer badly enough to go into a bar, knowing that to get a beer I must accept the TV programming that comes with it, because it's the reality today that bars have TVs. If I ultimately decide I'm through with bars, and even restaurants, because I'm no longer willing to make that trade-off, then the bar and restaurant industry loses the thousands of dollars over my lifetime that it would otherwise have earned from me, and I lose the enjoyment of having a beer in the company of others in a bar or having a meal in a restaurant.

As one person said in commenting on an anti-TV article by PBS commentator Mark Glaser, "I go out to eat to socialize and connect with my family and friends, not to watch their eyes dart from TV to TV as they shovel food in their mouths and offer mindless 'uh huh' replies to my attempts at conversation. I can get that at home (for much less money)."

In the world of beer and bars, and even of restaurants, having to make this trade-off is unfortunate but in the final analysis it's acceptable, because patronizing bars and restaurants remains a lifestyle choice, not a life necessity.

But that trade-off becomes less acceptable, or at least more complicated and problematic, in the world of grocery stores and gas stations because although these are private environments in which the owners are free to organize their business as they choose, when these industries are taken as a whole they comprise an essential resource that leaves me with little alternative if I'm to have a reasonably productive life as someone living in the developed world in 2009.

Since alternatives to these resources are scarce and practical alternatives virtually nonexistent, I essentially become a hostage to captive-audience environments once place-based TVs become the standard business practice in the places that I rely on, as all trend lines indicate they are.

To recall what Justice Douglas said in his dissent in the Washington, D.C., commuter train case, "Compulsion which comes from circumstances can be as real as compulsion which comes from a command."

To be sure, if demand is high enough for alternative resources — TV-free grocery stores and gas stations — then there will always be the maverick companies that cater to that minority market. And of course we always have the Internet. It's on account of these alternatives, as unsatisfactory as they are, that it's only fair to say that a world of TV-saturated grocery stores is unfortunate yet acceptable, but certainly more of a problem than a world of TV-filled bars and restaurants.

This dynamic changes entirely, though, when we turn from the private to the public sector, because here the public sector is the steward of our public space for all people, not just people who enjoy, or are at least willing not to challenge, being made captive to TV content.

It's with this civic responsibility in mind that public interest groups have taken up a call to roll back what they describe as the creeping captivity of our public spaces. "Governments exist to serve public ends," Gary Ruskin wrote to members of Commercial Alert a few years back in a declaration of the organization's mission. Commercial Alert is a responsible-media public interest group based in Washington. "Increasingly, corporations are capturing parts of government, and using them as tools for their own commercial ends. We seek to halt the conversion of government into a corporate advertising vehicle."

Among the prime targets of concern of Commercial Alert and other responsible-media groups is the rise of TV in publicly subsidized transit infrastructure like buses, subways, and airport terminals. "Public transit is public space," says Ruskin in a letter to his members. "Riders shouldn't be confronted at every turn with programming from intrusive television screens."

When the issue of transit TV first started surfacing, in the early 2000s, Commercial Alert sent a letter signed by two dozen cultural leaders to then-president George W. Bush with a call to curb the installation of TVs in public transit before it became widespread. "The precious quiet moments that people find in their busy days on public transit, for reading and study, are threatened," the letter says. "The [media] companies are starting with a pilot project. . . but say they want to deploy their compulsory television system in 'buses, rail, and other modes of mass transit' across the country — in other words, just about every kind of transportation in which people might want to take a few moments to read.... The government should not abet in any way the destruction of reading time. It should not help turn public transit into a commercial free-fire zone."

Among the signatories to the letter were many highly respected thought leaders on social and cultural responsibility, including Betsy Taylor, executive director of the Center for a New American Dream, Sut Jhally, founder and executive director of the Media Education Foundation, Paula Quint, president of the Children's Book Council, and George Gerbner, dean emeritus of the Annenberg School of Communication.

Given the almost overwhelming economic incentive for media companies to pursue TV on transit platforms and for the public transit authorities to subsidize their operations with commercial TV, it should comes as no surprise that the impact of this and other opposition campaigns has been modest at best.

Several years ago, when the Washington Metropolitan Area Transit Authority (WMATA) announced plans to install TVs on its subway cars, there was considerable vocal opposition to the plan and the outcry appeared to be a factor in slowing down implementation, but by 2008 WMATA continued to be publicly committed to moving forward.

This scenario — citizen push-back that seems effective in only slowing TV expansion plans but not in reversing them — has been played out over and over again in metropolitan areas throughout the country (and not just here but throughout the developed economies) over the last half dozen years or so, making it clear that citizen opposition is just one factor, and not the deciding one, that public authorities weigh in making their decisions.

Thus, for the foreseeable future, the conversion of public space into captive-audience environments seems assured. Unfortunately, the picture this paints for its critics isn't a pretty one. Consider what BAA, the private company that owns London's Heathrow Airport, did in developing its newest terminal at the airport, which opened for business in early 2008.

Known as Terminal 5, or T5, the $9 billion project opened with more than 200 TVs, all playing just commercials, strategically spaced throughout the terminal to eliminate any possibility of patrons being anywhere in the terminal without seeing a TV in close proximity.

In preparing for the massive TV installation, the company hired to oversee the program, Paris-based JCDecaux SA, studied the way travelers use other terminals — where they go, how long they stay, how they find their way around — in order to situate the TVs in the most strategically efficient space in the new terminal. The result: the typical traveler in Terminal 5 sees 120 TV ads — or one every three minutes — over the course of a typical stay, about two and a half hours, according to the company.

"This is the first time that digital is playing a really significant role" in an airport, says Jonathan Goldsmid-Whyte, chief executive of WPP Group PLC's Aviator, which buys ad space in airports for clients. Goldsmid-Whyte was quoted by

Aaron Patrick, who covered Terminal 5 on its opening in a piece called "Airport Advertising Takes Off."

Terminal 5 is clearly the poster child of TV excess, but travelers have been complaining about being made captive to TVs at airports for years. Mark Glaser, the PBS commentator, generated dozens of responses to a pair of commentaries he wrote a few years back about being "held hostage" to TV at airport terminals. The amount of feedback to those commentaries that he generated indicated the depth and breadth of concern that people have over being force fed TV.

"Televisions in public spaces are a nuisance — the visual version of the loud car stereos that boom past your house at two o'clock in the morning," one person wrote. "You're almost helpless to stop it and not lend your attention to it when it happens. . . . The problem with television lies in its flickering movement of color and shape that draw in the attention of even the unintentional viewer. We're designed to respond to movement, whether observing life from a seat at a cafe or as part of our fight or flight responses. These added stimuli in unexpected places add tension to the mind and body and information [overload] to our already stressed and saturated lives."

"If people wish to watch television in their own homes, that is their right," another commenter said. "However, forcing helpless, trapped people to listen to that swill in airports, restaurants, and waiting rooms is inexcusable."

PROFIT VS. RIGHTS

Importantly, the argument responsible-TV groups have been making over captive-audience environments has largely been based on rights, and that's the way it should be, because to address media captivity in any other terms — noise volume, light intensity — is to set up a false argument over acceptable levels of intrusion, which of course is irresolvable given the infinite variability of people's tolerance levels.

"While [noise] effects are an environmental health issue, its causes are tied to the issues of sovereignty," says Les Blomberg of the Noise Pollution Clearinghouse. "The noise maker has no claim to owning the air on which the noise travels. Therefore, they have no private property right to broadcast the noise. [Nor does anyone have] the right to do as he or she pleases [with regard to noise] because the air is common property owned by everyone. . . . Common property does not entail universal entitlement. In fact, such a policy leads to what is known as the 'tragedy of the commons.'

"The term 'tragedy of the commons' comes from the experience on common grazing fields in England; if everyone acts in his or her own self interest on common property (in the common grazing fields, that meant grazing your cattle as much as possible), the common resource is degraded (the field is overgrazed and therefore supplies only a fraction of the feed it otherwise could have)."

Anna McCarthy, a professor at New York University, does a good job in her book *Ambient Television* (2001: Duke University Press) capturing the rights issue as the core of the battle between private companies and the opponents of the companies' captive-audience platforms.

"Audience hostility generally centers on questions of rights and the control of space, expressed as a debate over the boundary between ambient sound and noise pollution," she says. "This concern with formal, or structural, properties rather than programming content noticeably differentiates this backlash from many other anti-media rhetorics, such as critiques of Hollywood TV's cultural imperialism or violent media imagery's effects, but it also couches the offense of place-based media very specifically as an offense against the individual."

McCarthy goes on to cite as a key example what is probably one of the earliest of present-day skirmishes over the captive-audience issue, and that's the backlash in 1997 against CNN's Airport Network subsidiary, which is the company responsible for the ubiquitous CNN news programming in airports throughout the country.

"The public rejection of the network was led by a newspaper columnist, Colin Campbell, who claimed that the network infringed on the rights of the individual," says McCarthy. "'In most public places, [Campbell argued] minorities as well as majorities retain certain rights. And apparently a substantial minority considers it intrusive to have to listen to the blare of repetitive TV news and ads.' Later he phoned the mayor's office to ask "why passengers are not permitted to play radio on city buses and subways?' The answer, he reported, was that it would probably be disturbing for others."

Today, the TVs are still on in the Atlanta system although, as with the three giant TVs on the street corner in Washington's Chinatown neighborhood, the CNN subsidiary made a concession and now reportedly plays the TVs in some parts of the airport at a reduced volume.

From the standpoint of the core issue of captivity, this can only be seen as an overwhelming victory for CNN and the entire place-based video media industry, and a huge loss for the individual, because the company succeeded in turning the question of rights into a question of tolerability levels, exactly the kind of outcome that obscures what's fundamentally at stake and goes against McCarthy's point about how people see the issue: as a question of rights.

Yet not all battles are ending in this unsatisfactory way for audience captivity opponents. In Toronto just a few years ago, the city's public transit authority had entered into a deal with a subsidiary of media giant Viacom to install TVs in the city's subway stations and trains. An initial effort by residents in opposition to the TVs failed when the transit board voted in favor of the plan, "even though public opinion was heavily opposed," according to the Toronto Public Space Committee (TPSC), a public interest group. However, after an additional eight months of opposition and "hundreds and hundreds of e-mails," the board held a second vote and the proposal was reshaped; TVs would be allowed in the stations but kept out of the cars.

"Let's hear it for the TPSC" was the response from an editorial in an online trade publication that monitors Toronto's outdoor advertising industry.

Even so, the issue will almost certainly return. The media company's contract with the transit authority ends in a few years, and when it does, the battle will begin all over again because the lure of revenue from TV advertisements for the transit authority is too strong to ignore.

As one developer of a subway TV platform says, in his application with the U.S. Patent Office for his system, "Mass transit systems such as subways are in need of extra sources of revenue to keep passenger fare structures at an afford-able level as operating costs rise, and to avoid decreased ridership as a result."

A similar back-and-forth has been playing out in Washington, D.C., for years as the Washington Area Metropolitan Transportation Authority, despite year-after-year increases in riders and revenue, looks for new sources of money. The look and ambiance of the agency's subway system, now close to 30 years old, has always been a sensitive topic among both the subway's supporters and its critics because of its uniqueness as the "nation's subway," so advertising has histori-cally been spare by the standards of other transit systems. Thus, when the agency about half a dozen years ago unveiled a plan for sweeping increases in the amount and types of advertising that would be permitted in the system, including on-board TVs, there was a predictable backlash.

"Our nation's capital is creating a new reason to stay outside its boundaries," ad critic Eric Martin said in an online commentary shortly after the announce-ment. "The Washington Metro, the second-busiest rail transit system in the United States and one that's been largely free of advertising and sales pitches throughout its existence, will likely become the most polluted, ad-ridden dump in the fifty states. Most horrifying of all, the board likes the idea of hanging video monitors that display commercials on buses, on trains, and inside rail stations."

The plan has since gone through several revisions but what hasn't changed is the agency's intention of turning some portion of the system into a TV-based captive-audience environment.

"We don't have any choice," said Carlton Sickles, a member of the Metro board at the time. "I've been prophylactically opposed to advertising. But I have to rec-ognize we need money. It's a thing we have to do."

Typical of the response to the plan is this comment, posted on the *Washing-ton Post*'s discussion board after it ran a piece in mid-2008 on what was in the works:

"We've become a society where there are no limits to advertising. The market-ers want our eyes and ears at all hours. It's just sick. And what's even more sick is that people and businesses devote so much time, energy, and money into creating these interactive ads — and yet we can't cure basic problems like lack of health care, the alienation of senior citizens, and poverty. What a joke."

In looking at these and other battles over who will own the mindscape of transit riders, despite concerns like the one expressed above, what's clear is that the supporters of captive-audience environments, not the people who are being held captive, are winning the day. In mid-2008, the number of publicly subsidized subway systems in the United States that either feature, or were planning to feature, a TV or other digital media platform was growing. Among them: Atlanta, Boston, and Denver.

And the push by TV networks into transit systems isn't limited to subways, although advertisers no doubt consider those systems to be the gold standard of public transit. Public bus systems, including school bus systems, are increasingly selling their space to captive-audience platforms.

The largest of the bus TV operators, Transit TV, has installed TVs in thousands of buses in Atlanta, Chicago, Orlando, and Milwaukee, among other metro areas. When the system launched in Milwaukee, in 2004, not all of the bus system riders celebrated. In writing about the new TVs the day after she had her first experience with them, local columnist Carrie Trousel said most riders found bus TV an invasion of their personal space. "People seem to find it intrusive," she said. One "Route 10 rider voices a typical complaint: 'I get irritated because I try to read and then get distracted by an announcement for a hair salon.'"

When TVs were introduced to Los Angeles buses, in 2006, one commenter called them a "torture device."

"As the bus gains speed, you suddenly are aware of an annoying intrusion of robotic sounding voices. It is called Transit TV and it broadcasts loudly into every Orange Line bus. There are advertisements for trade schools, banal weather and sports casters whose voice is automatically designed to increase in volume as the bus goes faster. You can no longer read your newspaper in peace or enjoy this brief moment of aloneness. You are a captive of Transit TV. There is something insidious, rude and completely disrespectful in allowing a private company to install televisions in a bus. It is the polar opposite of an iPod because you cannot escape the drivel, you must endure it. It would be like Metro installing open bags of foul smelling dog doo in every bus. You would try and hold your nose, but the smell would get worse until the bus ride ended and then you would jump out and thank the Lord."

"Splendid," another rider said. "Most of these buses are too crowded to begin with; now we're going to make them annoying, too."

"Who figured that riding the bus was 'boring' and that the only way to kill this boredom is to bring over TV sets?" another rider said. "This is a tragic move. People are watching enough crap. Let's leave them free from that crap at least for few minutes or hours. I don't have a car and take the bus. What I need is more frequency and more transfers; definitely not more ads."

Captive Children

Most egregious of all, at least from a critic's point of view, is the drive to put commercial radio on school buses, subjecting children — the most impressionable among us — to advertising content at a time when educators, lawmakers, and parents are pulling their hair out trying to get children to read or otherwise spend time in non-digital-related activity. Although the move to capture an audience of school children, by a company called BusRadio, uses radio instead of TV, the issue of captivity is the same.

"BusRadio is not a social service organization," Robert Weissman, Commercial Alert's chief since 2007, says in a letter the organization sent to a Florida school board when it was voting on a BusRadio proposal. "Its business model involves delivering captive and perfectly age-segmented markets to advertisers. Why would any school official want to be part of such exploitation of children? Advertising in schools and school property like buses is so inappropriate that even a majority of marketing professionals believes it is wrong. A 2004 Harris poll of youth advertising and marketing professionals found that only 45 percent 'feel that today's young people can handle advertising in schools.' Forty-seven percent believe that 'schools should be a protected area' and that 'there should not be advertising to students on school grounds.'"

Sen. Byron Dorgan (D-N.D.) called BusRadio "a low-grade form of child abuse that forces a captive audience to listen to commercial messages," and has been working to get the Federal Communications Committee to act on the issue, beginning with a study.

When the *Washington Post* covered BusRadio in late 2006, the story generated more than 285 comments in an online forum over the course of three weeks. The comments, when lined up one after another, take up 55 pages. About 90 percent of the comments are against BusRadio.

"I will drive my children to school rather than put them on a bus where they have no choice but to listen to "sponsored" programming. All this is designed to do (no matter what BusRadio may say) is to encourage children to want more and buy more. It is enough of a struggle without the school buses being involved. And I don't want to hear that this is just like listening to the radio at any other time, because it's not. If the only say I get is to let my child ride or not, then my child won't ride."

"School buses are to transport children, not inflict commercials on them. I would hope this issue never raises its head in North Carolina. Please let children talk to each other and just sit and read. They do not have to be entertained 24/7."

"What will be next, commercials between classroom lectures, big screen TVs in the cafeteria? Let the children be children."

"Children are exposed to so much mind conditioning already from TV, video games, and radio that it is criminal to force this marketing strategy on them in one of the last areas of protection they have."

"This company and the school have no right to force the children to listen to ads and products that some parents deem in direct conflict with their values. BusRadio takes away the parents' right to monitor what is played. I think this issue might just help fuel a culture war on values. I say no!"

"No wonder people want to send their children to private schools or home school. I hate to think of what today's children are going to be like when they grow up. And to think they are going to be our future leaders. If they are going to pipe anything into the school bus it should be something educational. I too wonder who is going to pay for this. Just leave the kids alone. They don't have to be busy all the time. Let the kids just think!"

I include a small selection of comments from parents on BusRadio in Appendix VII at the back of this book.

As of mid-2008, BusRadio was operating in some 10,000 school buses in 40 metro areas. One metro area in which it's not operating is New York City, which years ago banned advertising on school property, a ban that extends to its buses. In early 2008, lawmakers in South Carolina were considering legislation to impose a similar ban, specifically on school bus radio ads. Other states are considering advertising bands but it's not clear the bans would extend to radio ads on buses.

More than 50 parenting and other organizations, including the national PTA group, have formed a coalition to push *all* states and localities to ban the media intrusion on school buses. In a letter it has written to consumer products companies that market to children, the coalition makes an appeal to their conscious not to make children a captive audience.

"Whatever BusRadio advertises, children as young as six will have no choice as to whether to listen or not. Nor will their parents be able to exercise any control over their children's exposure. The sales pitches will fill the bus and interfere with those children who want to read, study, talk, pray, or do almost anything else other than listen to the programming. . . . We believe it is wrong for a company to use compulsory school attendance laws to force a captive audience of children to listen to advertising. As most practitioners in the field recognize, successful advertising depends on the willing participation of both advertiser and consumer. BusRadio . . . violate[s] this fundamental principle."

Although it's a big issue among parents, BusRadio remains a small-scale controversy when compared to the much older, and far more widely debated, issue over Channel One, the commercial in-school TV network that launched in 1990 and that was sold by its parent company in 2007 in part because of the heat it was taking from parents and opinion leaders.

The Channel One business model is widely known by many people. The company donates TVs and other audio and video equipment to cash-strapped schools in exchange for dedicated time in the classroom for its commercial programming. The company, which tells potential advertisers that it reaches 30 percent of U.S. teenagers in the classroom each school day, touts the educational value of its 12 minutes of daily programming.

"Our mission is to spark debate and discussion among teens, and also discussion between young people and their parents and educators, on the important issues affecting young people in America," the company says on its Web site.

But critics say the claim is hollow because the content is superficial, sensationalized, laced with thinly veiled tie-ins to the network's corporate sponsors, and in any case is accompanied by commercials for consumer products and services targeted to teens.

Ralph Nader has called Channel One "the most brazen marketing ploy in the history of the United States." The program, he says, promotes consumerism and "corrupts the integrity of schools and degrades the moral authority of schools and teachers."

Groups opposed to the company's business model have trained a portion of their fire on the consumer products and services companies that Channel One depends on for its advertising revenue. In one of several letters the groups have collaborated on and sent as a coalition over the years, the notion of media captivity is central to the message:

"Compelling impressionable children to view commercials during their limited school time is repugnant," the letter says. It goes on to cite a damning comment by Joel Babbit, a one-time president of Channel One, about why advertisers should like the in-school audience captivity: "The biggest selling point is . . . we are forcing kids to watch two minutes of commercials."

The coalition letter then points out the absurdity that has resulted from the inherent conflict between commercial programming and the classroom environment: "Last year," it says, "two Ohio children were sent to a juvenile detention facility for refusing to watch Channel One in school."

In concluding its plea, the coalition lists eight reasons why advertisers should think twice about allocating a portion of their spending to the in-school network:

1. Misuses the compulsory attendance laws to force children to watch ads
2. Wastes school time
3. Promotes violent entertainment
4. Wastes tax dollars
5. Promotes the wrong values to children
6. Bad for children's health

7. Corrupts the integrity of public education
8. Promotes television instead of reading

The more than 70 individuals, representing dozens of organizations, signing the letter comprise a Who's Who of parenting, education, civic, and religious organizations in the United States. Among the organizations represented are the American Academy of Pediatrics, the Consumer Federation, the Alliance for Childhood, the American Academy of Child and Adolescent Psychiatry, the American Family Association, the National Institute on Media and the Family, Focus on the Family, and the United Methodist Church.

The full text of the letter, which goes into detail on each of its eight arguments against the network, and the list of endorsing organizations, are included as part of Appendix VII.

It's hard to trace a direct cause-and-effect relationship between letters like this one and the strength of Channel One as a going concern, but it's reasonable to conclude that the unremitting criticism directed at the company at least helped discourage enough advertisers that Primedia, a New York-based media conglomerate that owned the company for several years, decided to sell it in 2007, after contemplating pulling the plug on the company in 2006.

When you combine the compulsory messaging children are exposed to on BusRadio on the way to and from school, and the compulsory messaging they're exposed to in the classroom from Channel One, the extent to which media captivity has inserted itself into our children's daily lives becomes apparent.

Chapter 4. Outdoor Rooms: When Memory Goes Missing

Media captivity isn't always intentional. Sometimes it's the side effect of the use of media by others, whether those others are our neighbors, our colleagues at work, or the people sitting next to us at the theater or driving down the street.

The use of digital media by others creates a captive-audience environment, albeit an unintentional one, because personal media technology respects no boundaries. In the same way that a TV on a subway car transmits its messaging to all riders equally, regardless of who among the ridership wants to consume that messaging, my TV, if I'm watching it in proximity to others, makes whoever is near me a captive to my media choices. Although I'm not trying to monetize my relationship with my neighbor, as commercial media companies are with captive-audience platforms, I nevertheless create an environment from which you can't escape because you have no choice but to watch what I'm watching, or listen to what I'm listening to, unless you either ask me to stop or you go somewhere else.

Of course, that sets up the conditions for conflict, the kind of conflict attendant on any situation when interests are competing for a scarce resource, in this case the viewscape or soundscape we share with others.

You might recall the widely reported story in 2008 of Curt Mann who erected a wind turbine outside his home in the leafy Grant Park neighborhood of Atlanta to help reduce his utility bills. The story was widely reported in the press because in erecting the turbine he set off a small firestorm of protest. The turbine stood 45 feet tall and was expected to cut Mann's monthly power bill by about $20. But to his neighbors the turbine was just an eyesore.

To many, the ungainliness of a wind turbine is a small price to pay to further a public good, but the neighbors' hostility isn't unreasonable; each of us is guilty at one time or another of putting our interests, no matter how trivial, before the common good. Remember what David Hume said about his finger: he'd rather see the world destroyed before he suffered a scratch on it.

In this particular case, the neighbors' concern over their viewscape (one neighbor called it the "public view") trumped the wider community's interest in encouraging alternative sources of energy.

Similar types of conflict arose a few years ago when some communities outlawed, or tried to outlaw, the residential use of clotheslines. In one of the most widely publicized cases at the time, a homeowner in Bend, Ore., was given what amounted to a cease-and-desist order from his homeowners' association because the covenants of the community in which he lived prohibited visible clotheslines.

From a practical standpoint the clothesline restriction makes no sense, because it restricts residents' ability to dry their clothes in an environmentally and economically practical way, but from an aesthetic one, it makes all the sense in the world.

A case can be made that many if not most conflicts between neighbors are fundamentally about the allocation of a scarce resource in a shared environment. If the conflict is over the derelict cars on the neighbor's front lawn, the issue concerns the neighborhood viewscape. There is only one viewscape of the neighborhood. If it's marred, it's marred for everybody. If the conflict is over the neighbor's loud stereo, the issue concerns the neighborhood soundscape. Again, there's only one soundscape for the neighborhood. If someone's playing music, everyone in that soundscape must listen to it.

When we thus consider that electronic media delivers its content in a shared environment, in contradistinction to print media, which delivers its content in a private environment, we see that the stage is set for a rise in the kinds of conflict that involve battles over the allocation of a scarce resource.

To be sure, it's possible to deliver digital content through a closed channel of communication. It's the ability to do this (ideally, although not always in reality) that makes the iPod and other personal media devices so popular. With these players, we can listen to or watch what we want without disturbing others (assuming we use the devices properly), thereby making our consumption of their content more like the closed-channel activity of reading, because our choices don't expand into the surrounding viewscape or soundscape.

But we don't want to confuse this personal consumption, in which we're overseers of our own choices, with the growing scarcity of environments in which our ability to choose is taken away from us. Any environment in which our autonomy is encroached upon creates the conditions for conflict.

It's with these notions of conflict in mind that we can look at a number of consumer trends that are setting the stage for increasing conflicts of the nature we see with the wind turbine and the clothesline. Among these trends is the rise in outdoor rooms, boom cars, and, in the workplace, desktop audio and video conferencing.

The rise in outdoor rooms is particularly troubling, not because people enjoying entertainment in their backyard is a bad thing. It's absolutely not, and indeed, people rightly feel they have an entitlement to use their private property as they see fit.

What makes the issue troubling is that it's precisely because this sense of entitlement sets up a painful conflict with one's neighbors, who feel an equally strong sense of entitlement to be able to enjoy *their* property as *they* see fit. So when the audio of your TV program, or when the flickering light and images from your outdoor screen, impact my ability to enjoy my own property in the way I want, a conflict of the most painful type arises, because it's a conflict that pits one neighbor against another.

These types of conflicts are truly among the most disturbing. We can see this when we look at how sensitive people are to the noise of others, and how upset they get — even murderously upset — when one person's noise invades the space of another.

No doubt there are more harrowing cases, but one case that was reported in the news, in 2005, involved a British Columbia woman who rammed her car into her neighbor's apartment in a fight over a loud television. Canadian police said the woman got into her 1985 BMW after becoming upset with her neighbor and drove the car across the lawn and through some patio furniture before smashing into the side of the building. The neighbor and a friend were inside the building watching television.

In another case, a Hong Kong resident bit the ear off his neighbor because of a noise dispute, and in another, a U.K. coroner pronounced "noise" as the cause of a Birmingham resident's suicide because he was driven over the edge by the incessant noise made by his neighbors.

For many of us, the idea of physically violating someone (or even ourselves) because of someone else's noise is scarcely thinkable, but at some level we nevertheless understand what drives such behavior. Sociologist Jack Levin has categorized fatal shootings over seemingly trivial disputes like noise "homicides over argument" and says they're rooted in primal feelings of disrespect.

This notion of disrespect is what David Staudacher of Vancouver's Right to Quiet Society has in mind when he talks about healthy social interaction, which can only thrive in an environment of mutual respect. "Noise destroys the sense of public peace and tranquility that nourishes healthy social interaction," he says. People can't relate to one another in a healthy, constructive manner because noise disputes are driven by this primal urge to be respected. Arguments over noise are really arguments over respect.

Journalists Mary Desmond Pinkowish and Ursula Sauter talk about the same thing in an *Alternet* piece on the health hazards of noise that they wrote in 2007. "Noise brings out the worst in human beings." Faced with noise outside their control, people experience "increased blood pressure and heart rate ... stress hormones surge into the bloodstream."

Thankfully, neighbor-on-neighbor conflict of the type by the British Columbia woman rarely escalates to such a violent point, but I mention it here to illustrate a point: we think of our home as an environment in which control resides with us and us alone. That's why we say a person's home is her castle, a place of refuge when everything outside the home gets to be more than we can bear. Thus, when someone else's media choices impinge on our ability to enjoy our home in peace, we get resentful and feel that primal pain of disrespect.

For this reason, we can only wonder about the wisdom of outdoor rooms.

What are outdoor rooms? If you watch HGTV or other home-oriented TV programming you're surely familiar with the outdoor room trend but if you're not, you will be shortly, because any time business leaders find a way to inject new growth into an old market, you know you better hold onto your hat because nothing exerts so strong a force as a vacuum being filled.

"Outdoor rooms" is a new term for something homeowners have always aspired to, and that's the transformation of their 1,100 square foot suburban home into a castle. What's new about outdoor rooms is, as with boom cars, the introduction of technology that empowers consumers but only at the expense of others.

To be sure, people have always been able to enjoy cooking, listening to the radio, and watching TV in their backyard, but thanks to the rise of technological innovation homeowners no longer need to rely on jerry-rigging to make everything work in an affordable, easy, and comfortable way; now products and off-the-shelf design solutions are available to make it a snap to re-create your indoor living experience in the comfort of your backyard.

"Just about anything you could have indoors now has an outdoor version," Deidra Darsa of the Hearth, Patio, and Barbeque Association says in a piece on remodeling Web site BobVila.com. "TVs and stereos, for instance, are becoming more popular for outdoor entertaining areas."

The reason? New materials and coatings, as well as the wireless revolution, now make it possible to keep sensitive electronics outdoors in all weather conditions.

"The moisture, dust or dirt that can get into the infrastructure of an indoor television will cause it to malfunction," Joe Pantel, CEO of Pantel Corp. in Garden Grove, Calif., says on Hometoys.com. For protection against the elements, Pantel TVs "are made with powder-coated aluminum, which allows them to easily ventilate so that they don't overheat and it prevents them from rusting as a result of bombardment by rain or any other moisture."

Pantel is speaking specifically about his own products, but innovation in coatings and other weatherization features apply throughout the outdoor electronic products industry.

"The bottom line," Pantel says in the Hometoys.com interview, "is that the elements that exist in an outdoor setting will cause our TVs no harm. The internal electronic components of our TVs are completely sealed off so that they are not brought into contact with the elements that could so easily damage an indoor television. Also, indoor TVs require that cables or wires be run from the TV unit to DVD players, cable or satellite boxes, and so on. Our TVs are made standard with wireless capabilities that allow for both an audio and video signal to be sent up to two-hundred feet away, wirelessly."

Other innovations tackle the longstanding usability issues that have tended to keep the enjoyment level of outdoor electronics down. Top among those limitations, as they apply to TVs, is glare, but advancements in high-resolution LCD screens coated with reflection-free glass have squelched that problem.

It probably doesn't hurt that the screens come in such large sizes now, too. It's not uncommon to see backyard TVs with 65-inch screens. For the real aficionados, though, the party only begins at 65 inches; screens can come in sizes as large as 100 inches, giving you in effect a mini movie theater that even your neighbors across the street will be able to enjoy.

The result of these advances is a surge in the exporting of TVs and stereos from indoor to outdoor spaces.

In 2007, two-thirds of American Institute of Architects members had seen an increased demand for outdoor living space, and shipments of outdoor furniture, which includes TVs and other entertainment systems, increased 140 percent in the past 10 year, according to the American Home Furnishing Alliance.

Everyone Deserves to Enjoy My Lifestyle

As with other innovations in personal technology, this growth is good for the person who's acting on his personal choices but it leaves out of the equation the people who share collaterally in that person's decisions. At the heart of the outdoor room movement is the introduction of sound and video images that don't respect property boundaries. As we've seen, for neighbors, that's a problem. Indeed, it's precisely their effort to escape this kind of intrusion into their lives that people migrate away from high-density living in multifamily buildings to our spread-out single-family suburbs.

This migration isn't hard to understand. What people are striving for in buying or renting a house with a bit of yard around it is autonomy. It's not enough to have walls around you; you want walls around you through which you can't hear your neighbor's TV, radio, and conversations.

Indeed, outside of physical safety, neighbor noise is generally the most frequent complaint of home owners and renters. As researchers put it in a recent study, called "Home sweet apartment: a text analysis of dissatisfaction with apartment homes," by University of Georgia researchers, "hearing noise through the walls, floor, or ceiling had the strongest negative impact on resident satisfaction of any characteristic."

The authors of that study point to research in 2007 published in the *Journal of Performance of Constructed Facilities* that found "violation of space separation by noise intrusion through walls, floors, or ceilings created dramatically negative effects" on residential satisfaction.

The number of other studies that come to a similar conclusion would be hard to quantify because there are so many of them, generated both in this country and abroad.

In a study by a U.K. researcher released in 2008, noisy neighbors are a chief reason homeowners would like to move if only economic and other constraints didn't stand in their way. Because of "high moving costs combined with the social and psychological costs of reestablishing a social network . . . many home owners may simply hunker down and stay put," the researcher, Diana Weinhold, says.

In a recent study on relationships between neighbors conducted in the Netherlands, 94 percent of households cited the playing of loud music (specifically, "pop" music) as either annoying or severely annoying, the highest of the complaints by far, and 76 percent cited neighbors' loud TVs or other audio as the second highest cause of annoyance.

A trade publication called *Rental Property Reporter* a few years ago analyzed tenant complaints from a Web site called Apartment Ratings and found noise the main problem of renters. A sampling of tenant comments:

"Your neighbor is like your unwanted roommate because you hear every step, every door open and close, every cabinet close, every word spoken, every phone conversation, every toilet flush, every TV program. . . ."

"The walls are so thin that you can hear every little thing that the neighbors do or say. My neighbors party every single day."

"The neighbors are extremely loud, constant loud . . . music vibrating my floor."

"You have been warned. Never live here. I have lived in other apartments in the area, and this one is the worst. Noise!"

What the University of Georgia report and the other research make clear is that people recoil from having to listen to their neighbors through their walls. Such intrusions feel like a violation of their right to be masters of their personal space.

"What bugs me is hearing somebody else's noise," an apartment resident says in an online community forum. "I hear trucks, fire engines, and people yelling outside, but if I hear my neighbor's TV . . . it bugs me. I'm a light sleeper and sensitive to noise, so that doesn't make it any easier."

There's little doubt that the noise issue is why "sound conditioning" is almost always a chief selling point of high-end condos and why buyers are willing to pay a premium to have it.

"Superb, quality tested sound conditioning assures you of the highest standards in both apartment construction and noise-free living," one Minneapolis apartment company advertises in its marketing material.

But sound-conditioned condos are a small slice of the market and sound conditioning is a luxury in the rental market, so it remains the escape from neighbor noise that continues to drive people's moves to the suburbs and the sanctuary of single-family homes.

What people are finding, though, is that the suburbs are increasingly not the sanctuary they once were. In a 2007 U.K. study, "antisocial" noise complaints in 100 municipalities jumped year-over-year by an average 22 percent, with the highest jumps taking place not in urban areas but in the *suburban* municipalities. The cause? Higher noise levels stemming from lifestyle changes that have led to increased invasiveness of loud music and large TVs. "Officials said the higher noise levels were due partly to changing lifestyles, with louder music . . . and larger TVs," said an article in the *Times* of London that looked at the findings.

In commenting on the findings, Brian Lamb, then acting director of the Royal National Institute for the Deaf, said this intrusion is overdue for a solution. "Noise pollution is one of the overlooked issues of our times," he told the *Times*.

Thus, given the role of autonomy in people's housing choices, the rise of outdoor rooms can only be seen as a massive case of social amnesia, because in turning on the full power of Western marketing muscle for the benefit of outdoor rooms, business leaders are setting the stage for the same kind of conflicts in our single-family-home sanctuary that people have been trying to escape in the conflict-ridden multifamily home world.

Karen Orr of the Florida League of Conservation Voters calls the invasion of TV and radio intrusions into people's lives the "new horror of suburban life" and says it's driving people in the suburbs to move even farther out, to the outlying exurbs, to put yet more space between themselves and their neighbors so they can maintain control over their personal environment.

"The 'outdoor entertainment' equipment pushed by the home electronics industry in the form of outdoor loudspeaker . . . and televisions for the porch and patio makes us wonder, what next?" Orr says in a *Tampa Bay Online* piece. "Mega bass boom systems for the riding lawnmower?"

"You used to reliably move to the suburbs and find peace and quiet," Les Blomberg of the Noise Pollution Clearinghouse in Montpelier, Vt., told the *Christian Science Monitor* in a piece it ran on the rise of noise-control laws throughout the U.S. But now "we've made our suburbs noisy. We can't all buy 1,000 acres and hide in the middle of it."

GOLDEN RAYS SHINING ON ME AT MY LEISURE

I talk about the rise of outdoor rooms as if this is a thought-out, coordinated effort on the part of business leaders to create a market by manufacturing a trend, but nothing is ever that simple. What's clear is that the technological innovations behind outdoor electronics have converged with a host of consumer trends, including the push for larger homes and more elaborate entertainment systems, in the last half dozen years to make "outdoor rooms" a buzzword in the real estate and consumer products industries. Once a buzzword enters the popular vernacular, it takes on a life of its own and over time becomes part of our consumer mindscape, entrenching it into our daily discourse, becoming part of the background of our lives, and taking on an air of inevitability so that *not* wanting an outdoor room becomes the kind of choice one expects only from eccentrics.

What we see in this trend are the planting of the seeds of a new wave of conflict. As entertainment writer Gregg Kilday says in one of his blog posts, what backyard TVs give us are "new status symbols: huge screens that rise out of the ground or hang from the patio awnings and speakers that are hidden around the yard in the landscaping," or, as he sums it up, "a new way to annoy the neighbors."

Lawmakers in Bonita Springs, Fla., might have had this new powerful technology in mind when they applied a local "special events" noise rule to even *residential* activities in a law they passed a few years ago. "The rule became that anything outdoors that had amplified music would need a permit and approval for the party from City Council," according to a *Naples Daily News* report on the law.

Other localities are scrambling to catch up now that technology is advanced enough to put into everybody's hands the means to control what everybody around them — whether in their home or in their car — listens to.

Pasco County, Fla., is a good example. It limits to 55 decibels at night (60 during the day) any noise created by radios, televisions, or exterior loudspeakers in its residential areas, with sound-level measurements taken at the property line of the home owner responsible for the noise.

"When some people choose not to be a good neighbor, laws must be passed to force neighborliness upon them," says Blomberg. "This is an unfortunate but all too common necessity in modern society. Laws forcing people to be good neighbors are much less desirable than people acting as good neighbors out of choice."

Without a doubt the availability of personal outdoor entertainment systems is nothing more than an extension of our time-honored quest to be masters in our own homes. Certainly marketers of these systems understand that aspiration and reflect it in their product pitches to consumers.

"Imagine relaxing outside, getting some much needed sun, while watching your favorite movie or television show in high definition," says marketing copy for Pantel Outdoor Weatherproof TVs on its Web site. "Watching a football game will never be the same again. Instead of missing the big play, while you are outside barbequing for your guests, now you can watch the game outside with them. Bring the game to you! Picture your teenagers and you taking a late night dip in the pool while watching *Jaws* in high definition. That would be an experience they would talk about for years. Family entertainment has reached a whole new level with fewer boundaries than ever before! Isn't this what life is all about, the memories and the time we share with the people that mean the most to us. At Pantel Corp, we believe it is, so bring the memories outside and breathe in the fresh air."

But as with boom cars, homeowners can only enjoy their outdoor rooms at the expense of others. Their personal consumption of media infringes on their neighbors' right to peaceful enjoyment of their own property, because noise and high-definition visual images don't respect property lines. The TV or stereo might be on my property, but its collateral effect doesn't stop at the border between my property and your property. My choices become your choices. It's a classic "tragedy of the commons" problem.

"Noisy neighbors do not care about their impact on others," says Blomberg. "They are the bullies in the schoolyard."

And noise isn't the only side effect of someone's media choices. People are increasingly taking stands against the use of large-screen outdoor media because high-definition technology is changing neighborhood viewscapes. In Northern Virginia a few years ago, residents created a huge backlash against a large-screen outdoor video monitor erected by George Mason University because of the intrusiveness of the sign's light. "It's like a big Jumbotron," one resident complained in a *Washington Post* piece on the conflict.

Similar conflicts have been sparked throughout the country. In Los Angeles, a large digital advertising sign erected in 2007 near a residential neighborhood sparked a backlash, although nothing was done about it. "My kitchen glows alternately red, blue and orange," one of the residents said in a *Los Angeles Times* article. "'[It's like] someone slapping your face with red," another said.

TV AND THE "ORIENTING RESPONSE"

It's not hard to understand the trouble people have with the introduction of large, bright screens to a spot within their site range. The light, colors, and movement of TV are notoriously hard to ignore. We can probably thank our biology for that. There's no shortage of evidence suggesting TV is particularly hard for us to ignore because of the way we're visually programmed to capture rapid movement. Researchers typically attribute our almost automatic attraction to TV screens to an "orienting response" that we exhibit whenever we're confronted with novel or sudden visual stimuli, something TV is especially well-suited to provide, particularly today with its big size, clear picture, and quick cuts and zooms. "It is part of our evolutionary heritage, a built-in sensitivity to movement" say researchers Robert Kubey and Mihaly Csikszentmihalyi in an article they wrote for *Scientific American* called "Television Addiction is No Mere Metaphor."

Judith Warner, a parenting columnist for the *New York Times*, attended a lecture by a neuropsychologist on this orienting response a couple of years ago, and she said the doctor, William Stixrud, described our biological fixation with TV this way:

"TV super-stimulates the brain by continually setting off its 'orienting response' — a primitive neurobiological process that keeps people alert. This orienting response is hard-wired; it's a survival thing, and, with a quickly changing screen, it kicks on again and again — kind of like my dog, who barks every time a truck goes by, or someone parks a car down the street, or a squirrel breathes, or someone opens a mailbox in Kansas. The experience of having your orienting response incessantly stimulated is draining. When it ends, you are exhausted, but also left with the memory of how much better you felt when it was happening. Dr. Stixrud talked about dopamine, attention and addiction and noted that watching TV violence puts people into a hyper-activated 'fight or flight mode' because the 'primitive' regions of our brains can't distinguish TV violence from a real threat."

In another paper of Kubey's, called "Television Dependence, Diagnosis, and Prevention," the researcher talks about the effect of watching television over time. People who watch a lot of TV do so to give themselves a break from negative thoughts, he says. In doing that, these TV watchers create a self-reinforcing feedback loop that they find increasingly hard to break away from over time. Kubey describes it as a "vicious circle, wherein the experience of negative moods and thoughts when alone and when unstructured, may interact with the ease with which people can quickly escape these feelings by viewing. As a result of many hours spent viewing television over many years, some people may become unpracticed in spending time alone, entertaining themselves, or even in directing their own attention."

"A television viewing habit," he goes on, "may be self-perpetuating, Viewing may lead to more viewing and may elicit what has been called 'attentional inertia,' i.e., 'the longer people look at television, the greater is the probability that they will continue to look.' Discomfort in non-committed, or solitary time, can lead to viewing, but after years of such behavior and a thousand hours or more of viewing each year, it seems quite possible that an ingrained television habit could cause some people to feel uncomfortable when left with 'nothing to do,' or alone, and not viewing."

You'll find more on these biological issues in Appendix IV, which reprints an article that includes a discussion of the influential Kubey and Csikszentmihalyi article, "Orienting response and TV addiction" as well as Kubey's paper.

To be sure, outdoor TVs remain rare enough today that they're off most people's radar screen and are hardly a problem for most of us, but the trend is clear and as demand for them increases and more companies enter the space the market will "democratize" and the TVs will become a must-have for homeowners all along the income scale. As that happens, outdoor entertainment will transition from a plaything of the rich to an entitlement for the middle class. Once outdoor rooms in general and outdoor TV in particular become ensconced in our culture, the window of opportunity for regulating personal outdoor entertainment in a way that works for everyone will have closed, and we'll be left with the same conditions that we have with our guns: if you want them removed, as Charlton Heston said so memorably, you'll have to pry them from our cold, dead hands.

An outcome like this is ludicrous, of course. Outdoor rooms make sense only in an environment in which their use won't impinge on others, and few of us live in such an environment. In our single-family communities we share our viewscape and soundscape with our neighbors, and as we know from the vitriolic conflict we have with them over barking dogs, early-morning lawn mowing and leaf blowing, all-night partying, and trash-strewn yards, we treat our shared soundscape and viewscapes as precious resources whose tainting we don't tolerate quietly. Conditions will get yet more volatile when we add outdoor rooms to the mix, effectively creating in our single-family neighborhoods the same conditions that drive people out of multifamily housing.

It's not the purpose here to vilify the companies that manufacture outdoor TVs and stereos or to question their free-market right to be as successful as they possibly can by providing products that clearly many people want and are willing to pay a lot of money for. They're proceeding in a rational, time-honored way by identifying a popular market niche and organizing their business around that niche as successfully as they can. But there's every reason to believe that their products will stir a backlash, at least among some people.

Chapter 5. Boom Cars: Funny as a Heart Attack

We see in boom cars the same conditions for conflict creation we see with outdoor rooms. If you're not familiar with "boom cars" in name you're likely familiar with them in experience. These are simply cars whose owners have tricked them out with a stereo capable of playing at the outer reaches of audio tolerance, particularly in the low, rumbling bass registers. The cars are vehicles of personal expression for their owners but for health officials they're a problem because of the danger they pose not just to people's hearing — the drivers' as well as the bystanders' — but to people's cardiac health. A London study that not long ago tied loud noises to cardiac damage in people exposed to them while asleep is just one in a long line of research pinning health risks to people exposed to rumbling noises like that of boom cars.

Like outdoor rooms, boom cars are a textbook case of how the rise of new technologies — in this case stereo components that represent a quantum leap in power output — create the conditions for the use of invasive media that didn't exist before, at least on a practical basis. But now that the technology is here, its exploitation has led to the creation of environments in which our ability to choose what media we do and don't consume is taken away from us.

These new environments raise the issue of autonomy. Do I or don't I have a say in whether someone else's personal music choices fills my soundscape? It's one thing for me to walk through an industrial area, where I know that, like having a beer at a bar, I must accept one thing (industrial noise) to get another thing (arrival at my destination). But it's another for me to have to accommodate what we might call the hyper-intrusive personal media of others without being given an opportunity for autonomous decision-making regarding the place of that media in my soundscape.

Trivially, you can look at my accommodation of someone else's media choices in the framework of what logicians call a hypothetical syllogism topped off with a modus ponendo ponens, $(p \rightarrow q + q \rightarrow r + r \rightarrow s + s \rightarrow t + p = t)$, an argument that arrives at a conclusion in which, basically, he whose personal choice is the loudest wins:

If Joe exercises his personal choice, he plays his boom-car stereo loudly.

If he plays his boom-car stereo loudly, he overpowers everything around him.

If he overpowers everything around him, he determines the quality of the environment for everyone around him.

If he determines the quality of the environment for everyone around him, he has de facto control over the personal choices of others as long as they're within his environment.

Joe exercises his personal choice.

Therefore, he has de facto control over the personal choices of others as long as they're within his environment.

The argument is obvious, but it reminds us that if we validate the life-style prerogative of boom-car owners, then we must allow that boom-car owners are entitled to live autonomously while the rest of us are not, because the boom car owner will always be able to do what he wants, regardless of what I do, while I can only do what I want depending on what the boom car owner does.

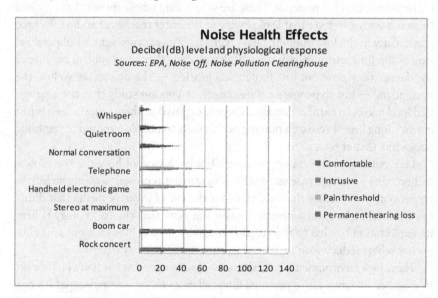

Noise Health Effects
Decibel (dB) level and physiological response
Sources: EPA, Noise Off, Noise Pollution Clearinghouse

But the issue of boom cars goes beyond autonomy to our personal health. As with secondhand smoke, when the personal choices of others impacts my health, then I have a vested interest in ensuring that it's me who decides whether to allow myself to be in harm's way. I'm the steward of my well-being.

What we know is that, with any loud noise, health issues are a genuine concern. At 60 decibels (the sound of a robust conversation), hormones are released into our bloodstream and our blood pressure, heart rate, breathing speed, and muscle tension increase. At 90 decibels (the sound of a power lawn mower), the tension in our muscles increase, and our organ systems weaken. Meanwhile, our blood pressure, heart rate, and breathing speed accelerate. And At 120 decibels (a rock concert), we're in pain (joyful pain, I guess, but pain nonetheless). One aspect of noise measurement that many people probably don't know about is that decibels (dB) are charted logarithmically, which means that for every increase by a certain interval, the value is doubled. Thus, for every increase in noise by three decibels, the impact of noise doubles. So, if you're listening to your stereo at 70 decibels and you increase it to 73 decibels, you've doubled the loudness of your music. When you consider this, the difference between listening to a radio in the background at 40 decibels and hearing someone's boom car stereo at 140 decibels is staggering, probably literally so.

Doctors say the facts are clear: noise causes, among other things, measurable increases in people's systolic blood pressure, even while they're sleeping, and these increases can lead to acute and chronic disabilities.

"Noise has been the Cinderella form of pollution and people haven't been aware that it has an impact on their health," Deepak Prasher, professor of audiology at University College London, says in *The Guardian*, in a piece on a World Health Organization noise report. "But new data provide the link showing there are earlier deaths because of noise. . . . Even when you think you are used to the noise, physiological changes are still happening."

The physiological impacts of noise are surely why militaries and police forces around the world have always used, and are continuing to use today, noise as a weapon, both on the battlefield and in the interrogation room. Perhaps the most memorable use of noise as a weapon, at least in recent decades, was during the ouster of Panamanian dictator Manuel Noriega in 1989. The U.S. military bombarded Noriega and his troops with rock music as a way to exert psychological pressure on the combatants and only ceased their bombardment after it caused an international outcry. The U.S. said it was only using the music to mask communications it didn't want to be picked up by Panamanians using parabolic microphones, but that wasn't enough to take the pressure off the military; even the Vatican protested.

Today, the use of "non-lethal" acoustic weapons and what are sometimes known as sonic weapons, including microwave noise guns, are being deployed with increasing frequency for a variety of aims, most notably crowd control.

One such use of sonic noise guns that's received considerable attention in just the last year or so involves high-pitched microwave noise guns — those that emit signals at a range above 20khz — because they're being used exclusively on troublesome teenage crowds. Apparently, the pitch is too high to be heard by people after a certain age because of physiological changes in people's hearing over time, but on youth the noise creates enough discomfort that it makes them disburse. Human rights organizations have protested the use of the weapons as an infringement on the rights of the victims.

The problem with using noise for crowd control, though, is that, while it might be non-lethal, it's not clear that it's harm-free. Researchers are increasingly convinced that sonic weapons can cause lasting neurological damage to people who are subject to them. "I would worry about what ... health effects [a new sonic weapon] is having," James Lin of the Electrical and Computer Engineering Department at the University of Illinois in Chicago said in an interview in mid-2008. He was referring specifically to a crowd-control device called MEDUSA ("Mob Excess Deterrent Using Silent Audio"), developed for the U.S. military and that remains under testing. "You might see neural damage."

The jury is still out on sonic weapons but what's clear is that noise, at certain pitches and volume, are far from neutral in our environment. Thus, as someone concerned about my health, boom cars make me nervous because they chart in at 140 decibels and sometimes they go up to 150 decibels. That's far above the threshold of what's considered safe.

The Loudest Urban Environment on Earth

It might be the regular breaking of the threshold for noise tolerance that residents of Cairo — by their own admission — are stressed out all of the time. A study by the Egyptian National Research Center found noise in the city to average 85 decibels from 7 a.m. to 10 p.m., about the same as standing 15 feet from a moving train, and in some areas the average is 95 decibels, making it what some have called the loudest urban environment on the planet.

Much of the noise is caused by residents using noise to block out other noise. One resident, in an interview in the *New York Times*, says he turns up the volume on his radio to block out the volume of his neighbors' radios. That's a reasonable strategy for him, but of course in doing that he's helping to worsen the problem he's reacting against.

"What are we going to do?" Essam Muhammad Hussein, a food-stand owner, asks rhetorically in his interview with the *Times*. "Where is the way out?"

According to the report, Cairo residents don't hesitate to attribute ill health, insufficient sleep, and chronic nervousness to their inability to escape to any place of quiet in the city. "The noise bothers me and I know it bothers people," a resident named Abdel Khaleq lamented to the *Times*.

"I can't do anything about it," another resident, Madbouly Omran, said. "It's forced on me."

Although it's standard for local governments to impose laws protecting their residents' right to peaceful enjoyment of public space, the impetus for many municipal sound ordinances enacted in recent years is less about rights than health concerns arising from loud noises, often specifically from boom cars.

Dozens of local jurisdictions have specifically addressed the boom car problem. In Freeport, Texas, boom car violators are fined $255 for a first offense, and in Bloomington, Ind., police slap fines up to $500 for each violation. To enforce the law, the police have stationed uniformed officers, and officers in unmarked cars, in areas where the complaints are concentrated.

New York City became the poster child of noise ordinances in 2004 when its mayor, Michael Bloomberg, pushed passage of a multifaceted approach to the city's colossal noise problem. New Yorkers have long called noise the city's number one problem and the city fields an average of 1,000 noise complaints a day, according to a *New York Times* article. What's interesting about the wide-ranging approach Bloomberg took at the time, for our purposes here, is the introduction of language on acceptable "bass level vibrations" that is specifically applicable to clubs but also captures boom cars.

Autonomy and health concerns aside, there's another dimension to the boom car issue that factors into the issues of captive-audience media: boom cars are not just about personal expression through media choices; they're also about the expressed communication of a *point of view* to others, a characteristic that leads to a blurring of the lines between the personal media choices of individuals and the intentional efforts to communicate by commercial and noncommercial interests that purposely seek to exploit captive-media environments.

When I say boom cars are about the expression of a *point of view*, I'm talking about someone's use of media not just for personal enjoyment but to communicate a message to someone else. In other words, as a boom car owner, I'm not just listening to a song that I like at high volume; I'm exerting influence over you by intentionally forcing you to listen to my song.

There's certainly nothing novel about the idea of people using media choices to exert influence over others. There's a reason why your local government hosting a July 4 fireworks display accompanies its show with patriotic music.

Let Me Tell You What I Think of You

With boom cars, the point of playing the music loudly is precisely to assert that you can. As a U.S. Department of Justice report says, "loud car stereos" are "an expression of rudeness and selfishness, or even a form of aggression — a blatant defiance of social etiquette and norms."

The DOJ goes on: "Police are confronting a popular and lucrative phenomenon. It is not easy to change the behavior of those who see loud car stereos as an important part of their lifestyle."

I reproduce much of the introductory portion of the DOJ report in Appendix V in the back of this book. Its discussion of what people don't like about noise, the role that "control" plays in people's feelings about it, and the impact of noise on people's ability to control aggressive behavior are illuminating and worth looking at in unedited form.

It's no doubt because of this attitude that anyone who confronts a boom car owner does so at his own peril, because a confrontation is precisely what the boomer wants. A few years ago a boomer in Cincinnati shot another driver in a gas station after the driver asked the boomer to lower the volume on his music. The two began arguing, and the driver who complained shut the car door on the boomer's leg, and the boomer responded by shooting him twice in the chest, killing him.

The car stereo industry, which is the technological underwriter of the boom car phenomenon, has been chest deep in promoting boom cars as forms of expression and not just personal media consumption. For years its members marketed their products to people precisely as a way to communicate an anti-social message.

One ad, from Boss, had the slogan, "Turn it down? I don't think so," and showed a defiant youth flipping off a critic. Another ad, from JBL, said, "Hate your neighbors," and made a joke about angering bystanders. Another ad, from Audiovox, said, "Put the over 40 set in cardiac arrest."

These ads, no longer as welcomed as they once were, go on and on. An anti-noise organization called Noise Free America maintains a collection of the most egregious of these ads and they number in the many dozens. One ad says, "Be loud. Be obnoxious." Another ad, called "Number one annoyance," says "Whatever" to a finding that boom cars are the number one annoyance of people over 40.

To give the car stereo industry some credit, its aware of, and increasingly concerned by, the backlash against boom cars. It's undoubtedly true the industry has seen the error of its ways and wants to make a peace offering. But it's also clearly worried about the increasing threat of regulation. The Mobile Enhancement Retailers Association, a group representing car-stereo stores, has launched a campaign to encourage industry self-regulation over the abusive use of car stereos. The organization makes material available to retailers to raise awareness with their customers about the negative attitude toward boom cars in an effort to neutralize the trend toward noise legislation around the country.

"It is in the best interest of the mobile enhancement community that promotions intended for consumers — whether from a retailer or vendor — be responsible," the organization says in its *Statement on Promotions*. "These promotions should not use symbols, messages or suggest behavior that would adversely affect the industry. Irresponsible promotion could negatively impact the perception of our industry by the public at large and could be used against us by activists or government to regulate our products and activities."

Boom-car owners and the car stereo industry paint any regulations against boom cars as a restriction of personal rights, and it's not uncommon for auto stereo retailers, both by themselves and collectively through their association, to lead efforts against local noise ordinances. In a St. Louis case a few years back, the Mobile Enhancement Retailers Association successfully led an effort against a proposed ordinance to single out boom car stereos for regulation. "Imposing steep fines and impounding vehicles just because of the type of audio system they contain would have been ridiculous," said Rick Mathies, MERA's executive director at the time.

It's not the place here to look at the competing claims about whose personal rights are being violated, the boom-car owners, who say they have a right to make as much noise as they want, even at the risk of harming others' health, or the people who are subjected to the noise against their will and who say they have a right to peaceful enjoyment of public space. Any time you have a conflict driven by the allocation of a scarce resource — in this case a content-neutral soundscape — the matter comes down to a test of competing claims of personal rights.

For the boom-car owners and the stereo industry, at any rate, although claims of personal rights are their main line of defense, the issue certainly is also economic. Stereo manufacturers have reportedly been hit hard by wireless technology, the improvement of stock radios in new cars, as well as by practices of the car manufacturers that make it difficult for independent companies to get their stereo products into new cars. Among the ways car manufacturers reportedly make life hard for the aftermarket car stereo industry is computerization; they link together unrelated car computer systems and restrict access to the computer data.

"The consumer and the aftermarket industry feel the pain," Vicki Scrivner, a past president of MERA, said a few years ago after meeting with a car manufacturer over the problem.

To a certain extent, then, the car stereo industry's boom car push can be seen as part of an effort to stay in the game by tapping the huge revenue potential of the small but enthusiastic subculture of boom car aficionados, for whom it's not uncommon to spend $7,000 or more on a stereo.

But you also have an economic incentive on the side of boom-car owners. They've invested those thousands of dollars in their systems, so any restriction on their ability to play their stereos in the way that they want creates for them a very real economic hardship.

One boom car enthusiast in Orlando, Fla., who'd been ticketed several times for noise violations, said in early 2008 in an Orlando *Sentinel* report that he had no intention of curbing his stereo use because the tickets were a small price to pay when weighed against what he spent on his equipment. "It doesn't matter how much the fine is," he said. "If I want to hear my music, I want to hear my music."

That's one of the reasons NoiseFree America, the advocacy group that maintains the database of egregious boom car ads, has been calling for steeper penalties for violations. At $70 — which is a typical amount for a noise violation fine — violators are paying "about the same as for jaywalking or spitting on the sidewalk," Ted Rueter, founder and executive director of the group, told the *Sentinel*. "The systems that produce this noise cost tens of thousands of dollars. I can't imagine any boom-car user is going to be affected by such a minimal fine."

Undercurrent of Anger

What's notable about the growing boom car controversy is its vehemence. Combatants on both sides are digging in their heels and the battle is getting ugly. The attitude of boom-car owners is one of vitriolic defiance, and their attacks on people who promote noise ordinances are merciless. The invective and mean-spiritedness that characterize their attacks, which are often *ad hominem*, are enough to make anyone think twice about taking them on.

Probably the most instructive case in point is the war being waged against Michael Wright, at one time a particularly vocal critic of boom cars. Wright became the target of a relentless hate-mail campaign that included death threats by boom-car owners for his advocacy of noise control laws.

On his Web site, Wright publishes a selection of the hate mail he receives, and what's breathtaking after viewing a sampling of the letters is the depth of unfocused anger among the boom-car owners.

> "You are one sad case making a website about boom cars?" one person writes. "What the ** is a boom car anyway? You are one sad man, i bet you get hundreds of these emails as 1/7 people are affected (bull) most people dont care, but 6/7 people want one or do it.......next time im going through a quiet neighbourhood im gonna drop the m*&! clutch, choons up full and cause the loudest i can at the earliest time JUST FOR YOU."

Other letters:

> "I am going to kill you, you mother –r."

> "Stop your war on audio, or you will be killed. We have your address."

> "i think you are pathetic,M Whats wrong with you? Trying to outlaw people with loudsystems.

> I think someone is insecure over their pinto. HA HA HA HA, LOOSER, WHY DONT YOU CONGRESS THIS"

"You realize how much of a ** ** you are, right? people like you need to DIE and rot in hell. what are your hobbies? i am so ** irate at your display of compelet idiacy i cant even put it into words! its people like you that make living on this earth unbearable. and how ** dare you compare us to TERRORISTS!! "The combined destructive power of the many thousands of boom cars blasting their way across America cities is far greater than the power of McVeigh's bomb. In the long run, unless these monsters are controlled, the number of victims killed slowly by the effects of sleep deprivation, stress, and vibroacoustic illness will far exceed 168. In boom car land, it's Oklahoma City every day. F* YOU YA STEROTYPICAL **!!"

This anger is a rich subject for psychologists and sociologists to mine, but what's more important for our purposes here is the letters make clear that boomcar owners intentionally use their stereos for anti-social purposes. This isn't just about personal media enjoyment. Although they like to listen to their music loud, much of what's driving their use of the stereos is the explicitly acknowledged satisfaction they derive from angering other people, as the DOJ report makes clear. In effect, these car stereos have given them a tool for touching people in a negative way that they haven't had before. Yesterday they might have initiated a fist fight in a bar; today they can drive down a street and leave a sidewalk full of angry people in their wake.

Wright isn't the only advocate for boom car regulation who has suffered personal attacks. I interviewed Ted Rueter of Noise Free America a few years ago and during our conversation he shared with me the criticism that's been directed at him over the years. "Boomers think they'll beat us down into submission," he told me. "This is their lifestyle. Their culture is violent, vicious, and hate-filled. It's about disturbing the peace."

I'm lingering here on the back-and-forth between boom-car owners and their critics because it makes concrete what conflicts over scarce resources can look like when taken to an extreme. What's underwriting the conflict between boomcar owners and others are three principles:

One, although the boom car owner is making a personal media choice in playing his music loud, I'm a captive to his action because what he's chosen to listen to consumes the soundscape that he shares with me. Two, when he deliberately uses his personal media choice to force me into the soundscape of his choosing (as opposed to not being aware that his music is bothering me), he's attempting to assert his dominance over me. In this case, there's no substantive difference between his playing his radio and other acts of dominance such as turning my radio off against my will. Either way it's a violation of my personal sovereignty. Thus, he's setting the stage for a battle over dominance. And three, when his personal media choices threaten my health, then the issue is no longer a benign conflict over a scarce resource — our shared soundscape — but a matter of self-preservation. To put it in the most dramatic terms, we've gone from a fight over dominance to one over survival.

There's a fourth aspect to the boom car issue and it has to do with the self-contradictory nature of dominance — any form of dominance. The boom car culture, if carried to its logical conclusion, creates a self-contradiction of the type enumerated by Immanuel Kant in his seminal writings on ethics. If each of us took the liberty to antagonize others with our boom car, the broader community in which we all live would be made uninhabitable because it would collapse into self-inflicted chaos.

A boom car enthusiast, in other words, can only exist in a world in which most people are *not* boom car enthusiasts. Once everyone becomes a boom car enthusiast, society can no longer organize itself into a community and therefore it must descend into chaos. Thus, the boom car owner takes on the character of a parasite living off the stability of its host while sucking the life from it. And that's really what Kant's ethics is all about. Any behavior that collapses into self-contradiction is parasitic because it can only sustain itself if the community as a whole doesn't engage in the behavior. It's a free-rider problem.

One way to see the free-rider problem in sharp relief is to think about traffic intersections. It's easy and relatively safe for anyone to violate the rules of a traffic intersection as long as everyone else at the intersection is obeying the rules. If everyone else is obeying the rules, the violator can exploit that orderliness because all the pieces in the equation are known. Thus, if everyone heading south is properly stopped at the red light, then the violator knows he can pull out into the intersection against the light because the cars heading south are safely outside the intersection box. Thus, disorder depends on order. The equation changes dramatically, however, if nobody can be counted on to follow the rules systematically. In this case, the intersection collapses into chaos as each driver tries to pass through it without regard to traffic rules, and then no one is safe. And so it is with boom cars. Violators are exploiting a luxury afforded them by the civility of others.

What's helpful about the boom car issue for our purposes is its clarity. Although some people aren't bothered much by boom cars, and many people who are bothered by them don't feel it's their place to ask the enthusiasts to lower the boom, it's a safe bet that few people outside of the boom car subculture are glad the noise is part of their world. If given a choice, at no personal cost, most people would vote the enthusiasts off the island. That seems clear from the DOJ study and other research on the topic. In a sense, voting the boom-car owners of the island is already happening in many communities, in the form of noise regulations that are specific in their target. Although noise control advocates complain the rules are only superficially enforced, the trend toward regulation in any case is clear. Over time, more such regulations will be passed, and as they are, enforcement can be expected to get more serious, too, particularly as the health effects of loud noises become more widely talked about in the mainstream media and by lawmakers. The momentum is in favor of the community because the threat to the public good is clear.

What's problematic, though, is that lawmakers tend to couch the boom car problem in terms of its health risk rather than as a violation of our autonomy. This is understandable but unfortunate. It's understandable because health risks are measurable, so lawmakers have an objective basis on which to argue the case for noise ordinances. That's presumably why it took so long for the anti-smoking movement to catch on; nothing could happen until measurable evidence of the health risk from secondhand smoke had been assembled to give lawmakers a case for restricting where people can smoke. It was never enough simply to couch the issue in terms of autonomy.

But the autonomy issue is really at the heart of the noise problem posed by boom cars, or any form of media consumption that's used intentionally to impact others. The problem is the fact of the violation, not that the violation becomes so severe that people start suffering heart attacks. If we always wait until there's evidence of a health impact, our shared environments risk becoming irresolvable battlegrounds of competing claims for a scarce resource.

Chapter 6. You Hear Me, Therefore I Am

Thanks to the rise of all types of personal media, the kind of conflict we've seen with outdoor rooms and boom cars is poised to erupt throughout the many environments in which we spend our time. Unfortunately, that includes our workplace, the environment we spend the bulk of our time outside our home.

The prominence of noise as a workplace problem makes sense for the same reason it tops renters' and homeowners' complaints. It's about personal autonomy, and that autonomy is being threatened by the explosive growth in open work environments at the same time that the use of digital media — TV and podcasts on computers, video conferencing, and speaker phones — in employees' work stations is growing. In essence, open-space design and the rise of technology like desktop video and audio conferencing are seeding the grounds of conflict.

"A decade's worth of downsizing and real estate cuts, coupled with a desire to improve adjacencies by putting entire groups together, has led to greater densities of people and equipment on floors," says a report on workplace privacy that was released in 2000, when open-space designs were just gaining traction in office settings. "In any given work area there are likely to be more people talking and laughing, more telephones ringing, more keyboards clacking, and more printers whirring. With each new wave of technological tools — speaker phones, pagers, videoconferencing, to name a few — comes another array of sounds."

The result is a lack of what the report terms acoustical privacy, which office workers say is necessary to function at peak productivity. Indeed, with cubicles, office workers arguably have the worst of all possible worlds: they're confined in terms of space but exercise no control over noise. "A major shortcoming of cubicles is walls that define an individual's boundaries but do little to stop disruptive noises," says a white paper on the subject by Emory University.

As a result, office workers don't enjoy what an Emory University researcher, Andrea Hershatter, calls "incubation," the privacy cocoon that knowledge workers need to perform at their best. "Incubation as a means of creative problem-solving works best when the person is free to relax and contemplate openly," Hershatter says. "It works like meditation, creating a state that's simultaneously relaxed yet aware."

When you consider that between 60 and 75 percent of the U.S. workforce, depending on whose numbers you use, are desk-bound white-collar workers, the absence of incubation for the bulk of this workforce is a genuine problem, especially in light of the fact that the productivity of white collar workers is tied to their ability to concentrate on complex, or at least abstract, tasks.

In a survey sponsored by the American Society of Interior Designers and conducted in partnership with office-interior manufacturers, more than 70 percent of office workers say noise is their biggest distraction and more than 80 percent say they could be more productive in a quieter environment.

"People may be more bothered by sounds they can't control or don't expect," the report says. A sound "can be bad if it's distracting people who are concentrating on a task."

In an online forum on office etiquette conducted in late 2008, an office worker complained about coworkers who take all their calls on speaker phone without regard to the effect the conversation has on those around them.

"There's the employee who sits in a cubicle and uses the speaker phone incessantly, whether it's a business or personal call," the office worker says. "I went up to this brain donor and said, 'If you feel you must use the speaker phone, please use one of the conference rooms. It's hard to concentrate when you do that.' He just looked at me. The very next phone call, he didn't use the speaker phone but he talked even louder than usual. The surrounding employees were audibly sighing and groaning at his inconsiderate behavior. There have been a few times where I've actually gone over to a conference room filled with people who are listening to Muzak on the speaker phone, waiting for the conference call to begin,, to politely close the door. Rarely do I hear, 'Oh, I'm sorry,' or, 'My bad!'"

Perhaps because of the rise of office conflict, Peter Post, the director of the Emily Post Institute and an etiquette guru, addressed the issue of office noise in general, and speaker phone use in particular, in a 2004 *Boston Globe* column. "The speaker option [on phones] should not be used as a hands-free device for the benefit of one person," he says. "Speaker phones in shared work areas are distracting and annoying. If you need to have a meeting using a speaker phone, hold it in an office or a conference room where the phone won't disturb others."

A number of studies conducted in the late 1990s and early 2000s, just when the use of open office environments was taking off and technology was making work stations nosier, go far in explaining what's behind the exasperation expressed by office workers when they're forced to listen to their colleagues as they hold their conversations on speaker phones.

In one study, researchers found a correlation between elevated noise in offices and increased levels of cortisol in the people subjected to it. Cortisol is probably one of the better known hormones among non-scientists because it gets a lot of press attention as "the stress hormone." It's the hormone that releases sugar into the blood, increases blood pressure, and lowers the body's immune response. Thus, when you step back and look at what's happening, open offices — which management justifies on the grounds of team-building but probably has as much to do with saving money on real estate — appears to extract a high physiological cost from office employees in return for saving their company money.

According to the authors of the high-cortisol study, the open-office noise "produced behavioral after-effects [such as fewer attempts at unsolvable puzzles], indicative of motivational deficits. Participants were also less likely to make ergonomic, postural adjustments in their computer work station while working under noisy, relative to quiet, conditions [hunkering down, in other words]. Postural invariance is a risk factor for musculoskeletal disorder."

In an interview after the study came out, Gary Evans, one of the researchers, said the findings are significant in part because they show that noise problems aren't caused by how loud the noise is but how distracting it is, which doesn't always correlate to volume.

"Our study is one of the few to look at low-intensity noise," he says in the interview, which was conducted by the online health Web site WebMD. "Yet our findings resemble those in studies of very noisy environments in that we found that realistic, open-office noise has modest but adverse effects on physiological stress and motivation."

In another study, the findings attributed other physiological problems with higher office noise, namely "increased fatigue, difficulty in concentrating, and decreased work-rate by 3 percent."

Perhaps it's with findings like this in mind that in 2008 a network of universities established as part of their video conferencing protocol a rule that participants host a conference call only if they book a separate room and not conduct it at their desk.

"You need a location where you will not disturb others, ideally a single-person office or similar," the group says in its guidelines. "This is because you will be talking, probably quite loudly, at your computer. Also it may be difficult to concentrate on what others are saying in the meeting if there are other people in the room with you having their own conversations. It is strongly recommended that attendees do not share computers — each should be at their own computer in a separate room — otherwise annoying echoes are again likely to result."

Today, of course, the issue just isn't speaker phones and video conferences in the office but TV as well. Catching the latest episode of your favorite sitcom while at work is increasingly common thanks to the networks' accommodative policy of making many of their most popular shows available over the Internet. Weekdays between Noon and 2 p.m. are when network shows receive their highest online viewership, according to a Nielson release. That means it's a favorite pastime during an extended lunch period. "The number of people watching these half-hour or hour-long shows online during lunch hours is 50 percent higher than the average of all other times," says a *Wall Street Journal* item on the Nielson release posted online in early 2008. Thus, you can add episodes of *The Office* to the mix of noise in the office.

CELL PHONES: MINE IS INDISPENSABLE; YOURS IS INSUFFERABLE

Moving out of the office and into the world at large, the near-universal use of cell phones is creating its own conflict dynamic.

The irritation we have over other people's cell phone conversations by now is part of our popular culture. It seems as if every lifestyle and editorial writer in the United States has written the obligatory essay on why people's use of cell phones is inconsiderate of others and why cell phones have become a symbol of all that is wrong with our culture's obsession with digital communications. Typical of the genre is this piece by Al Neuharth, founder of *USA Today*, who talked up a 2002 initiative to host an annual cell phone courtesy month in his paper:

"What really makes my mouth water is the possibility of more courteous cell phone users. National Cell Phone Courtesy Month is the brainchild of etiquette expert Jacqueline Whitmore, who runs The Protocol School of Palm Beach, Fla. She thought it up when she consulted for Sprint PCS and realized how many rude cell phone users there are. This is the first year cell phone Courtesy Month is being observed. Here's why it's important: There are 137 million cell phones in use in the United States. Millions of them go off menacingly every day. In theaters, restaurants, libraries, museums, classrooms, churches. Even at funerals. Many public places have put in rules against incoming cell phone calls. More are considering it. As a lifelong advocate of free speech, free spirit and free press, I'm reluctant to side with those who want to curb cell phone use. But most cell phone culprits inherently are ill-mannered underachievers. Getting a phone call in a public place and carrying on a long, loud conversation gives these wannabes a feeling of importance.... But those who misuse cells, or encourage their misuse, should heed the wake-up call during this cell phone Courtesy Month. If they don't, free speech and free spirit may become victims of their oafishness."

Joe Howry, editor of the Ventura County, Calif., *Star*, discusses civility and cell phones particularly eloquently in an editorial he ran in late 2007:

"For all the good cell phones have brought into our lives, there has been a down side. Actually, there have been several down sides, depending on a person's perspective, but the most obvious is the decline in good manners. In the cell-phone culture, it is perfectly acceptable to take a phone call in the middle of a conversation, while standing in line anywhere, while walking down the street, while at the movie theater, doctor's office or even a funeral. In fact, there isn't any place it seems where it isn't acceptable to take a call. Empowered with a cell phone, we've become more important than anybody or anything else. Even when politely asked to turn off their cell phones for a short period of time so as to not interrupt someone else, people won't do it. The ring tones of cell phones, which in and of themselves at times can be rude, punctuate every meeting, get-together, function, festival and social gathering. Often, any attempt to silence the activity is met with, in its mildest form, a quick dismissal and, at the worst, scorn, ridicule and that most ancient form of communication: an obscene gesture. The bad behavior is not limited to the younger generation. In fact, they can hardly be blamed for this phenomenon because they don't know better. Those who do know better either have forgotten good manners or have forsaken them in favor of their own convenience and sense of self-importance. Either way, common courtesy is not something that should be sacrificed in the name of progress."

It's not the place to here to rehash cell phone use and civility because the conflict has become so thoroughly entwined in our popular culture that it's now part of late-night comedy routines. What the issue does, though, is give a high profile to the issue of control. As the research on low-frequency noise disturbances in offices shows, the loss of control that people feel due to someone's intrusive use of media isn't about intensity, or noise level. It doesn't matter how loud an intrusion is. It's about people's feeling of self-respect and fairness.

Self-respect and fairness are issues rooted in perception: how one perceives something determines how they react to it, whether negatively, positively, or neutrally. Research conducted in the U.K. a few years ago highlights the role of perception in people's response to conversations held in their vicinity. What's key is that volume is essentially immaterial to people's perceptions of intrusiveness.

In their summary of the findings, the researchers said "mobile phone conversations were significantly more noticeable and annoying than face-to-face conversations at the same volume when the content of the conversation is controlled. Indeed this effect of medium was as large as the effect of loudness."

Clearly, cell phone use is too integral to our world today to give serious consideration to any form of curtailment, and in any case curtailment isn't the issue; civility is. But people's irritation over the use of cell phones by others is in fact a component of the broader issue of scarcity, an issue that encompasses audience captivity, outdoor rooms, boom cars, and the whole panoply of personal technology that beeps, plays music, streams video, and channels conversations.

Chapter 7. Creating a New World of Stress

In 2005, the National Academies Institute of Medicine published a widely cited study on childhood obesity called *Preventing Childhood Obesity: Health in the Balance.* It was among several studies that had been released between 2005 and 2007 on the obesity trend lines in the United States and helped confirm what many people were already aware of at least anecdotally: the country was becoming dangerously overweight.

What grabbed people's attention about the Academies study was its conclusion explicitly linking TV viewing to the epidemic in obesity.

"Media now have a more central role in socializing today's children and youth than ever before," the report says. "Virtually all children ages 2–18 years now live in households with a television, and more than half of today's children and youth report that their families have no rules for television viewing.... Before a certain age, children lack the defenses, or skills, to discriminate commercial from noncommercial content, or to attribute persuasive intent to advertising. Children generally develop these skills at about age 8 years, but children as old as 11 years may not activate their defenses unless explicitly cued to do so. Concern about young children's limited ability to comprehend the nature and purpose of advertising, and about the appropriateness or impact of food marketing to which younger children might be exposed, led to a Federal Trade Commission (FTC) rulemaking process in the late 1970s on the question of whether advertising to young children should be restricted or banned as a protective measure."

The report goes on to talk about the relationship between the "dramatic augmentation of strategic tools and vehicles for marketing activities" and "the rapid growth of childhood obesity in the United States."

For "dramatic augmentation of strategic tools" you can probably substitute "new ways of using TV and other electronic media for reaching children." Channel One is the perfect case in point.

Another study, this one undertaken by the American Academy of Pediatrics and released a few years before the Academies report, linked TV viewing to the rise in attention deficit disorders in children. In the study of more than 2,000 children, the lead researcher, Dimitri Christakis of the Child Health Institute at Children's Hospital and Regional Medical Center in Seattle, Wash., found that for every hour watched at age one and age three, the children had almost a 10 percent higher chance of developing attention problems that could be diagnosed as attention deficit hyperactivity disorder by age seven.

"The insistent noise of television in the home may interfere with the development of 'inner speech' by which a child learns to think through problems and plans and restrain impulsive responding," says Jane Healy, psychologist and child brain expert, in a comment on the study.

TV is also associated with sleep disorders in children, with the condition thought to be related to the effect of light before bedtime. "One theory is that television may have an actual physiologic impact on its viewers," say the authors of a 2005 study on the issue that appeared in the journal *Pediatrics*. "It may be that the bright light of the television before sleep affects the sleep-wake cycle through suppression of the release of melatonin."

Michael Breus, a sleep specialist, says the light appears to make it difficult for people to wind down. "The actual light emanating from the screen can disrupt your body's ability to prepare for sleep," he says.

Other reasons TV might make it hard for children to get to sleep is simply content-based: they watch programs that disturb them or are otherwise more than they can process.

"Children may watch programs that are developmentally inappropriate for their ages or have violent content," authors of the 2005 *Pediatrics* study say. "Violent programming has been shown to have a negative impact on children's behavior and may also inhibit the relaxation necessary for sleep induction, although this has not been demonstrated."

The list of studies linking TV viewing to any number of troubling childhood conditions, including increased levels of violence and declining mastery of reading, and even autism, is too extensive to list here and the findings of the major ones are surely already well known to many people. I mention these studies only to paint in bold relief what's at stake as we prepare to enter the brave new world of pervasive "compulsory" TV throughout the environments in which we live out our lives. And, as we've seen, compulsory media isn't limited to TV platforms; it includes all digital audio and video media that respects no boundaries. I focus on TV here, though, because it has been around the longest and its impact has received the most study.

Given the empirical linkage between heavy TV viewing and violence as well as obesity and attention deficit and all the other maladies we see on the rise in the modern world, for us to embark on a quantum expansion of TV consumption, particularly in environments expressly designed for activities other than TV viewing that make people — willingly or unwillingly — captives of TV and other digital media, is to embark on an experiment of which we can probably guess the outcome.

To be sure, there is no shortage of studies on the other side of the issue suggesting TV viewing can be an important educational tool for children, and few people would challenge the positive role of *Sesame Street* and other groundbreaking children's shows like *Mr. Rogers' Neighborhood* on children's development.

But what so many of these studies look at is the content of the TV programming, not the medium itself. A good example is the 1970s study on TV and child development by L.K. Friedrich and A.H. Stein, which found differences in TV content to be integral to differences in child behavior. "The results of their experiment indicate that *Mister Rogers' Neighborhood* [for example] led to an increase in tolerance of delay (waiting for materials or adult attention). They hypothesize the critical factors were aggressive content producing negative effects and helping pro-social content producing positive effects."

But what this and the many other studies like it that paint a favorable or at least neutral picture of TV don't look at is the impact of TV itself, and certainly not TVs in environments outside the home. When the issue is framed by the formal question of TV v. no TV rather than the specific issue of content, the overwhelming evidence is in the other direction.

TV DOESN'T MAKE YOU NOT DUMB

That's not to say there are no studies looking at the formal issue of TV that come out on the side of TV. There are such studies, but they are few and far between. One such study released relatively recently, a 2006 review of household TV data from the late 1940s and early 1950s, called "Does Television Rot Your Brain?" is from two university of Chicago researchers. They found no difference between school performance between children in Seattle, who had access to early TV, and those in Denver, who didn't.

It's worth pausing a minute to look at the study because on close examination its findings raise as many questions as they answer.

The study rests on the premise that, if TV harmed cognitive development, then children who were first exposed to TV in the late 1940s, when they were under five years of age, would perform more poorly in school than children who were not exposed to TV until the early 1950s, when they were already at least five years old. In other words, the Seattle kids had a five-year head start on TV watching, so they should do more poorly than the Denver kids, when the school performance records of the two sets of children were analyzed in a target year, which was set at 1965. In the Chicago researchers' conclusion, the early TV watchers didn't under-perform academically compared to the later TV watchers, so there appears to be no adverse TV impact.

And yet the data used in the study fails to provide solid support for that conclusion. It relies solely on the findings published in a 1961 book, *Television in the Lives of Our Children* (Stanford University Press: 1961), by Wilbur Schramm, Jack Lyle, and Edwin Parker. Those findings were culled from surveys conducted in the late 1950s involving 6,000 children and 2,000 adults in 10 cities. The bulk of the data applies to elementary school-aged children, not the preschool children who are the focus of the Chicago researchers' study. The entire data set applicable to preschool-aged children is from a single survey, conducted in 1958, on TV viewing habits of preschool children in San Francisco. In that survey, three-year-olds watched TV during the week a median of 42 minutes a day, four-year-olds, 1.6 hours a day, and five-year-olds, 2.3 hours a day, for an average viewing time of roughly 1.5 hours a day. Viewing amounts were somewhat higher for the three age groups on the weekend.

The weakness on building an entire study on such a thin data set must be clear. First, since all of the data came from a single source, the Chicago university researchers have no way of validating the accuracy of the findings because they have no other data sets with which to make a comparison, so the data could be way off and no one would have any way to independently show that. As it is, other researchers have questioned the quality of the data that was used. In the book *Mass Communication Theory* (Thomson Wadsworth: 2005), Stanley Baran and Dennis Davis say the researchers compiling the TV viewing data published in that 1961 book conducted their surveys "without using a single well-articulated theoretical framework" and instead relied on "a welter of empirical generalizations."

Second, the data set is relatively small to represent all preschool children's viewing habits since it involves only 600 children if you assume that the San Francisco survey represents one-tenth of the 10-city survey universe. Third, and perhaps most importantly, the survey results are from 1958, yet they're being used to illuminate the viewing habits of children in Seattle 10 years prior to that, when the quality of TV, both in picture resolution and programming content, was much different and certainly far more limited.

Even setting these concerns aside, any data on TV viewing from the late 1940s and early 1950s, when TV meant "family time" around a single TV with a grainy black and white picture after dinner to watch *Father Knows Best*, can have only limited application to today's world of hundreds of cable channels, virtually unlimited DVD selections, Web TV, plus personal video devices, minivan TVs, children's bedroom TVs, and TVs on buses, trains, planes, subways, elevators, taxis, restaurants, bars, doctor's offices, coin laundries, gyms, school cafeterias, hotel lobbies, street corners, gas stations, and on through the list.

It's clear what we need to take away from the preponderance of evidence about the undesirable effects of television is this: where there's smoke there's fire. For every study that finds TV viewing positive or at least neutral when it comes to behavior and development, there are two or three, if not more, that reach the opposite conclusion.

Without regard to the relative merits and weaknesses of each of the studies, on both sides of the issue, what surely is clear is that something is going on, even if we can't quite pin down exactly what, and this uncertainty is important given the massive expansion of captive-audience environments we face. We're embarking on an uncharted journey into social engineering that no one fully understands or controls but one that will nevertheless bring about change in our relationships to information and even to other people.

There's a moral dimension to this expansion. If we grant there's a correlation between TV and negative behavior or health effects, at least in some people and to different degrees, then like the issue of secondhand smoke, the spread of captive-audience environments can't be seen as a morally neutral development. We can't on the one hand agree with the many studies linking heavy TV viewing to obesity, attention deficit disorder, increased violence, poor school performance, autism, sleep disorders, and all the other maladies and social pathologies that have been linked to it, while on the other sit back and do nothing as TV spreads from the living room to the children's bedroom to the backseat of the SUV to the backyard to the street corner to the bus to the train to the plane to the subway to the taxi to the elevator to the office lobby to the dentist's office to the gym to the coin laundry to the restaurant to the bar to the grocery store to the school cafeteria and to the gas station.

Given this moral dimension, it's not surprising that public interest groups like Commercial Alert, the TV Project, the TV Turnoff Network, Noise Pollution Clearinghouse, Noise Free America, and Screen Time Awareness, among others, have assumed advocacy roles on behalf of consumers, and that private groups like White Dot have started weighing in. White Dot has even developed a turnkey campaign for community groups to wage protests against TVs in public places.

"Show owners of restaurants and cafes that TV may be losing them customers," says the organization in the material on its campaign. "Start a conversation about noise pollution, image pollution, and public spaces. Suggest to owners they use a TV-free atmosphere to attract customers. Show that ordinary customers are wise to the way TV is being pushed at them. Tell people about the new and growing industry in 'captive-audience television.' Show that ordinary customers hate being a captive audience."

What these groups like White Dot have done is put two and two together to challenge the unrestrained growth of captive-audience environments. The groups say TV isn't a cognitively neutral way to deliver information to people but is a medium linked to developmental problems in children and possibly even in adults. On the basis of these connections they make clear that it's the height of irresponsibility for anyone with an interest in the quality of life in the public sphere to sit back and permit the unrestrained growth of TV in the common spaces that we rely on most — buses, stores, gas stations, elevators, and so on, because to do so is to relinquish our right to exercise autonomy in our common spaces.

The Wrong Way to Fight

Whatever side of the issue you fall on, the kind of activism represented by Commercial Alert and other public interest groups on behalf of our quality of life in the public sphere is healthy. No one would take issue with people's right to organize and educate others about the balance of rights that are at stake when people are being exposed to electronic content they've not asked for.

But not all is productive in the approach being taken by responsible-TV advocates.

The problem advocates face going forward is a loss of the moral high ground as more people, taking the battle against captive-audience environments into their own hands, use morally ambiguous methods of protest. I'm thinking specifically of the popular rise of the "empowerment" or "annoyancetech" gadgets we talked about early on, TV-B-Gone and other devices like it, that enable people rightly upset over the encroachment of TV to take matters into their own hands.

TV-B-Gone is arguably the most well-known of these universal remote devices that empower people to shut off many types of TVs from a distance, and clandestinely. For people in a captive-audience environment, the device gives them a powerful — and tempting — way to fight back. You take away from us (our autonomy) and we take away from you (your control). And certainly the huge popularity of TV-B-Gone should be, if anything, a wake-up call to media companies and their clients that trouble is brewing. If the rise of these empowerment devices doesn't alert them to the negative effect their systems have on people, then they're proceeding with very dangerous blinders on.

Almost entirely on the basis of word of mouth, TV-B-Gone since its introduction only a handful of years ago has sold more than a million units in North America and Europe, and its inventor, Mitch Altman, has become a popular speaker at schools and anti-TV events around the country and abroad and has become something of a folk hero.

"Thank you for giving me the power to control what pops on other people's TV while I have my kids with me," says one enthusiast in a testimonial on the TV-B-Gone Web site. "Bless you!"

"I can turn off the continuous pharmaceutical ad video that runs in [my doctor's] waiting room on the big screen TV that nobody watches," another person says. "That's one of many annoying TVs I encounter that I can now do something about, thanks to your product."

"The thrill of going into a mall and being able to shut up the TVs will be a ... delight," another person says.

But the use of the device must give pause to even fierce opponents of captive-audience environments because in its use one is effectively fighting one incursion into someone's rights with another, and in doing that anti-TV activists risk ceding the moral high ground to their detractors. Think of environmental activists who torch new-home developments in the outlying suburbs. Although their tactics are clearly of a different magnitude (destructive violence against property vs. the harmless turning off of a TV), the two activities represent violations of people's property rights.

While many people would agree with the environmental activists' concerns over the destruction of unspoiled land to accommodate large, look-alike houses, the radical tactics of the activists victimizes the developers and turns people's sympathies away from the activists' legitimate concerns. Not only is such activism wrong but it represents bad PR.

In the same way, whatever one thinks of a business owner's decision to mount TVs in his restaurant dining room, it's simply a violation of the owner's rights to turn off his TV. As one critic said in an online debate with a TV-B-Gone supporter, use of the device is a passive-aggressive attack on the personal property rights of another. In fact, the person said, the only legitimate response to invasive TV in a private-property setting is to ask permission — from the owner or manager and from other patrons — if there are any objections to turning the TV off.

You're "very much a coward for using a device to turn off TVs secretly instead of having a conversation with the people who are authorized to turn it on or off," the commenter said. "It's not your property; you have no right at all to manipulate it. If you don't want to be exposed to it, remove yourself from the situation."

Nor would looking at the conflict in a public setting like a subway car or a bus rather than a private setting like a restaurant change the moral dynamic of using of the device, because the same issues apply. The public entity that governs the space is empowered by the people it represents to manage that space as it deems fit in its wisdom, and when its actions are deemed in fact not to be wise, the only appropriate recourse by its constituents is to effect change in the public entity and its policies, through voting and advocacy efforts, not to take what you might call "extra-legal" action by what amounts to vandalizing the TVs.

To its credit, the company that makes TV-B-Gone makes clear that, although people might use it for "philosophical or practical" reasons, the device is for amusement and the company encourages people to use it in that spirit.

The use of universal remotes like TV-B-Gone as a defense mechanism against intrusive media is a minor point today, but it won't be tomorrow. As we've seen, the use of such devices is rising rapidly, and so too are the patent applications for more such devices. As we talked about earlier, some 400,000 "annoyancetech" applications were submitted to the U.S. Patent Office just in 2006, according to a report in *The Wall Street Journal*. The report said that that number represents a doubling over 10 years. "These devices are ... a way for people to bridge the gap between the birth of a new form of annoyance ... and the point at which lawmakers finally organize a response," the article says.

So, the stage is being set for something like a guerrilla war, in which on the one hand you have for-profit and nonprofit interests deploying captive-audience platforms to force their messaging onto people while on the other hand you have people in increasing numbers wielding a clandestine device to sabotage these efforts. Thus, incursion is being used to fight incursion. This is not the way to address this mounting conflict.

Chapter 8. What It All Boils Down to: Users v. Stewards

There's no shortage of reports lamenting the drop in visits to our national parks and other open spaces by families. With their fingers pointing to television, the Internet, video games, and personal digital devices like the iPhone Touch, the critics say children today are losing touch with the natural world because of the compelling attraction of the virtual one.

"One little boy said the reason he preferred playing indoors was that's where all the electrical outlets are," says Richard Louv, author of *Last Child in the Woods* (Algonquin Books: 2005). "I heard that kind of thing over and over. And the parents were saying, 'I don't understand — how come the kids won't go outside?'" Louv was interviewed in *Grist*, an environmental news journal.

But there are two groups of constituents who still flock to the national parks and other public open space: the lovers of the outdoors looking for solace in the trails that wind their way through acres of unspoiled land, and their nemesis, the adventurers looking for excitement in tearing through the unspoiled land in their all-terrain vehicles.

The conflict between these two users of our public land is legion. Countless articles have been written and bookshelves of reports have been filed on how to manage our public parks and forests in a way that meets the needs of these two very different — and always conflicting — constituencies.

Mike Eisenfeld, an environmentalist interviewed by the *Washington Post* in mid-2008 for a piece on the topic, says the problem has gotten so bad in national parkland that it's a good day when conflict *doesn't* erupt. "If you're out there, just about every time you'll run into off-road vehicle conflict," he says.

"Anything goes," a U.S. Bureau of Land Management official says in the same article.

I mention this tension because this type of conflict represents a textbook case of what happens when you have competing claims to a scarce resource. On the one hand you have the "users," the adventurers who say the land is there for the public to enjoy and their choice is to enjoy it from the seat of an ATV, and on the other hand you have the "stewards," who say the noise from the ATV and its destructive wear and tear on the land prevents others from enjoying the environment.

We see this same dynamic between users and stewards when it comes to boom cars and outdoor rooms. The boom-car owners, like the ATV riders, are living life large and "consuming" the shared resource of our soundscape for their own ends but in the process impeding the ability of others to use that resource. Theirs is a lusty attitude toward what they're doing, calling someone who takes umbrage at their actions a "sad case," as one of the critics of anti-boom car activist Michael Wright called him in an e-mail. In a word, their response to every objection is the same: get over your problem with what we're doing or go somewhere else.

The same idea about "consuming" a shared resource can be said of the owners of outdoor rooms, because if I'm watching TV on a 65-inch screen with the volume set high enough for me to hear the program from across my swimming pool, then I'm "consuming" the viewscape and soundscape that I share with you, my neighbor, even though you might find the picture and the sound distracting while you try to garden or read a book.

What's different about the captive-audience business model is that it institutionalizes this user-steward conflict over shared resources by holding out a financial reward to those who commandeer the resources for commercial or institutional ends. By adding in this financial incentive, it sets the stage for an intractable split between users and stewards because now the stakes aren't just personal — my lifestyle over your lifestyle — but economic: my livelihood over your lifestyle. As media executive William Jeakle has said, "Even if people complain about [audience captivity], that wouldn't be enough to shut it down, because it meets your advertisers' target audience." Jeakle helped develop the CNN Airport Network, the company that provides the content for the TVs that are ubiquitous in airport gates.

To be clear, commercialization of space that we share in common with others is not at issue when we talk about concerns over captive-audience environments. Commercialism and common space have long coexisted peacefully and will continue to coexist peacefully for as long as people will need information about products and services. Captive-audience environments are different altogether because they succeed precisely by making such coexistence impossible.

THE USURPATION OF AUTONOMY

In 1953, a year after the U.S. Supreme Court voted to allow commercial radio on public transit in Washington, D.C., with William O. Douglas dissenting and Felix Frankfurter abstaining, Ray Bradbury published his story "The Murderer" in an anthology called *The Golden Apples of the Sun*. The story is about a man, driven to the edge of sanity, living in a transparently familiar world in which piped-in music, TV, and other electronic media play in every corner of the world. It's only after the man begins destroying the media devices as he comes across them, gets arrested, and then is sent to an isolation cell that he regains his equanimity. By the time a psychiatrist questions him, the man is perfectly content to live out his life in his cell, because as the only media-free environment left, it's the only place in which his mind can be free.

Brock: *"I am that thing called a minority. I did join fraternities, picket, pass petitions, take it to court. Year after year I protested. Everyone laughed. Everyone else loved bus radios and commercials. I was out of step."*

Psychiatrist: *"Then you should have taken it like a good soldier, don't you think? The majority rules."*

Brock: *"But they went too far. If a little music and 'keeping in touch' was charming, they figured a lot would be ten times as charming"* — Brock and the psychiatrist in "The Murderer," by Ray Bradbury.

It's probably not a coincidence that the Supreme Court decision and Bradbury's story came out a year apart from one another. What "The Murderer" suggests is that Bradbury saw what the court, with the exception of Justices Douglas and Frankfurter, clearly could not: that audience captivity is an issue about liberty in the broadest sense. In a world in which captive-audience media is accepted in one environment, it is accepted in all environments, because the two debates that govern audience captivity — what constitutes a voluntary environment and what constitutes acceptable content — are irresolvable. To open the door to any captive-audience media platform is thus to open the door to all of them, and we see the result of that open door today with even children in public schools and on public school buses not exempt from media captivity.

The world that Bradbury foreshadows is indeed upon us, as regular business travelers to our big metropolitan areas already know. After riding to the airport in a cab with TV, you wait beneath a TV at the terminal gate, sit before a TV in the airplane, are welcomed to the hotel by a TV in the lobby, watch TV in the elevator up to your room, are given more TV at the lounge or restaurant at dinner, and then are welcomed to the office the next day for a meeting by another TV in the building lobby.

The life-pattern marketing talked about by Monte Zweben of SeeSaw Networks is clearly far along in the business travel industry, and it is steadily making its inroads into every other facet of consumer, business, and social life today.

It's hard to imagine that the Boston office employees, when they gave their okay to Captivate Network's elevator TV field test in 2001, or when consumers voted favorably for Premier Retail Network's checkout TV in 2007, knew that they were giving their endorsement to TV at all times and in all places.

It is similarly hard to imagine that the commuters who had a favorable opinion of commercial radio on Washington, D.C.'s rail system in 1953 anticipated that the door would one day be open to audience captivity where they shop for groceries, buy their shoes, get their shirts laundered, do their banking, and walk their dog. Would they have been so sanguine about it had they reason to believe in the inevitability of Bradbury's darkly rendered world?

SIGNING THE ULTIMATE PACT

We take it for granted that escape from unwanted media is just a personal decision away, that we have it within our control to choose, as many successful businesspeople, cultural leaders, and individuals have, to turn off the TV and start living.

Indeed, the literature of people who've given up TV and other immersive media and found a renewed sense of life and purpose is extensive.

"People are often surprised when I tell them that (one of my best decisions) was my decision to quit watching TV," says Jeffrey Strain, who with a partner launched a popular personal finance Web site a few years ago and now talks extensively about how much income people lose by spending their downtime in front of the television. "For most people, TV is a habit that costs in excess of $1 million over a lifetime, or the equivalent of a healthy retirement account."

"What's TV worth? Nothing," says David Piccione, a project manager in Vancouver, B.C., who's written about pulling the TV plug. "I don't miss it in the least. What's changed is that my nights are longer, I've been much more productive, I've spent more time with my son, I've read more, and I've had some great Scrabble games."

Yet the pervasiveness of TV and other digital media platforms throughout the places in which we conduct the business of our lives makes a mockery of the idea that we control our destiny when it comes to media consumption.

The business model of place-based TV and other captive-audience media is precisely to take this self-empowerment away from us. As the one CBS executive has said, "We're looking for places we can be intrusive," where "you can't turn us off."

In a sense, people have become only too good at avoiding TV and so now the media companies have armed themselves with their out-of-home strategies so they can take their TV messages to where the people are.

"We are the one unavoidable medium," says Stephen Freitas of the Outdoor Advertising Association of America. "There is no mute button, no off switch.

You can't change the channel. We're there. It's a medium that isn't controlled by consumers."

"You cannot not look," says video signage consultant Lyle Bunn.

On its face the idea of capturing people and holding them hostage while force-feeding them content is a morally dubious business plan, to say the least. To give them their due, though, supporters of audience captivity say that all they're trying to do is give people relevant content in a place where people can be expected to be receptive to it. "Let's face it, in some of the places [where placed-based TV is located] it's boring," Fred Margolin, a media company executive, says in a *TV Week* interview. "We are entertaining them." He was speaking about TVs in cafeterias and restaurants, but his point applies to all place-based TV environments.

Aside from the patronizing character of this view, it's worth wondering if place-based media executives ever consider that some people enjoy the company of their own thoughts, and indeed don't find media-free environments boring for just that reason? As one critic says of TVs in the checkout lines at grocery stores, "I'd much prefer to zone out or scan the tabloids than have some obnoxious advertising blaring at me. Can't we go anywhere and have it be QUIET? Sometime I like to hear my own thoughts, amazingly enough."

But be that as it may, people do like their electronic media. Indeed, when you consider that people watch TV on average 4.5 hours a day, a strong case can be made that people *love* their TV (or at least are addicted to it, as Robert Kubey and Mihaly Csikszentmihalyi suggest they might be) and certainly they seem to prefer it far more than reading. So, when it comes to moving TV outside the home and into the world at large, what's not to like?

But even more importantly, supporters say, each of us is ultimately in control of whether we consume the content or not. As William Jeakle of CNN Airport TV has put it, some people will be "putting on headphones and listening to their iPods and reading the *Wall Street Journal*" rather than tuning into the TVs.

A *Wired* reader in an online forum goes one step further than Jeakle by saying responsibility to block out unwanted distractions in today's distracting world is the responsibility of each of us:

"City noise is 'real-people' noise. Deal with it. If you are not sophisticated enough to carry your own personal society-blocking devices such as headphones, earpieces, and hand-held distraction devices, than you deserve to be emotionally upended by the chaos that is modern civilization. Society is numerous and expansive. You are only one. No one is stopping you from shutting it out by carrying a personal seclusion system. But going without one and opening yourself up to the rawness that is the urban-suburban experience is your choice. There is no default. You must choose. Do not expect the world to make you happy and change on your whim. You must intervene and choose how the experience of the world infiltrates you, be it loud and unadorned or filtered through headphones, iPhones, and euro-glasses."

Without addressing whether carrying an iPod must now become a civic duty, it remains the case that people *can't* simply tune this content out because of the invasive nature of the medium. As researchers have made clear, people are biologically disposed *not* to tune out a highly visual medium like TV, which is why so many people find the medium so compelling and even addicting and why media companies are pouring so much money into moving it outside the home. To say that people can simply tune out the unwanted electronic media is to pretend an entire body of empirical research on our involuntary "orienting response" to it doesn't exist.

Supporters also say people are at any rate free to leave a captive-audience environment and go where there are no TVs or audio streaming, but of course that claim is disinguous on its face when you're talking about airport terminals, commercial restrooms, doctors' offices, or transit systems. These and other environments are attractive to media companies precisely because the opportunity cost to avoid them is so high that people put up with the invasive character of the media because they can't afford the cost of finding an alternative environment. There are only so many choices for people who are taking a flight or using a transit system or even using a restroom in a restaurant.

At the end of the day, what the growth projections for captive-audience environments tell us is that much of the world in which we do the bulk of our living is being systematically turned over to media companies — companies like NBC Everywhere, CBS Outernet, and the CNN Airport Network — who by their own admission are seeking to exploit people's inability to tune them out, and it doesn't take a leap of imagination to see where this is going. Yes, I can turn off the TV in my home — as former President George W. Bush encouraged us to do in a 2004 speech and as Democratic presidential nominee Barack Obama did on the campaign trail in 2008. I can also spend TV-free time at a public park with my children as our cultural and religious leaders encourage us to do.

But once I leave these enclaves and move into the part of the world where much of my public and commercial life takes place, the freedom to make that choice is increasingly withheld from me.

If this intrusion on my autonomy was limited to the places where I'm willing to consider a trade-off — a bar for a beer — then I would have to agree with captive-audience supporters that I should stop wringing my hands and just enjoy the program.

But in the years to come, when we can no longer do much of our business in a TV-free environment, then the price we'll be paying to just enjoy the program will be too high for us to accept, because that price will be a Mephistophelean pact with chaos.

For people like Jean Lotus, the White Dot founder, or others who've made a personal choice to give up or limit TV, I doubt that's a pact they would be willing to sign.

In the end, it's unlikely they'll have to. What we've seen is that, over time, stewards don't remain passive for long in the face of egregious consumption of scarce resources by users. The laws regulating secondhand smoke that swept the U.S. and Europe in the last decade are certainly a highly visible and recent example of stewardship winning out over consumption. The growth of in-house policies on cell phone use is another example. Here it's not government so much as private businesses like movie theaters and restaurants that are imposing restrictions in response to complaints of their customers. Even the growth in laws regulating boom cars and other invasive noises, like leaf blowers and lawn mowers, attest to the compelling case stewards are able to make over time.

Thus, the pattern that emerges is fairly clear: the users have their way only while the most sensitive complain about the loss of a shared resource, but once a critical mass of people sensitive to that loss is reached, the tide turns and the momentum shifts from the users to the stewards. We see this pattern writ large in our conflicts over the environment, from air quality to water quality to endangered species, and we see it writ small in our conflicts over our neighborhood viewscapes and soundscapes.

We are sure to see this pattern emerge yet again as more of us realize the extent to which places free of electronic content have become an increasingly scarce resource in our world.

Chapter 9. What Does a Responsible-Media Environment Look Like?

In a perfect world, people would not be forced to consume audio or video media they haven't asked for. Yet even the most strident critic of audience captivity must realize we've come awfully far as a society to realistically hope we can go back. When so much technical innovation is moving in one direction, the idea of compelling society to apply the brakes and dismantle the rapidly expanding infrastructure of captive-audience media must seem naive. Too many billions of dollars have been invested, too many people are too habituated to consuming intrusive media, and too much of our country's economic growth in the years ahead is organized around growing out-of-home media networks. To stop it suddenly is, if not pure fantasy, then at least a very complicated and controversial proposition. In the same way that our world has become organized around the automobile and all that goes with it, our world increasingly is organized around audio–video communication and the pressure for that communication to spread to every nook and cranny of our world is too great to stop. In short, increasingly we're a society of addicts of audio–video media and our world is organizing itself to accommodate that habit.

Yet to acknowledge this reality isn't to accept defeat. Rather, it's to take a first step toward moderating it.

We don't have to face an either–or situation. Thanks to many of the same innovations that made growth of captive-audience media platforms possible, we have today the technological tools to restrict "push" media to those who want it while respecting the wishes of those who don't. Mixing this technology with reasonable regulations will go a long way to accommodating everyone in a world of media everywhere.

THE NEW WORLD OF CONSENSUAL CAPTIVITY

When the Central Wisconsin Airport in Mosinee, Wis., replaced obsolete advertising kiosks in its terminals two years ago, it did something that not only opened up additional doors for advertisers but surely made at least some harried passersby breathe a sigh of relief. Although the new kiosks actually tripled the number of digital advertisements, each with its own audio, they did so while limiting the audio footprint to just a small area immediately before the screens. The result: the audio is available only to those who want it. The technological innovation underwriting this new approach is what engineers call directional audio.

Directional audio is just one of a host of technological tools that are coming on the market today that promise to change the audience captivity dynamic significantly. These technologies include not only directional audio but privacy filters, dual-view screens, and active noise cancellation transducers, among others. These tools used in combination with one another offer a way for us to control what we see on a screen and hear from a speaker. When incorporated into platforms for captive-audience media, they make it possible for both sides of the communication equation to get what they want: with those doing the communicating getting their messaging out and those being communicated to deciding whether or not to consume that messaging. Thus, the balance between message and audience is restored to a "pull" media dynamic similar to what we have with print media, in which control appropriately returns to the audience.

To be sure, engineers are looking at years of effort to refine what's available today, but it is important that all of the technologies underlying what we might call consensual captivity platforms are already in place today. There is nothing hypothetical about any of these solutions:

Privacy Filters

Imagine you are a marketing executive for a software firm and that you're under the gun to finish a presentation about an application your company has under development. Your presentation is sensitive; there are dozens of companies that would love to know how far along your company is, because they're in the same market. For that reason, finishing the presentation on your laptop while in-flight to a meeting poses risk, yet not to have it completed isn't an option. What do you do?

Well, these days you can cover your laptop screen with a film so that anyone looking at your screen from an angle sees nothing but black, while your view is normal.

"Shuffle sideways and the screen quickly starts to darken to obscurity at its far extremity," says technology writer Tony Smith, who's taken the technology for a test drive. "The whole thing [goes] dark before your viewing angle is 45 degrees from full-on."

The film, which uses what its manufacturer calls "microlouver" technology, is comprised of two thin layers: one to absorb light and the other, like a louver in a window, to control it. 3M, the big Minnesota technology company that holds the patent, has been marketing the film for laptop privacy for years. But the product's applications are as infinite as the imagination and as our reliance on screens outside the home increases, the stage is set to multiply the ways this technology is used.

Already the film is migrating to desktop units, including those with wide screens, as well as to handheld devices. And since the film has no effect on screen clarity from the front, it can be seamlessly applied to out-of-home video monitors. When applied to screens in common spaces, the film makes it possible for a room to be organized into viewing space (in front) and non-viewing space (off to the sides).

Dual-View Screens

Closely related to this filtering is dual-screen technology that Sharp and other companies rolled out a few years ago, primarily to increase the usability of video screens in cars. Although the dual screens take an entirely different approach (hard-wired into the system rather than applied as a film), the effect can be very much the same. What you see on the screen depends on the angle from which you view it. In Sharp's version of the technology, the screen uses what it calls a parallax barrier mounted in front of the LCD panel. The barrier splits the direction of the backlight illumination on a per-pixel basis. "By arranging the 'parallax barrier,' it is possible to display more than three different images," a write-up in the technical trade journal *Tech Japan* says.

The screens are set to become fixtures in cars in just a few years; Mercedes and BMW have announced plans to offer them in some of their models as early as 2010. But what's important for our purposes isn't how the car manufacturers are using the screens. They're just making it possible for the GPS navigation screen to remain visible to the driver while a video shares the screen for the benefit of the passengers. Of broader interest is the availability of this technology for reaching the same end as the privacy filter: keeping screens in common areas dark when viewed at an angle and visible when viewed from the front.

Other uses are already in the works:
- a living room display that shows a PC screen from the left and a TV image from the right
- a display that shows a presentation to customers while showing internal information to a salesperson
- a display that shows one set of advertisements to passers-by from the left and a different set to those from the right
- a display that shows upper floor information to those going up an escalator and lower floor information to those going down

Add to this list the ability to black out the screens from an angle (Sharp already enables this in what it calls its "veil-view" application) and we may be on the road to screen technology that respects non-viewers as much as viewers.

Directional Audio

Of course, screen filtering is only half the equation. For critics of captive-audience media, the audio is equally unwelcome. This is where the directional audio technology that is in use at the Central Wisconsin Airport comes into play.

Directional audio works very much like a light beam, only with noise vibrations: Sound is projected in a narrow band and aimed at a target, so the audio is available to those directly in front of or beneath a speaker but not to those on either side of the speaker.

The audio beam generates super thin sound waves (ultrasonic) that vibrate at a range below what can be heard by the human ear. These silent sound waves can be controlled to vibrate at different levels, including levels that reach the threshold of audibility, about 20 Hz (or "Herz").

By determining which waves to vibrate at that threshold, engineers can direct the audio outward from the source while keeping it from expanding into the wider environment. It's not that there are no sound waves radiating out beyond the core of the sound beam; there are. But these waves vibrate at a rate below 20 Hz, outside the range of human hearing; only the waves directly in front of the source are fluctuated to vibrate above that threshold for audibility.

Thus it is possible to combine visual privacy filtering with directional audio to create a media platform that's engineered from the start with two audiences in mind: those who want the content and those who don't.

Audio writer Philip Hirz describes sound-beam technology this way: "Step into the beam, and the projected sound fills your ears; step out again, and you hear nothing."

Panphonics, a Finnish company that's deeply involved in directional audio and that provided the audio component to the advertising kiosks in the Wisconsin airport, is marketing its technology mainly as a way to combine multiple audio streams in a small space, as in the ad kiosk, without them drowning one another out, but it's also touting the technology as a way to keep surrounding areas quiet.

Directional audio can be focused to particular areas in open spaces, e.g., children's entertainment centers, the company says. The "elements can be used to complement other in-store media systems [such as] flat TV-screens; the directional audio can be focused only to the direct proximity of the screens."

For marketers, directional audio must be seen in every sense as an enhancement to anything they're doing today, even though it enables people to opt out of the audio environment, because the audio experience is structured to be much richer. Not only is the audio clarity capable of being far above the traditional audio experience, but the audio field can be engineered to keep other noises out, so the immersive character of the marketing experience can be far greater.

"Directional audio incorporated into the advertisements or screens significantly improves the stopping power of the visual advertisements," the company says in a white paper. "Due to the directivity of the sound, there are much less unwanted reflections and the overall audio environment can be made much more pleasant."

Active Sound Cancellation

Closely related to directional audio is new active sound cancellation technology, which, unlike traditional sound dampening (absorbent surfaces), restricts sound not by obstructing it but by using noise to turn itself off.

The idea of using what engineers call "anti-noise" to counteract noise has been around for years, but moving from the theoretical stage to the practical stage has not been easy and even today the technology hasn't caught up with its potential. But, importantly, the technology has evolved enough that companies are beginning to roll out commercial applications that point the way to a more peaceful future than what we face today.

To cancel out noise, engineers create the same noise in mirror-image form. That sounds abstract, but all it means is that new noise is created that has the identical amplitude of the old noise while also moving in opposite phase to the old noise. Amplitude refers to oscillations in atmospheric pressure (the sound waves we talked about in the part on directional audio), and phase is about timing. When the unwanted noise's oscillation is up, you want the oscillation of the mirror-image noise to go down, and vice versa. Noise cancellation is total when the noise and its anti-noise are in perfect opposition to one another.

The difficulty for audio engineers is creating a system in which perfect opposition in noise is maintained over time when the unwanted noise is infinitely variable. Thus, in a laboratory, it's not hard to create perfect opposition to a simple an unchanging noise, like a hum. But when the system is moved into the real world, where noise is ever-changing, both in amplitude and in phase, then the challenge is obvious.

Given the limited availability of solutions, audio companies have been using a mix of active and traditional passive elements to create a hybrid form of noise cancellation. This approach is used today in the high-end headphones and ear buds for personal stereos. In these hybrid approaches, active sound cancellation is used for noise at certain audio frequencies (such as 50 Hz and above) while passive noise dampening (the absorbent-padding approach) is used for more extreme frequencies (such as those above 500 Hz).

Although not perfect, these hybrid noise control solutions, when they're applied in combination with directional audio, provide the pieces to create dramatically more comfortable audio environments. In a captive-audience media setting, crystal clear audio can be made available to those who want it while an audio-neutral environment is there for those who don't. Not only is a portion of the area kept audio free, but the audio in the area designated for audio is free of intruding ambient noise, thereby giving the audio even more impact. Thus, it's a win for marketers and at the same time a win for consumers who prefer quiet.

APPLYING RULES TO SEED SOLUTIONS

The benefits of these technologies seem clear, and yet, left to their own devices, the media companies driving the introduction of captive-audience media platforms are unlikely to jump on them any time soon. It's safe to say that their business models depend on expanding their viewership as much as possible. Indeed, Arbitron and Nielsen, the audience-counting companies, both launched programs in the past couple of years to measure out-of-home media audiences, enabling networks to show advertisers just how large their audiences are. These media companies are not likely to suddenly shift way from full-throttle growth to accommodate non-viewers, even if a case can be made that it's in their long-term interest to make their platforms compatible with the preferences of non-viewers as well as those of viewers.

Yet it's best to be cautious before suggesting a regulatory approach to address audience captivity. As we saw, the Supreme Court is split on the issue: In the commuter train case it found that audience captivity is okay because consent is given tacitly, while in the sound truck case it found that such captivity isn't okay — or, at least, is appropriately subject to local regulation without running afoul of the Constitution — because consent is never given, tacitly or otherwise.

That said, the rules for restricting secondhand smoke certainly serve as a model if we want to press for regulatory changes. Today, states have laws on the books restricting where people can smoke, and we can extrapolate from there. Indeed, advocates for a number of causes have pointed to secondhand-smoke restrictions in pushing for rules for curbing any number of nuisances, including those that involve bottled water (which depletes public aquifers and chokes landfills), perfume (to which many people are allergic), and flights over urban areas (they make a lot of noise).

While the details of each situation will vary, it's clear that, unless and until hard data are available to show the harmfulness of exposure to unwanted noise — both audio noise and visual noise — in environments in which people can't escape except at steep opportunity cost, no secondhand-smoke type regulation is going to be enacted. It took lawmakers decades, reams of empirical data, class-action lawsuits, and, at least according to one critic,* a little stretching of the truth to rein in secondhand smoke; to expect lawmakers to tackle audio and visual noise — a far more subjective ill — without the scale of support for con-

---

*Christopher Snowdon in *Velvet Glove, Iron Fist: A History of Anti-Smoking* (2009: Little Dice) looks at instances in which advocates ramped up arguments in linking ills to secondhand smoke.

trolling secondhand smoke — is unrealistic. This is particularly the case in the private sector: the day that restaurant owners are told to rein in the TVs just isn't coming, nor should it necessarily be coming.

As such, any nod to critics of captive-audience media from restaurant owners and others in the private sector will have to come voluntarily. Only when it's clearly seen to be in their best interests will restaurant owners and others integrate consensual captivity technology into their captive-audience platforms. Nothing speaks louder than consumers taking their business elsewhere. That, and only that, will spur change.

And yet there are environmental pockets in which it's appropriate for the public sector to step in. Let's take a look at just a few of them as a way to get a sense of what possible solutions are available to us, not just for explicit, commercial captive-audience platforms but for all types of captivity, including inadvertent captivity posed by the personal media technology we looked at earlier, such as outdoor rooms.

Public Space: Where My Tax Dollars Are at Work

Imagine for a moment that on a drive across the country you come to a stretch of highway in which your radio automatically tunes to a station playing a mix of sports, music, entertainment, and commercials. A sign overhead explains that the revenue from the commercials is necessary to help pay for upgrades to that stretch of highway. Facing a shortage of federal highway funds, state lawmakers had issued bonds to raise capital and now those bonds need to be repaid.

There's nothing wrong with the programming; by any measure it's pretty innocuous stuff, if a bit pointless, not unlike much of the media noise that fills our environment. And of course we can always just ignore it. We can turn the radio off, listen to a CD instead, or just talk over it. Just because it's playing doesn't mean we have to attend to it.

Acceptable? Of course not. Few of us would allow the commandeering of our radio in this way to pay for a public project no matter how reasonable the purpose. There are too many alternatives, including tolls and taxes, to attain the same end, and in any case there's something unholy about the public sector using its power to issue mandates to privilege not only certain programming but also certain commercial interests.

And yet we acquiesce to this commandeering of our public space whenever we're forced to share space with TV or other commercial programming while waiting for a plane or while riding public transit.

To be sure, public environments are characterized by a multitude of media, not just what's playing on the overhead TV. At airports, people listen to music on personal stereos, watch videos on their laptop, and read the newspaper. But when all that is stripped away, the scenario is the same as in the car; the only difference is what you might call the optics. The airport environment gives the appearance of choice not because you have alternatives to the privileged programming but because other media are available to help you block it out. It's like being at a theater and being offered not a choice of movies but the option of reading a book, listening to your iPod, or watching a video on your laptop if you don't like what's playing. To have a real choice, you would need to be given the option of watching this movie or another movie.

To emphasize: blocking out privileged media is not the same as having alternatives to it; it's fighting noise with noise and, as in Cairo, that leads to only one endpoint: chaos.

People generally recognize the unholiness of privileging media in publicly subsidized settings. That's why that 1952 commuter bus case went all the way to the Supreme Court. It wasn't just that commuters were being held hostage to commercial programming but that the commercial programming was being broadcast on a publicly subsidized system. There's something wrong with the public sector giving its imprimatur to any kind of content that's not related without ambiguity to a public purpose.

It's for this reason that the one environment in which captive-audience media can and should be regulated is the public environment. That includes any type of transit environment that receives public money: airports as well as systems for buses, trains, and subways. It also includes streets and sidewalks, bus stops and other public "street furniture," parks, public buildings, including elevators, public works facilities, and publicly subsidized development projects such as stadiums and convention halls.

These settings clearly differ from one another in meaningful ways, and because of that, regulating captive-audience media in them must necessarily take different forms. But we can divide the different forms into two categories:

Those in which willing audiences and non-willing audiences can be equally accommodated and those in which they can't.

Equal Accommodation

The kinds of technology solutions we looked at above — privacy screen filters, dual-view screens, directional audio, and active sound cancellation — can appropriately be applied in settings where different audiences can be equally accommodated. Thus it makes sense to apply restrictions in the following settings:

Airports, including terminals and gates. Public regulation appropriately applies only to airports receiving public subsidy, so private airports would be excluded. And since the public subsidy applies to the airport facility and not to the airlines themselves, it would be inappropriate, and no doubt subject to challenge in court, to apply restrictions to the airlines themselves.

Bus, train, and subway systems. The mandated accommodation would be applicable to the stations as well as to the buses and cars. Private systems would be excluded.

Arenas and convention centers. Mandated accommodation would apply to these types of development projects only to the extent they're publicly subsidized. Accommodation would apply to concession areas, exhibit and performance space, restrooms, and the other settings in which people congregate.

Public office buildings. Lobbies would have to accommodate non-willing audiences, and elevators would have to be kept free of force-fed media because accommodating different users wouldn't be possible without segregating elevators, and that's impractical.

What would accommodation look like? Facility operators would be mandated to use consensual captivity technology such as privacy filters and directional audio to apportion space between willing and unwilling audiences, and this mandate would be applicable to any setting with captive-audience media. In an airport gate, content on TVs would be visible and audible only to persons seated in front of the sets. In a bus, it would be visible and audible only to persons in a designated row.

Which level of government would regulate? The appropriate level would be dictated by the source of the public subsidy. When subsidies come from multiple levels, as is the case in many transit systems and big-dollar projects, the jurisdiction would follow the same hierarchy as the rules for the subsidies.

What about the constitutionality question? After all, the commuter bus case was decided in favor of the captors, not the captives. The constitutionality of mandating accommodation is a decision for the High Court to decide. But what's clear is that the environment has changed considerably since 1952. Then, the issue was a single, novel instance of audience captivity. Today we're looking at audience captivity evolving into a principle of how we organize space. The differences are so extreme as to constitute substantively different things. What's more, today the technological means exist to accommodate willing and non-willing audiences. That's new.

Impractical Accommodation

Where accommodation of non-willing audiences isn't practical, it's appropriate to prohibit audience captivity entirely. Thus, captive-audience media would be prohibited on streets, sidewalks, bus stops and other street furniture, as well as in elevators in public and publicly subsidized buildings.

The argument against prohibition is that people can always go elsewhere or just cross the street but that's actually to argue the point rather than against it. Here you have pure public space: a public sidewalk or street. To dismiss the concerns of unwilling audiences is to relegate them to second-class citizenship. If you can't accommodate both, how can you justify making the one class go elsewhere and not the other? The only way to accommodate both is to prohibit it. We managed to live for generations without digital media on our streets; we can live for generations more without it. Any argument in favor of privileging audio and video media for willing audiences ultimately comes down to the law of the jungle: Might makes right. That may represent reality, but let's not pretend it's anything other than majority rules. There's no principle at work.

Inadvertent Captivity

Suggesting restrictions on captive-audience media when it touches upon individuals rather than institutions is always a sour task. The vitriol that answered the Oklahoma anti-boom car activist is a case in point. Anything that has even a whiff of nannyism is widely greeted with derision, dismissal, and hostility among critics, and it makes no difference that the goal — trying to accommodate a plurality of people — is positive.

Really, the only effective rule for accommodating people of different needs and sensitivity is common courtesy borne out of empathy. There has been a rash of articles in the major media in the last couple of years, many coming in the wake of disturbing acts of random violence, suggesting that empathy is on the wane. That's for others to decide, but in a world in which we can't take for granted courteous use of highly intrusive media, it's at least worth advocating for the appropriate use of consumer advisories.

We're already seeing some of this happening. In some examples we looked at earlier, USA Today publisher Al Neuharth is championing a cell phone courtesy month, the Mobile Enhancement Retailers Association is cautioning its members against encouraging the inflammatory use of boom car audio promotions, and private business owners are instituting policies on the use of personal media devices in theaters and restaurants, among other settings.

These and other examples show that popular sentiment eventually catches up to abusive uses of personal media, although it can take a while.

I would suggest that the next area to attract popular attention is outdoor rooms. Although outdoor rooms are off most people's radar screens today, as more people watch TV and listen to powerful stereos in the comfort of their backyards, the opportunity for conflict with neighbors escalates and the stage is set for the issue to gain popular attention in the same way rude cell phone use has.

If this conflict over outdoor rooms is inevitable, then the time to suggest a better way is now. It shouldn't be inappropriate to expect manufacturers of outdoor media hardware — TVs and stereos — to advise their customers to consume their media in a way that's sensitive to their neighbors. That's not asking much, yet it can accomplish a lot: making people aware that their media consumption doesn't happen in a vacuum.

AFTERWORD

History is written by the winners. Fifty years from now, when TV is everywhere and our population is comprised of children today who were weaned on TV in the backseat of their parents' car, the concern of responsible-TV advocates will be relegated to a footnote in some text on a media history Web resource. Or will it?

As Nassim Nicholas Taleb says in his insightful book *The Black Swan* (Random House: 2007), the most important elements in forecasting are the things we can't predict — the unknown unknowns, as U.S. Defense Secretary Donald Rumsfeld said during the early days of the Iraq war. Today, TV and other forms of electronic media are expanding to fill every nook and cranny with someone's messaging, and by all appearances will continue to do so into the foreseeable future. But tomorrow might be a different story. What I found from talking to people about this issue and researching it online and in print is that there are a lot of people unhappy with this trend. I can't imagine how you can profit long from a business model that causes people to describe their engagement with it as "torture" or "hell." That is not the way to build a loyal base of constituents.

We in the west have tasted freedom and would never tolerate despotic leaders who governed without democratic legitimacy. Why, then, would we tolerate despotic media that waits until we can't get away and then tells us which toothpaste to buy? Today media executives and other supporters of captive-audience environments are talking as if the battle for consumer attention is about to be won, but I suspect the battle really hasn't been joined yet because for most people it's not on their radar screen. But audience captivity could very well be on their radar soon.

Appendix I. Channel Inefficiencies: A Theory of Communication

I talk a lot about the differences between print and digital communications and why in the former the reader is in control of the communications while in the latter it's the communicator. How you feel about the contention that captive-audience environments are of a questionable moral character will likely depend on your view about autonomy in a communications relationship. To help further clarify the notion of autonomy in that relationship, I want to set out what to me is at the heart of communications, and what's at stake as we move from a print to a digital culture.

Confrontation with unwanted communications is a fact of life, a function of living with other people. What's different today is the explosion in tools that puts into our hands the means to encroach upon others at will with our communications and media choices. I can't encroach upon you by handing you a magazine, because you decide whether you'll read it or not. I can, however, encroach upon you if I play a radio or a TV near you, because the radio or TV content plays regardless of whether you want it to.

You can say that what underlies the difference between these two types of media is the channel in which they're consumed. The channel is closed for print, open for TV and radio (or any form of audio, for that matter).

The difference between a closed and open channel is one of degrees, not of kind, because print can be structured in such a way that it starts to resemble communications in an open environment, and TV or radio can be transmitted in a way that it resembles a closed environment.

For example, a large, illuminated print advertisement in an otherwise dim and uninteresting environment will share the characteristics of communications in an open environment because of the way it attracts attention involuntarily. It's virtually impossible for anyone in the environment to ignore it. By the same token, TV or radio that's played through headphones or ear buds will share the characteristics of communications in a closed environment because the content is only available to the person wearing the headset, assuming they're wearing the headset properly and keeping the volume at an appropriate level.

Of course, wearing a headset or a pair of ear buds only creates a closed channel of communication if the devices are worn properly or the volume is kept to a reasonable level, otherwise the audio spills out and creates the conditions characteristic of an open channel of communication. A letter by an unhappy commuter in the *Washington Post* on New Year's Day in 2009 illustrates this point nicely:

> "I've been riding Metro [the Washington, D.C., subway rail] for five years....While the vast majority of passengers are considerate of others, there are some who, while strictly following the rules ("use headphones with all audio and video devices") show no consideration for other passengers. They listen to such loud sounds ... through their headphones that anybody within three meters can hear their choice of music. I've seen Metro staff members ignore the offenders, but this is probably best, since who knows what could set someone off these days?"

— From "Wishes for 2009," *Washington Post*, Jan. 1, 2009, p. A12

What we might call channel *excess* and channel *insufficiency*, two terms we'll talk about presently, are features of both closed and open channels of communication, and it can be said that the marketing profession is the science of exploiting channel excess and avoiding channel insufficiency.

When marketers talk about ways of breaking through the clutter or noise with their message, they're essentially talking about ways to use channel excess to reach people in an open or a closed channel of communication and to avoid the danger of channel insufficiency.

Channel excess is the degree to which content spills out of the channel between itself and its consumer and reaches other people; channel insufficiency is the degree to which content fails to reach its consumer.

An example of channel excess can be seen on a bicycle trail. A bicyclist calling out "passing on your left" to another bicyclist sends a message in a relatively closed channel of communication. The message is only intended for the bicyclist being passed and, depending on how loudly the passing bicyclist calls out the message, it may only be heard by the intended recipient.

That's an efficient communication, because the message is transmitted only to its intended recipient. There's no overage or channel excess.

But if the bicyclist rings a bell on his handlebars instead of calling out "passing on your left," and if the bicycle bell is so loud that it makes other nearby bicyclists think the signal is intended for them, then you have a case of channel excess. The communication is inefficient, because it spills out of its intended channel (it was only meant for the one bicyclist) and reaches people for whom it wasn't intended. There's too much communication, you can say.

Channel insufficiency is inefficiency in the other direction, when a communication fails to reach its intended recipient. A good example is this book you hold in your hands. I've written this book to reach readers interested in media and its place in society. Regardless of how well or how poorly I've approached my topic, if no one obtains this book, opens it, and reads what's in it, my communication is insufficient because no one receives the content. In a sense, the communication channel is too closed; no information gets through.

From the standpoint of someone trying to send a message, whether that someone is a marketer promoting a brand of toothpaste or a writer advancing a theory of media and society, the better type of inefficiency, at least on its face, is excess rather than insufficiency. Why not err on the side of reaching as many people as possible? The only downside is that you'll alienate a portion of the people who find the communication an intrusion. By erring on the side of reaching too few people, by contrast, your only advantage is that the people you do reach will be favorably disposed to your communication, or at least not negatively disposed toward it, because their consumption of the message was driven entirely by themselves. That's a better environment for having people consume your message.

Regardless of which is the better approach, what's clear is that with the rise of digital communications the trend line is pointing in the direction of more channel excess rather than more channel insufficiency. That's because channel insufficiency is the hoary bugbear of print culture, the inescapable character of a communications ecology that is dominated by closed channels of communication, while channel excess is the hoary bugbear of digital culture, because digital culture is the culture of audio and video streaming anytime, anywhere, for any reason. And that is the inescapable character of a communications ecology that is dominated by open channels of communication.

We can say with some certainty, then, that if our past was all about getting people to read something, our future will be all about getting people to stop encroaching on us with things to watch and listen to. Hence the new scarcity, as we find it more difficult each day to find peace from the din of people whose communication encroaches upon us in ways over which we have no control.

APPENDIX II. DISSENT: JUSTICE DOUGLAS IN PUBLIC UTILITIES COMMISSION OF THE
DISTRICT OF COLUMBIA ET AL. V. POLLAK ET AL. *[343 U.S. 451 (1952)]*

The issue of audience captivity has been around for just about as long as popular mass media has been around, which says something about the universality of the desire of media companies to get their content in front of a captive audience. The issue came to a head in 1952, when the U.S. Supreme Court heard a case involving piped-in commercial radio on publicly funded commuter trains in Washington, D.C.

As I mention in the text, the issue was very much like today's issue over Bus-Radio, with the difference being that the latter involves children on school buses and the former the general commuting population.

Most people in a poll conducted at the time of the controversy favored continuation of the radio programming, which was mainly entertainment and announcements (only about 5 percent consisted of commercials), but the issue wasn't over the character of the content but over the constitutionality of subjecting the programming to the minority of people opposed to it. The question before the court was whether the radio constituted free speech and due process violations.

The court concluded that the programming didn't constitute such violations, but Associate Justice William O. Douglas put forth an eloquent dissent.

Also, Associate Justice Felix Frankfurter abstained on the grounds that he couldn't be objective because turning commuters into a captive audience, while apparently not unconstitutional, was abhorrent to him. As he says, "My feelings are so strongly engaged as a victim of the practice in controversy that I had better not participate in judicial judgment upon it."

For Douglas, the issue was about the meaning of liberty and whether subjecting people to media content over which they exercised no control constituted a violation of their liberty. In his mind, when liberty is construed in its broadest terms, it does. Here's his dissent in its entirety:

> This is a case of first impression. There are no precedents to construe; no principles previously expounded to apply. We write on a clean slate.
>
> The case comes down to the meaning of "liberty" as used in the Fifth Amendment. Liberty in the constitutional sense must mean more than freedom from unlawful governmental restraint; it must include privacy as well, if it is to be a repository of freedom. The right to be let alone is indeed the beginning of all freedom. Part of our claim to privacy is in the prohibition of the Fourth Amendment against unreasonable searches and seizures. It gives the guarantee that a man's home is his castle beyond invasion either by inquisitive or by officious people. A man loses that privacy of course when he goes upon the streets or enters public places. But even in his activities outside the home he has immunities from controls

bearing on privacy. He may not be compelled against his will to attend a religious service; he may not be forced to make an affirmation or observe a ritual that violates his scruples; he may not be made to accept one religious, political, or philosophical creed as against another. Freedom of religion and freedom of speech guaranteed by the First Amendment give more than the privilege to worship, to write, to speak as one chooses; they give freedom not to do nor to act as the government chooses. The First Amendment in its respect for the conscience of the individual honors the sanctity of thought and belief. To think as one chooses, to believe what one wishes are important aspects of the constitutional right to be let alone.

If we remembered this lesson taught by the First Amendment, I do not believe we would construe "liberty" within the meaning of the Fifth Amendment as narrowly as the Court does. The present case involves a form of coercion to make people listen. The listeners are of course in a public place; they are on streetcars traveling to and from home. In one sense it can be said that those who ride the streetcars do so voluntarily. Yet in a practical sense they are forced to ride, since this mode of transportation is today essential for many thousands. Compulsion which comes from circumstances can be as real as compulsion which comes from a command.

The streetcar audience is a captive audience. It is there as a matter of necessity, not of choice. One who is in a public vehicle may not of course complain of the noise of the crowd and the babble of tongues. One who enters any public place sacrifices some of his privacy. My protest is against the invasion of his privacy over and beyond the risks of travel.

The government may use the radio (or television) on public vehicles for many purposes. Today it may use it for a cultural end. Tomorrow it may use it for political purposes. So far as the right of privacy is concerned the purpose makes no difference. The music selected by one bureaucrat may be as offensive to some as it is soothing to others. The news commentator chosen to report on the events of the day may give overtones to the news that please the bureau head but which rile the streetcar captive audience. The political philosophy which one radio speaker exudes may be thought by the official who makes up the streetcar programs to be best for the welfare of the people. But the man who listens to it on his way to work in the morning and on his way home at night may think it marks the destruction of the Republic.

One who tunes in on an offensive program at home can turn it off or tune in another station, as he wishes. One who hears disquieting or unpleasant programs in public places, such as restaurants, can get up and leave. But the man on the streetcar has no choice but to sit and listen, or perhaps to sit and to try not to listen.

When we force people to listen to another's ideas, we give the propagandist a powerful weapon. Today it is a business enterprise working out a radio program under the auspices of government. Tomorrow it may be a dominant political or religious group. Today the purpose is benign; there is no invidious cast to the programs. But the vice is inherent in the system.

Once *privacy* is invaded, privacy is gone. Once a man is forced to submit to one type of radio program, he can be forced to submit to another. It may be but a short step from a cultural program to a political program.

If liberty is to flourish, government should never be allowed to force people to listen to any radio program. The right of privacy should include the right to pick and choose from competing entertainments, competing propaganda, competing political philosophies. If people are let alone in those choices, the right of privacy will pay dividends in character and integrity. The strength of our system is in the dignity, the resourcefulness, and the independence of our people. Our confidence is in their ability as individuals to make the wisest choice. That system cannot flourish if regimentation takes hold. The right of privacy, today violated, is a powerful deterrent to anyone who would control men's minds.

You can read the case in its entirety online at *http://caselaw.lp.findlaw.com/scripts/getcase.pl?court=us&vol=343&invol=451.*

APPENDIX III. DECISION: KOVACS V. COOPER *[336 U.S. 77 (1949)]*

Just a few years prior to the commuter train ruling, the dissent from which is reproduced above, the U.S. Supreme Court ruled on an equally important but quite different type of captive-audience case, and in this instance decided in favor of the captives rather than the captors.

The court said the city of Trenton, N.J., had acted within the constitution when it imposed an ordinance prohibiting the use of sound trucks (any vehicles with external loudspeakers) as a method for delivering content to city residents. The court made it clear that the prohibition doesn't violate our right to free speech because what's being regulated isn't the content of the speech but the mode of delivery. Allowing anyone at any time to drive around town to broadcast their "speech" would create intolerable conditions for residents, because unlike with printed material, such speech doesn't allow for people to decide whether or not they want to consume it.

As the court says, "The unwilling listener is not like the passer-by who may be offered a pamphlet in the street but cannot be made to take it. In his home or on the street, he is practically helpless to escape this interference with his privacy by loudspeakers except through the protection of the municipality."

You can say that, unlike in the commuter train case, residents haven't given their tacit agreement to be made captive to the content, so the force-fed communication isn't unconditionally protected under the constitution. Thus, from the standpoint of captive-audience media, the ruling is clear that consent is required before you can push out your content to people.

Here's the decision in its entirety with references and footnotes removed.

U.S. Supreme Court
Kovacs v. Cooper, 336 U.S. 77 (1949)
Submitted October 11, 1948
Decided January 31, 1949

Syllabus

An ordinance of Trenton, New Jersey, forbids the use or operation on the public streets of a "sound truck" or of any instrument which emits "loud and raucous noises" and is attached to a vehicle on the public streets.

Held: As applied to the defendant in this case, it does not infringe the right of free speech in violation of the First Amendment, made applicable to the states by the Fourteenth Amendment.

Appellant was convicted in police court for violation of an ordinance of Trenton, New Jersey.

The New Jersey Supreme Court upheld the conviction, and the Court of Errors and Appeals affirmed by an equally divided court. On appeal to this court, affirmed.

Mr. Justice Reed announced the judgment of the court and an opinion in which the chief justice and Mr. Justice Burton join.

This appeal involves the validity of an ordinance provision of the city of Trenton, New Jersey. It reads as follows:

"That it shall be unlawful for any person, firm or corporation, either as principal, agent or employee, to play, use or operate for advertising purposes, or for any other purpose whatsoever, on or upon the public streets, alleys or thoroughfares in the city of Trenton, any device known as a sound truck, loudspeaker or sound amplifier, or radio or phonograph with a loudspeaker or sound amplifier, or any other instrument known as a calliope or any instrument of any kind or character which emits therefrom loud and raucous noises and is attached to and upon any vehicle operated or standing upon said streets or public places aforementioned."

The appellant was found guilty of violating this ordinance by the appellee, a police judge of the city of Trenton. His conviction was upheld by the New Jersey Supreme Court, and the judgment was affirmed without a majority opinion by the New Jersey Court of Errors and Appeals in an equally divided court.

We took jurisdiction to consider the challenge made to the constitutionality of the section on its face and as applied on the ground that §1 of the Fourteenth Amendment of the United States Constitution was violated because the section and the conviction are in contravention of rights of freedom of speech, freedom of assemblage, and freedom to communicate information and opinions to others. The ordinance is also challenged as violative of the Due Process Clause of the Fourteenth Amendment on the ground that it is go obscure, vague, and indefinite as to be impossible of reasonably accurate interpretation. No question was raised as to the sufficiency of the complaint.

At the trial in the Trenton police court, a city patrolman testified that, while on his post, he heard a sound truck broadcasting music. Upon going in the direction of said sound, he located the truck on a public street near the municipal building. As he approached the truck, the music stopped and he heard a man's voice broadcasting from the truck. The appellant admitted that he operated the mechanism for the music and spoke into the amplifier. The record from the police court does not show the purpose of the broadcasting, but the opinion in the Supreme Court suggests that the appellant was using the sound apparatus to comment on a labor dispute then in progress in Trenton.

The contention that the section is so vague, obscure and indefinite as to be unenforceable merits only a passing reference. This objection centers around the use of the words "loud and raucous." While these are abstract words, they have through daily use acquired a content that conveys to any interested person a sufficiently accurate concept of what is forbidden. Last term, after thorough consideration of the problem of vagueness in legislation affecting liberty of speech, this court invalidated a conviction under a New York statute construed and applied to punish the distribution of magazines "principally made up of criminal news or stories of deeds of bloodshed or lust so massed as to become vehicles for inciting violent and depraved crimes against the person."

As thus construed, we said that the statute was so vague that an honest distributor of tales of war horrors could not know whether he was violating the statute. But in the Winters case, we pointed out that prosecutions might be brought under statutes punishing the distribution of "obscene, lewd, lascivious, filthy, indecent or disgusting" magazines. We said, "The impossibility of defining the precise line between permissible uncertainty in statutes caused by describing crimes by words well understood through long use in the criminal law—obscene, lewd, lascivious, filthy, indecent or disgusting—and the unconstitutional vagueness that leaves a person uncertain as to the kind of prohibited conduct—massing stories to incite crime —has resulted in three arguments of this case in this court."

We used the words quoted above as examples of permissible standards of statutes for criminal prosecution. There, we said: "To say that a state may not punish by such a vague statute carries no implication that it may not punish circulation of objectionable printed matter, assuming that it is not protected by the principles of the First Amendment, by the use of apt words to describe the prohibited publications. . . . Neither the states nor Congress are prevented by the requirement of specificity from carrying out their duty of eliminating evils to which, in their judgment, such publications give rise."

We think the words of §4 of this Trenton ordinance comply with the requirements of definiteness and clarity, set out above.

The scope of the protection afforded by the Fourteenth Amendment, for the right of a citizen to play music and express his views on matters which he considers to be of interest to himself and others on a public street through sound amplification devices mounted on vehicles, must be considered. Freedom of speech, freedom of assembly, and freedom to communicate information and opinion to others are all comprehended on this appeal in the claimed right of free speech. They will be so treated in this opinion.

The use of sound trucks and other peripatetic or stationary broadcasting devices for advertising, for religious exercises, and for discussion of issues or controversies has brought forth numerous municipal ordinances. The avowed and obvious purpose of these ordinances is to prohibit or minimize such sounds on or near the streets, since some citizens find the noise objectionable and to some degree an interference with the business or social activities in which they are engaged or the quiet that they would like to enjoy. A satisfactory adjustment of the conflicting interests is difficult, as those who desire to broadcast can hardly acquiesce in a requirement to modulate their sounds to a pitch that would not rise above other street noises, nor would they deem a restriction to sparsely used localities or to hours after work and before sleep—say 6 to 9 p.m.—sufficient for the exercise of their claimed privilege. Municipalities are seeking actively a solution. Unrestrained use throughout a municipality of all sound amplifying devices would be intolerable. Absolute prohibition within municipal limits of all sound amplification, even though reasonably regulated in place, time and volume, is undesirable and probably unconstitutional as an unreasonable interference with normal activities.

We have had recently before us an ordinance of the city of Lockport, New York, prohibiting sound amplification whereby the sound was cast on public places so as to attract the attention of the passing public to the annoyance of those within the radius of the sounds. The ordinance contained this exception:

"Public dissemination, through radio loudspeakers, of items of news and matters of public concern and athletic activities shall not be deemed a violation of this section provided that the same be done under permission obtained from the chief of police."

This court held the ordinance "unconstitutional on its face," because the quoted section established a "previous restraint" on free speech with "no standards prescribed for the exercise" of discretion by the chief of police. When ordinances undertake censorship of speech or religious practices before permitting their exercise, the constitution forbids their enforcement. The court said in the Saia case: "The right to be heard is placed in the uncontrolled discretion of the chief of police. He stands athwart the channels of communication as an obstruction which can be removed only after criminal trial and conviction and lengthy appeal. A more effective previous restraint is difficult to imagine."

This ordinance is not of that character. It contains nothing comparable to the above-quoted §3 of the ordinance in the Saia case. It is an exercise of the authority granted to the city by New Jersey "to prevent disturbing noises," nuisances well within the municipality's power to control. The police power of a state extends beyond health, morals and safety, and comprehends the duty, within constitutional limitations, to protect the wellbeing and tranquility of a community.

A state or city may prohibit acts or things reasonably thought to bring evil or harm to its people.

In this case, New Jersey necessarily has construed this very ordinance as applied to sound amplification. The Supreme Court said, "The relevant provisions of the ordinance apply only to (1) vehicles (2) containing an instrument in the nature of a sound amplifier or any other instrument emitting loud and raucous noises and (3) such vehicle operated or standing upon the public streets, alleys or thoroughfares of the city."

If that means that only amplifiers that emit, in the language of the ordinance, "loud and raucous noises" are barred from the streets, we have a problem of regulation. The dissents accept that view. So did the appellant in his statement as to jurisdiction and his brief. Although this court must decide for itself whether federal questions are presented and decided, we must accept the state courts' conclusion as to the scope of the ordinance. We accept the determination of New Jersey that §4 applies only to vehicles with sound amplifiers emitting loud and raucous noises. Courts are inclined to adopt that reasonable interpretation of a statute which removes it farthest from possible constitutional infirmity. We need not determine whether this ordinance so construed is regulatory or prohibitory. All regulatory enactments are prohibitory so far as their restrictions are concerned, and the prohibition of this ordinance as to a use of streets is merely regulatory. Sound trucks may be utilized in places such as parks or other open spaces off the streets. The constitutionality of the challenged ordinance as violative of appellant's right of free speech does not depend upon so narrow an issue as to whether its provisions are cast in the words of prohibition or regulation. The question is whether or not there is a real abridgment of the rights of free speech.

Of course, even the fundamental rights of the Bill of Rights are not absolute. The Saia case recognized that in this field by stating "The hours and place of public discussion can be controlled." It was said decades ago in an opinion of this court delivered by Mr. Justice Holmes, that, "The most stringent protection of free speech would not protect a man in falsely shouting fire in a theatre and causing a panic. It does not even protect a man from an injunction against uttering words that may have all the effect of force."

Hecklers may be expelled from assemblies, and religious worship may not be disturbed by those anxious to preach a doctrine of atheism. The right to speak one's mind would often be an empty privilege in a place and at a time beyond the protecting hand of the guardians of public order.

While this court, in enforcing the broad protection the constitution gives to the dissemination of ideas, has invalidated an ordinance forbidding a distributor of pamphlets or handbills from summoning household-ers to their doors to receive the distributor's writings, this was on the ground that the home owner could protect himself from such intrusion by an appropriate sign "that he is unwilling to be disturbed." The court never intimated that the visitor could insert a foot in the door and insist on a hearing. We do not think that the Struthers case requires us to ex-pand this interdiction of legislation to include ordinances against obtain-ing an audience for the broadcaster's ideas by way of sound trucks with loud and raucous noises on city streets. The unwilling listener is not like the passer-by who may be offered a pamphlet in the street but cannot be made to take it. In his home or on the street, he is practically helpless to escape this interference with his privacy by loudspeakers except through the protection of the municipality.

City streets are recognized as a normal place for the exchange of ideas by speech or paper. But this does not mean the freedom is beyond all con-trol. We think it is a permissible exercise of legislative discretion to bar sound trucks with broadcasts of public interest, amplified to a loud and raucous volume, from the public ways of municipalities. On the business streets of cities like Trenton, with its more than 125,000 people, such dis-tractions would be dangerous to traffic at all hours useful for the dissemi-nation of information, and in the residential thoroughfares, the quiet and tranquility so desirable for city dwellers would likewise be at the mercy of advocates of particular religious, social or political persuasions. We can-not believe that rights of free speech compel a municipality to allow such mechanical voice amplification on any of its streets.

The right of free speech is guaranteed every citizen that he may reach the minds of willing listeners, and to do so, there must be opportunity to win their attention. This is the phase of freedom of speech that is involved here. We do not think the Trenton ordinance abridges that freedom. It is an extravagant extension of due process to say that, because of it, a city cannot forbid talking on the streets through a loudspeaker in a loud and raucous tone. Surely such an ordinance does not violate our people's "concept of ordered liberty" so as to require federal intervention to protect a citizen from the action of his own local government. Opportunity to gain the public's ears by objectionably amplified sound on the streets is no more assured by the right of free speech than is the unlimited opportunity to address gatherings on the streets. The preferred position of freedom of speech in a society that cherishes liberty for all does not require legisla-tors to be insensible to claims by citizens to comfort and convenience. To enforce freedom of speech in disregard of the rights of others would be harsh and arbitrary in itself. That more people may be more easily and cheaply reached by sound trucks, perhaps borrowed without cost from some zealous supporter, is not enough to call forth constitutional protec-tion for what those charged with public welfare reasonably think is a nui-sance when easy means of publicity are open. Section 4 of the ordinance bars sound trucks from broadcasting in a loud and raucous manner on the streets. There is no restriction upon the communication of ideas or discussion of issues by the human voice, by newspapers, by pamphlets, by dodgers. We think that the need for reasonable protection in the homes or business houses from the distracting noises of vehicles equipped with such sound amplifying devices justifies the ordinance.

Affirmed.

Mr. Justice Murphy dissents.

Mr. Justice Frankfurter, concurring.

Wise accommodation between liberty and order always has been, and ever will be, indispensable for a democratic society. Insofar as the constitution commits the duty of making this accommodation to this court, it demands vigilant judicial self-restraint. A single decision by a closely divided court, unsupported by the confirmation of time, cannot check the living process of striking a wise balance between liberty and order as new cases come here for adjudication. To dispose of this case on the assumption that the Saia case, decided only the other day, was rightly decided, would be for me to start with an unreality. While I am not unaware of the circumstances that differentiate this case from what was ruled in Saia, further reflection has only served to reinforce the dissenting views I expressed in that case. In the light of them, I conclude that there is nothing in the constitution of the United States to bar New Jersey from authorizing the city of Trenton to deal in the manner chosen by the city with the aural aggressions implicit in the use of sound trucks.

The opinions in this case prompt me to make some additional observations. My brother Reed speaks of "the preferred position of freedom of speech," though, to be sure, he finds that the Trenton ordinance does not disregard it. This is a phrase that has uncritically crept into some recent opinions of this court. I deem it a mischievous phrase if it carries the thought, which it may subtly imply, that any law touching communication is infected with presumptive invalidity. It is not the first time in the history of constitutional adjudication that such a doctrinaire attitude has disregarded the admonition most to be observed in exercising the court's reviewing power over legislation, "that it is a constitution we are expounding." I say the phrase is mischievous because it radiates a constitutional doctrine without avowing it. Clarity and candor in these matters, so as to avoid gliding unwittingly into error, make it appropriate to trace the history of the phrase "preferred position." The following is a chronological account of the evolution of talk about "preferred position" except where the thread of derivation is plain enough to be indicated.

1. "The power of a state to abridge freedom of speech and of assembly is the exception, rather than the rule, and the penalizing even of utterances of a defined character must find its justification in a reasonable apprehension of danger to organized government. The judgment of the legislature is not unfettered. The limitation upon individual liberty must have appropriate relation to the safety of the state."

2. United States v. Carolene Products Co. set forth in the margin. A footnote hardly seems to be an appropriate way of announcing a new

constitutional doctrine, and the Carolene footnote did not purport to announce any new doctrine; incidentally, it did not have the concurrence of a majority of the court. It merely rephrased and expanded what was said in Herndon v. Lowry, and elsewhere. It certainly did not assert a presumption of invalidity against all legislation touching matters related to liberties protected by the Bill of Rights and the Fourteenth Amendment. It merely stirred inquiry whether as to such matters there may be "narrower scope for operation of the presumption of constitutionality," and legislation regarding them is therefore "to be subjected to more exacting judicial scrutiny."

The Carolene footnote is cited in Thornhill v. Alabama, in an opinion which thus proceeds:

"Mere legislative preference for one, rather than another means for combatting substantive evils, therefore, may well prove an inadequate foundation on which to rest regulations which are aimed at or in their operation diminish the effective exercise of rights so necessary to the maintenance of democratic institutions. It is imperative that, when the effective exercise of these rights is claimed to be abridged, the courts should 'weigh the circumstances' and 'appraise the substantiality of the reasons advanced' in support of the challenged regulations."

It is cited again in the opinion of the court in American Federation of Labor v. Swing, together with the Herndon and Schneider cases, in support of the statement that the "right to free discussion" "is to be guarded with a jealous eye." The Carolene footnote was last cited in an opinion of this Court in the passage of Thomas v. Collins, quoted below.

"In every case, therefore, where legislative abridgment of the rights [freedom of speech and of the press] is asserted, the courts should be astute to examine the effect of the challenged legislation. Mere legislative preferences or beliefs respecting matters of public convenience may well support regulation directed at other personal activities, but be insufficient to justify such as diminishes the exercise of rights so vital to the maintenance of democratic institutions. And so, as cases arise, the delicate and difficult task falls upon the courts to weigh the circumstances and to appraise the substantiality of the reasons advanced in support of the regulation of the free enjoyment of the rights.

"Moreover, the likelihood, however great, that a substantive evil will result cannot alone justify a restriction upon freedom of speech or the press. The evil itself must be 'substantial,' Brandeis, J., concurring in; it must be 'serious." And even the expression of 'legislative preferences or beliefs' cannot transform minor matters of public inconvenience or annoyance into substantive evils of sufficient weight to warrant the curtailment of liberty of expression.

"What finally emerges from the 'clear and present danger' cases is a working principle that the substantive evil must be extremely serious, and the degree of imminence extremely high, before utterances can be punished."

This formulation of the "clear and present danger" test was quoted and endorsed in Pennekamp v. Florida. A number of Jehovah's Witnesses cases refer to the freedoms specified by the First Amendment as in a "preferred position." The phrase was apparently first used in the dissent of Chief Justice Stone in Jones v. Opelika. It reappears in [other cases].

West Virginia State Board of Education v. Barnette, "The test of legislation which collides with the Fourteenth Amendment, because it also collides with the principles of the First, is much more definite than the test when only the Fourteenth is involved. Much of the vagueness of the due process clause disappears when the specific prohibitions of the First become its standard. The right of a state to regulate, for example, a public utility may well include, so far as the due process test is concerned, power to impose all of the restrictions which a legislature may have a 'rational basis' for adopting. But freedoms of speech and of press, of assembly, and of worship may not be infringed on such slender grounds. They are susceptible of restriction only to prevent grave and immediate danger to interests which the state may lawfully protect.

"For these reasons, any attempt to restrict those liberties must be justified by clear public interest, threatened not doubtfully or remotely, but by clear and present danger. The rational connection between the remedy provided and the evil to be curbed, which in other contexts might support legislation against attack on due process grounds, will not suffice. These rights rest on firmer foundation. Accordingly, whatever occasion would restrain orderly discussion and persuasion, at appropriate time and place, must have clear support in public danger, actual or impending. Only the gravest abuses, endangering paramount interests, give occasion for permissible limitation."

This is perhaps the strongest language dealing with the constitutional aspect of legislation touching utterance. But it was the opinion of only four members of the Court, since Mr. Justice Jackson, in a separate concurring opinion, referred to the opinion of Mr. Justice Rutledge only to say that he agreed that the case fell into "the category of a public speech, rather than that of practicing a vocation as solicitor." In short, the claim that any legislation is presumptively unconstitutional which touches the field of the First Amendment and the Fourteenth Amendment, insofar as the latter's concept of "liberty" contains what is specifically protected by the First, has never commended itself to a majority of this court.

Behind the notion sought to be expressed by the formula as to "the preferred position of freedom of speech" lies a relevant consideration in determining whether an enactment relating to the liberties protected by the Due Process Clause of the Fourteenth Amendment is violative of it. In law, also, doctrine is illuminated by history. The ideas now governing the constitutional protection of freedom of speech derive essentially from the opinions of Mr. Justice Holmes.

The philosophy of his opinions on that subject arose from a deep awareness of the extent to which sociological conclusions are conditioned by time and circumstance. Because of this awareness, Mr. Justice Holmes seldom felt justified in opposing his own opinion to economic views which the legislature embodied in law. But since he also realized that the progress of civilization is to a considerable extent the displacement of error which once held sway as official truth by beliefs which, in turn, have yielded to other beliefs, for him, the right to search for truth was of a different order than some transient economic dogma. And without freedom of expression, thought becomes checked and atrophied. Therefore, in considering what interests are so fundamental as to be enshrined in the Due Process Clause, those liberties of the individual which history has attested as the indispensable conditions of an open, as against a closed, society come to this court with a momentum for respect lacking when appeal is made to liberties which derive merely from shifting economic arrangements. Accordingly, Mr. Justice Holmes was far more ready to find legislative invasion where free inquiry was involved than in the debatable area of economics.

The objection to summarizing this line of thought by the phrase "the preferred position of freedom of speech" is that it expresses a complicated process of constitutional adjudication by a deceptive formula. And it was Mr. Justice Holmes who admonished us that "To rest upon a formula is a slumber that, prolonged, means death." Such a formula makes for mechanical jurisprudence.

Some of the arguments made in this case strikingly illustrate how easy it is to fall into the ways of mechanical jurisprudence through the use of oversimplified formulas. It is argued that the constitution protects freedom of speech: freedom of speech means the right to communicate, whatever the physical means for so doing; sound trucks are one form of communication; ergo, that form is entitled to the same protection as any other means of communication, whether by tongue or pen. Such sterile argumentation treats society as though it consisted of bloodless categories. The various forms of modern so-called "mass communications" raise issues that were not implied in the means of communication known or contemplated by Franklin and Jefferson and Madison. Movies have created problems not presented by the circulation of books, pamphlets, or newspapers, and so the movies have been constitutionally regulated. Broadcasting, in turn, has produced its brood of complicated problems hardly to be solved by an easy formula about the preferred position of free speech.

Only a disregard of vital differences between natural speech, even of the loudest spellbinders, and the noise of sound trucks would give sound trucks the constitutional rights accorded to the unaided human voice. Nor is it for this court to devise the terms on which sound trucks should be allowed to operate, if at all. These are matters for the legislative judgment controlled by public opinion. So long as a legislature does not prescribe what ideas may be noisily expressed and what may not be, nor discriminate among those who would make inroads upon the public peace, it is not for us to supervise the limits the legislature may impose in safeguarding the steadily narrowing opportunities for serenity and reflection. Without such opportunities, freedom of thought becomes a mocking phrase, and without freedom of thought, there can be no free society.

Mr. Justice Jackson, concurring.

I join the judgment sustaining the Trenton ordinance because I believe that operation of mechanical sound-amplifying devices conflicts with quiet enjoyment of home and park and with safe and legitimate use of street and market place, and that it is constitutionally subject to regulation or prohibition by the state or municipal authority. No violation of the Due Process Clause of the Fourteenth Amendment by reason of infringement of free speech arises unless such regulation or prohibition undertakes to censor the contents of the broadcasting. Freedom of speech for Kovacs does not, in my view, include freedom to use sound amplifiers to drown out the natural speech of others.

I do not agree that, if we sustain regulations or prohibitions of sound trucks, they must therefore be valid if applied to other methods of "communication of ideas." The moving picture screen, the radio, the newspaper, the handbill, the sound truck and the street corner orator have differing natures, values, abuses and dangers. Each, in my view, is a law unto itself, and all we are dealing with now is the sound truck.

But I agree with Mr. Justice Black that this decision is a repudiation of that in Saia v. New York.

Like him, I am unable to find anything in this record to warrant a distinction because of "loud and raucous" tones of this machine. The Saia decision struck down a more moderate exercise of the state's police power than the one now sustained. Trenton, as the ordinance reads to me, unconditionally bans all sound trucks from the city streets. Lockport relaxed its prohibition with a proviso to allow their use, even in areas set aside for public recreation, when and where the chief of police saw no objection. Comparison of this, our 1949 decision, with our 1948 decision, I think, will pretty hopelessly confuse municipal authorities as to what they may or may not do.

I concur in the present result only for the reasons stated in dissent in Saia v. New York.

Mr. Justice Black, with whom Mr. Justice Douglas and Mr. Justice Rutledge concur, dissenting.

The question in this case is not whether appellant may constitutionally be convicted of operating a sound truck that emits "loud and raucous noises." The appellant was neither charged with nor convicted of operating a sound truck that emitted "loud and raucous noises." The charge against him in the police court was that he violated the city ordinance "in that he did, on South Stockton Street, in said city, play, use and operate a device known as a sound truck." The record reflects not even a shadow of evidence to prove that the noise was either "loud or raucous," unless these words of the ordinance refer to any noise coming from an amplifier, whatever its volume or tone.

After appellant's conviction in the police court, the case was taken to the Supreme Court of New Jersey for review. That court, composed of three judges, stated with reference to the ordinance and charge:

"In simple, unambiguous language, it prohibits the use upon the public streets of any device known as a sound truck, loudspeaker or sound amplifier. This is the only charge made against the defendant in the complaint."

That this court construed the ordinance as an absolute prohibition of all amplifiers on any public street at any time and without regard to volume of sound is emphasized by its further statement that "the ordinance leaves untouched the right of the prosecutor to express his views orally without the aid of an amplifier." Thus, the New Jersey Supreme Court affirmed the conviction on the ground that the appellant was shown guilty of the only offense of which he was charged—speaking through an amplifier on a public street. If, as some members of this court now assume, he was actually convicted for operating a machine that emitted "loud and raucous noises," then he was convicted on a charge for which he was never tried.

"It is as much a violation of due process to send an accused to prison following conviction of a charge on which he was never tried as it would be to convict him upon a charge that was never made."

Furthermore, when the conviction was later affirmed in the New Jersey Court of Errors and Appeals by an equally divided court, no one of that court's judges who voted to affirm expressed any doubt as to the correctness of the New Jersey Supreme Court's interpretation; indeed, those judges wrote no opinion at all. One of the six who voted to reverse did base his judgment on the fact that there was not "a scintilla of evidence that the music or voice was loud or raucous," and that, under the wording of the ordinance, such proof was essential. In construing the statute as requiring a proof of loud and raucous noises, the dissenting judge made the initial mistake of the majority of this court, but he conceded that, under this construction of the statute, there was a fatal absence of proof to convict. The other five judges who were for reversal concluded that the ordinance represented "an attempt by the municipality under the guise of regulation, to prohibit and outlaw, under all circumstances and conditions, the use of sound amplifying systems."

It thus appears that the appellant was charged and convicted by interpreting the ordinance as an absolute prohibition against the use of sound amplifying devices. The New Jersey Supreme Court affirmed only on that interpretation of the ordinance. There is no indication whatever that there was a different view entertained by the six judges of the Court of Errors and Appeals who affirmed the conviction. And it strains the imagination to say that the ordinance itself would warrant any other interpretation.

Nevertheless, in this court, the requisite majority for affirmance of appellant's conviction is composed in part of justices who give the New Jersey ordinance a construction different from that given it by the state courts. That is not all. Affirmance here means that the appellant will be punished for an offense with which he was not charged, to prove which no evidence was offered, and of which he was not convicted, according to the only New Jersey court which affirmed with opinion. At the last term of court, we held that the Arkansas Supreme Court had denied an appellant due process because it had failed to appraise the validity of a conviction "on consideration of the case as it was tried and as the issues were determined in the trial court." I am unable to distinguish the action taken by this court today from the action of the Arkansas Supreme Court which we declared denied a defendant due process of law.

The New Jersey ordinance is, on its face and as construed and applied in this case by that state's courts, an absolute and unqualified prohibition of amplifying devices on any of Trenton's streets at any time, at any place, for any purpose, and without regard to how noisy they may be.

In Saia v. New York, we had before us an ordinance of the city of Lockport, New York, which forbade the use of sound amplification devices except with permission of the chief of police. The ordinance was applied to keep a minister from using an amplifier while preaching in a public park. We held that the ordinance, aimed at the use of an amplifying device, invaded the area of free speech guaranteed the people by the First and Fourteenth Amendments. The ordinance, so we decided, amounted to censorship in its baldest form. And our conclusion rested on the fact that the chief of police was given arbitrary power to prevent the use of speech amplifying devices at all times and places in the city without regard to the volume of the sound. We pointed out the indispensable function performed by loud-speakers in modern public speaking. We then placed use of loudspeakers in public streets and parks on the same constitutional level as freedom to speak on streets without such devices, freedom to speak over radio, and freedom to distribute literature.

In this case, the court denies speech amplifiers the constitutional shelter recognized by our decisions and holding in the Saia case. This is true because the Trenton, New Jersey, ordinance here sustained goes beyond a mere prior censorship of all loudspeakers with authority in the censor to prohibit some of them. This Trenton ordinance wholly bars the use of all loudspeakers mounted upon any vehicle in any of the city's public streets.

In my view, this repudiation of the prior Saia opinion makes a danger-ous and unjustifiable breach in the constitutional barriers designed to insure freedom of expression. Ideas and beliefs are today chiefly dissemi-nated to the masses of people through the press, radio, moving pictures, and public address systems. To some extent, at least, there is competi-tion of ideas between and within these groups. The basic premise of the First Amendment is that all present instruments of communication, as well as others that inventive genius may bring into being, shall be free from governmental censorship or prohibition. Laws which hamper the free use of some instruments of communication thereby favor competing channels. Thus, unless constitutionally prohibited, laws like this Tren-ton ordinance can give an overpowering influence to views of owners of legally favored instruments of communication. This favoritism, it seems to me, is the inevitable result of today's decision. For the result of today's opinion in upholding this statutory prohibition of amplifiers would surely not be reached by this court if such channels of communication as the press, radio, or moving pictures were similarly attacked.

There are many people who have ideas that they wish to disseminate but who do not have enough money to own or control publishing plants, newspapers, radios, moving picture studios, or chains of show places. Yet everybody knows the vast reaches of these powerful channels of communication, which, from the very nature of our economic system, must be under the control and guidance of comparatively few people. On the other hand, public speaking is done by many men of divergent minds with no centralized control over the ideas they entertain so as to limit the causes they espouse. It is no reflection on the value of preserving freedom for dissemination of the ideas of publishers of newspapers, magazines, and other literature, to believe that transmission of ideas through public speaking is also essential to the sound thinking of a fully informed citizenry.

It is of particular importance in a government where people elect their officials that the fullest opportunity be afforded candidates to express and voters to hear their views. It is of equal importance that criticism of governmental action not be limited to criticisms by press, radio, and moving pictures. In no other way except public speaking can the desirable objective of widespread public discussion be assured. For the press, the radio, and the moving picture owners have their favorites, and it assumes the impossible to suppose that these agencies will at all times be equally fair as between the candidates and officials they favor and those whom they vigorously oppose. And it is an obvious fact that public speaking today, without sound amplifiers, is a wholly inadequate way to reach the people on a large scale. Consequently, to tip the scales against transmission of ideas through public speaking, as the court does today, is to deprive the people of a large part of the basic advantages of the receipt of ideas that the First Amendment was designed to protect.

There is no more reason that I can see for wholly prohibiting one useful instrument of communication than another. If Trenton can completely bar the streets to the advantageous use of loudspeakers, all cities can do the same. In that event, preference in the dissemination of ideas is given those who can obtain the support of newspapers, etc., or those who have money enough to buy advertising from newspapers, radios, or moving pictures. This court should no more permit this invidious prohibition against the dissemination of ideas by speaking than it would permit a complete blackout of the press, the radio, or moving pictures. It is wise for all who cherish freedom of expression to reflect upon the plain fact that a holding that the audiences of public speakers can be constitutionally prohibited is not unrelated to a like prohibition in other fields. And the right to freedom of expression should be protected from absolute censorship for persons without, as for persons with, wealth and power. At least such is the theory of our society.

I am aware that the "blare" of this new method of carrying ideas is susceptible of abuse, and may, under certain circumstances, constitute an intolerable nuisance. But ordinances can be drawn which adequately protect a community from unreasonable use of public speaking devices without absolutely denying to the community's citizens all information that may be disseminated or received through this new avenue for trade in ideas. I would agree without reservation to the sentiment that "unrestrained use throughout a municipality of all sound amplifying devices would be intolerable." And, of course, cities may restrict or absolutely ban the use of amplifiers on busy streets in the business area. A city ordinance that reasonably restricts the volume of sound, or the hours during which an amplifier may be used, does not, in my mind, infringe the constitutionally protected area of free speech. It is because this ordinance does none of these things, but is instead an absolute prohibition of all uses of an amplifier on any of the streets of Trenton at any time that I must dissent.

I would reverse the judgment.

Mr. Justice Rutledge, dissenting.

I am in accord with the views expressed by my brother Black. I think it important, however, to point out that a majority here agree with him that the issue presented is whether a state (here a municipality) may forbid all use of sound trucks or amplifying devices in public streets, without reference to whether "loud and raucous noises" are emitted. Only a minority take the view that the Trenton ordinance merely forbids using amplifying instruments emitting loud and raucous noises.

Yet a different majority, one including that minority and two other justices, sustain the ordinance and its application. In effect, Kovacs stands convicted, but of what it is impossible to tell, because the majority upholding the conviction do not agree upon what constituted the crime. How, on such a hashing of different views of the thing forbidden, Kovacs could have known with what he was charged or could have prepared a defense, I am unable to see. How anyone can do either in the future, under this decision, I am equally at loss to say.

In my view, an ordinance drawn so ambiguously and inconsistently as to reflect the differing views of its meaning taken by the two groups who compose the majority sustaining it, would violate Fourteenth Amendment due process even if no question of free speech were involved. No man should be subject to punishment under a statute when even a bare majority of judges upholding the conviction cannot agree upon what acts the statute denounces.

What the effect of this decision may be, I cannot foretell, except that Kovacs will stand convicted and the division among the majority voting to affirm leaves open for future determination whether absolute and total state prohibition of sound trucks in public places can stand consistently with the First Amendment. For myself, I have no doubt of state power to regulate their abuse in reasonable accommodation, by narrowly drawn statutes, to other interests concerned in use of the streets and in freedom from public nuisance. But that the First Amendment limited its protections of speech to the natural range of the human voice as it existed in

1790 would be, for me, like saying that the commerce power remains limited to navigation by sail and travel by the use of horses and oxen in accordance with the principal modes of carrying on commerce in 1789. The constitution was not drawn with any such limited vision of time, space and mechanics. It is one thing to hold that the states may regulate the use of sound trucks by appropriately limited measures. It is entirely another to say their use can be forbidden altogether.

To what has been said above and by Mr. Justice Black, I would add only that I think my brother Frankfurter demonstrates the conclusion opposite to that which he draws, namely, that the First Amendment guaranties of the freedoms of speech, press, assembly and religion occupy preferred position not only in the Bill of Rights, but also in the repeated decisions of this court.

Source: http://supreme.justia.com/us/336/77/case.html

Appendix IV. Noise and Sovereignty

So much of what we think about noise and noise pollution centers on degrees of impact. By this way of thinking, loud noise is considered bad and not-so-loud noise is considered less bad, but intuitively we know this way of looking at noise fails to capture the nature of the problem. To be sure, if noise is bad than loud noise is worse, but for each of us not all noise problems come down to matters of volume; in many cases not-so-loud noises are just as irritating or distracting or even unhealthful as loud noises. Recent research that looks at people's perceptions of noise rather than the noise itself backs this up. We touch on some of this research in Chapter 6. More intuitively, what we think of as noise problems are really more accurately described as problems of autonomy. We really can't be free without control over our ability to access quiet. Anybody who's been held hostage to someone else's noise (unwanted sound) for an extended period of time understands this. As we saw in Chapter 4, it's this notion of being free to control one's auditory environment that makes single-family residency so attractive to people living in a multifamily environment. It's not enough to have walls round you; to feel like you're really master of your own environment you need to have some degree of control over what you hear and when you hear it.

In the article that follows, Les Blomberg, head of the Noise Pollution Clearinghouse, addresses this notion of autonomy directly, although he uses the term sovereignty. The piece does a good job of taking the focus away from volume and putting the problem of noise in its proper context, and I reproduce it in its entirety here.

Noise, Sovereignty, and Civility

by *Les Blomberg*

Noise is unwanted sound. It causes hearing loss, stress, high blood pressure, sleep loss, lost productivity, and a general reduction in the quality of life and opportunity for personal and collective tranquility. Noise is caused by people and businesses claiming rights, usually property rights, to emit noise into the air, and by people who do not possess the civility to be good neighbors. While its effects are an environmental health issue, its causes are tied to the issues of sovereignty (who owns the air?) and civility (how should we treat our neighbors?).

Together, environmental health, sovereignty, and civility are the three pillars that support noise activism. Through the work of the League for the Hard of Hearing, Arline Bronzaft, Gary Evans, Alice Suter, and many others, the public is starting to grasp the health issues related to noise. Noise activists, likewise, are starting to grasp the full implications of their work and the importance of sovereignty and civility. We are coming to the realization that combating noise requires addressing the underlying causes of the problem, of which sovereignty and civility are at the center.

Sovereignty

Much of the noise pollution we experience results from individuals and businesses who believe that it is their right or freedom to make noise. The most common right claimed is a property right. They claim that they should be free to use their property as they see fit without interference from others. The second most common right cited is that of prior occupation. People often assume that if the noise source "was there" before the complainant, that the noise is permissible. Finally some people claim that they should be free to act as they wish without interference from others or the state, or they claim specific rights such as the freedom of speech.

Each of these claims shows a fundamental misunderstanding of noise, ownership, and the western tradition of freedom. Persons making the first claim, that it is their property right, are wrongly assuming that they own the air over and around their neighbors. If the noise was limited to their property their case would be slightly stronger. Even then, however, it is not an absolute right. Smoking, for example, is prohibited in many public places by the states, even though the pollution is limited to air within private property.

In the case of noise heard on public property or another's private property, the noise maker has no claim to owning the air on which the noise travels. Therefore, they have no private property right to broadcast the noise.

Another version of the property rights argument claims that because the air is common property owned by everyone, everyone has the right to do as he or she pleases. This too is clearly a flawed argument. Roadways are also common property, but no one has the right to drive left of the yellow line or park their car in the middle of the street. Common property does not entail universal entitlement. In fact, such a policy leads to what is known as the "tragedy of the commons."

The term "tragedy of the commons" comes from the experience on common grazing fields in England. If everyone acts in his or her own self interest on common property (in the common grazing fields, that meant grazing your cattle as much as possible), the common resource is degraded (the field is overgrazed and therefore supplies only a fraction of the feed it otherwise could have).

The antidote to the tragedy of the commons is an ethic of the commons: common property needs to be managed so that uses that do not degrade or detract from others' use and enjoyment are encouraged, and uses that detract from others' use and enjoyment are discouraged. With respect to noise, that means encouraging quieter uses and discouraging noisy ones.

The claim of prior occupation clearly does not provide justification for noise pollution. One way to see the weakness in this argument is to realize that the argument is not used in reverse. Communities do not give neighbors the right to prohibit the introduction of new noises in their neighborhood because the prior use was quiet. People lived near almost all major noise sources before those sources existed. Moreover, there were people living there before the source was expanded. At some point there were no motorized boats on lakes, no airports, no jets, yet there have always been people seeking quiet.

The claim of freedom from government interference seems to overlook the very nature and development of the concept of freedom in western cultures. Even at the height of laissez-faire attitudes in the 18th century, philosopher John Stuart Mill, one of the greatest defenders of the freedoms of individuals, recognized that people ought to be free to do as they please so long as they do not harm others. This is a concept well understood in America today. My right or freedom to swing my fist ends at your nose. My right to make noise ought to end at your ear.

The effort to control noise is part of a greater effort to protect that which is held in common by the public from abuse and degradation. Other efforts to protect the commons are concerned with protecting our public lands and parks; air, airways, water, and waterways; habitat, species, and biodiversity. What these efforts share is the recognition that our well-being is enhanced when the commons is used to maximize opportunities for everyone, and degraded when the commons is used to maximize profits or opportunities for a few, or to maximize only a few opportunities.

Combating noise is part of a larger struggle to politically and legally establish sovereignty and control over common or public property. People working to reduce noise are environmentalists seeking an ethic of the commons. Our success is tied directly to other environmental causes. The battle against noise is strengthened when other environmentalists succeed, and weakened when they fail. As the term sovereignty suggests, it is inherently a political struggle. This has several implications for persons seeking to effectively control noise. In addition to the obvious one, supporting efforts to reduce noise, friends of quiet should:

- Support initiatives that treat noise as a pollutant (for example, efforts to reopen the EPA's noise office, stronger regulation of transportation related noise, etc.).
- Join forces with environmentalists and build coalitions with environmentalists to educate them about noise.
- Support environmental causes unrelated to noise such as efforts to control global warming, acid rain, smog, etc.
- Support environmentally concerned candidates and initiatives.
- Work against property rights and "wise use" movement candidates and initiatives.

Civility

Noise, more than most pollutants, is closely related to manners. Good neighbors keep their noise to themselves; bad neighbors don't.

Noisy neighbors do not care about their impact on others. They are the bullies in the schoolyard. The Noise Pollution Clearinghouse receives more than 100 inquiries a week from people impacted by noise. The most common source of the noise is a business: a racetrack, grocery store with early morning garbage pickup, a building with very noisy refrigeration or air conditioning equipment, a bar, a gun range.

As director of the Noise Pollution Clearinghouse, it has become obvious to me that the typical noise-making bully in America today is a business. Most people would have thought the "neighbor from hell" would be an intimidating bully who lives next door. While they exist, businesses eclipse individuals for the title of "neighbor from hell" by an order of magnitude.

The reason businesses are☐ the worst offenders is that political power is on their side. Local governments are unwilling or unable to challenge them, while they do crack down on individuals. If the noise polluter were a teenager with a boom box playing half as loud as the noise of the business, the boom box would probably be confiscated. If the noise polluter were a college student hosting a late night party, the party would be shut down. But if the noise polluter is a business, nothing is done.

It is difficult to understand any justification for these differences, especially in the cases of the most egregious acts of incivility reported to the Noise Pollution Clearinghouse. It is not uncommon for people who call the Noise Pollution Clearinghouse to be kept awake for a couple hours at night, or to be awakened three times a night, five nights a week. The defining characteristic between the teen or college student who are dealt with swiftly and the business that is allowed to pollute is that the business is making money. It is absurd that just because someone is making money they can also make noise.

Businesses are not the only bullies in our communities. Sharing some of the claim to "worst noise polluter" is the average normal person. The two most common sources of noise pollution are highways and airports — places that most Americans use quite frequently. Normal people tend to noise pollute when they have some sense of anonymity and when they lack connection to their community — when they are literally zipping by. The same people who would never honk their horn at midnight in a residential community will fly over the same homes at midnight, to the very same effect: families can't sleep.

Understanding just who the noise polluters are and that they include us is both enlightening and disturbing. It should not be surprising, however, that minorities and the poor are most often the noise polluted. Minorities and the poor have the highest exposure to many environmental pollutants, and this is clearly the case with noise. Low-income neighborhoods are much more likely than wealthier ones to suffer from excessive airport and aircraft noise. The U.S. Census reports that families who rent their homes are twice as likely to list noise as a major neighborhood problem as those who own their homes. Similarly, African Americans, Hispanics, and persons living below the poverty level are significantly more likely to list noise as a major neighborhood problem.

When some people choose not to be a good neighbor, laws must be passed to force neighborliness upon them. This is an unfortunate but all too common necessity in modern society. Laws forcing people to be good neighbors are much less desirable than people acting as good neighbors out of choice. The Noise Pollution Clearinghouse has developed a Good Neighbor Policy to use as a guideline for respect within a community. Obviously, it can be modified for different communities depending on their needs.

Noise, Sovereignty, and Civility

Just as noise cannot be heard in a vacuum, noise activism does not succeed in a vacuum. Environmental and community consciousness is the medium of noise activism. Friends of quiet need to be part Rachel Carson and part Miss Manners. We need to demand that common property be protected, that our air remains clean, free of noise, smog, acid rain, etc., and that others be treated respectfully and in a manner we would wish for ourselves.

Average people definitely share some responsibility for using the highways and airports. The airline, motorcycle, car, and truck industries, the Federal Aviation Administration, and the Federal Highway Administration deserve much more of the blame for making almost no attempt to reduce the impact of noise. With the exception of the car industry (specifically many high end and Japanese cars), these industries have historically made no effort to quiet their products unless forced to by regulations. And since government regulations of all these industries and products is very lax, lagging way behind European standards, almost no progress is being made.

Good Neighbor Policy

The Purpose of the Good Neighbor Policy is to protect the comfort, quiet, repose, health, peace, and quality of life of people. At a minimum, everyone should reasonably expect:

1. To be protected from adverse impacts on their quality of life due to noise;
2. Not to have their sleep disturbed by noise;
3. Not to hear someone else's noise in their home.

The Good Neighbor Policy is based on the principal "Good neighbors keep their noise to themselves." We ask neighbors to agree to the following. With respect to:

Lawn and garden equipment
- Use a reel mower and rake whenever possible.
- Use power lawn and garden equipment between 9 a.m. and 6 p.m.
- Do not use a leaf blower for health and noise reasons.
- Whenever possible, avoid the outdoor use of power tools on Sunday.
- Avoid the use of power lawn equipment if your neighbors are in their yards.
- Establish a schedule for motorized outdoor lawn and garden work with your neighbors (e.g. even-numbered days only).

Loudspeakers, sound amplifiers, public address systems, musical instruments, and outdoor events
- Limit outdoor nighttime noise (between 9 p.m. and 9 a.m.) to levels quieter than typical conversation.
- Ensure that nighttime noise is not audible within neighbor's homes.
- Ensure that maximum daytime noise levels on neighbor's property does not exceed typical conversation levels.
- Commercial and industrial establishments should use pagers or radios instead of PA systems.

Shared walls, floors, and ceilings
- Walk lightly, especially on hardwood floors.
- Keep music to conversational levels, site speakers away from common walls, and limit bass volume.
- Respect your neighbor's sleep schedule.
- Lay rugs in heavily traveled areas and hallways.

Trash removal

- Schedule trash pickup between 9 AM and 5 PM.

Barking dogs and other animal noises

- Train dogs not to bark.
- Ensure that dogs and other animals are not left unattended and in situations where they may bark or otherwise disturb neighbors.

Cell phones and pagers

- Turn cell phones and pagers off, or use them in "silent mode" in public places such as, parks, beaches, trains, restaurants, theaters, and concert halls.
- When using a cell phone, move to a private place where you will not disturb others.
- Air conditioning, refrigeration, heating systems and other permanent outdoor appliances
- Purchase only the quietest air conditioning, refrigeration, and heating equipment.
- Locate air conditioning, refrigeration, and heating systems as far as possible from neighbors and screen central heating and air conditioning systems with a solid fence.
- New appliances and equipment
- Buy quiet. Purchase products that are among the quietest in their class.

Consumerism

- Buy local. Purchase products that require the least shipping,

Construction

- Perform noisy construction work only between 9 AM and 5 PM, Monday-Saturday. Noisy construction work usually includes activities such as hammering or the use power tools outdoors.

Commercial and industrial operation within 1,000 feet of residential property

- Limit noisy operations such as outdoor loading, unloading, use of power tools, to 9 AM to 5 PM, Monday to Saturday.
- Ensure that any noise spilling over onto neighbor's property is less than typical conversational levels.
- Turn off trucks and auxiliary equipment if vehicle is stationary for more than 2 minutes.

Automobiles, trucks, and motorcycles

- Maintain exhaust and muffler systems in good working condition.

• Do not use straight pipes, cutouts, or other noisier modifications of exhaust systems.

• Maintain stereo volume levels so that noise is not audible 25 feet from vehicle.

• Do not use air compression brakes (Jake Brakes).

• Use a horn only for emergencies.

• Buy smaller vehicles with smaller tires and drive at slower speeds (noise is proportional to tire size and vehicle speed--avoid SUV's and speeding)

Alarms and car alarms

• Rely on silent alarms and devices that disable vehicles to protect cars.

• Do not leave valuables in passenger compartments of cars.

• Do not purchase cars that use the horn to let the driver know when the doors are locked.

Off-road vehicle use

• Use standard equipment or better mufflers.

• When operating off-road vehicles, maintain at least 1,000 feet distance from residential property, parks, or public or private beaches.

• Do not use ORV's in remote or pristine areas.

Thrill craft (Jet Skis)

• When operating thrill craft, maintain a distance of at least 2,000 feet from shoreline and islands.

• When leaving or returning to shore, maintain a 2,000 foot "no wake" zone.

• Maintain at least 1,000 feet from non-motorized watercraft.

• Do not jump waves or go in circles.

• *Watercraft*

• Do not remove mufflers or use cutout devices.

• Maintain a 1,000 feet from shoreline "no wake" zone.

• Limit boat stereo levels.

Aircraft

• Whenever possible, use quieter, more efficient forms of transportation.

• Book all flights to take off and land between the hours of 8 AM and 8 PM.

• Pilots should avoid flying over urban or residential areas and parks.

• Pilots should maintain a minimum of 2,500 feet from residential areas, parks, and beaches.

• Do not take tour flights.

Overnight deliveries requiring nighttime air flights
- Ship next day packages only in cases of emergencies.

Firearms
- Do not discharge firearms within 2,500 feet of residential property.

Notification
- Notify all potentially affected neighbors if an activity may interfere with their use and enjoyment of their property and arrange to control and eliminate any possible interference.

Exemptions
- Emergency construction or operations necessary to protect safety of persons or property.

Special community-sponsored events
- Modifications of the Good Neighbor Policy based on mutual agreement of all affected neighbors.

— Les Blomberg is executive director of the Noise Pollution Clearinghouse.

Reprinted with permission. "Noise, Sovereignty, and Civility" originally appeared in *Hearing Rehabilitation Quarterly*, Vol. 25, No. 1, published by the League for the Hard of Hearing, New York City

APPENDIX V. TELEVISION ADDICTION

There are several pieces of research that have helped draw attention to the unusually strong hold that TV has over us. The research is important because it helps take the debate out of the realm of gut feeling and into the more solid realm of empirical analysis. The studies don't end the debate over whether TV is like a drug, as some people contend. Rather, they give the debate a solid place to begin talking about what makes TV so hard to ignore.

What follows is an article by Ron Kaufman, a Philadelphia educator and the publisher of TurnoffyourTV.org. In his piece, he touches on what has become something of a landmark article on TV addiction, "Television Addiction is No Mere Metaphor," by Robert Kubey and Mihaly Csikszentmihalyi, which appeared in the Feb. 2002 issue of *Scientific American*. That article has become one of the most widely cited on TV addiction and it builds on research on the interaction between TV and our brain by Byron Reeves of Stanford University and Esther Thorson of the University of Missouri.

Television Addiction Identification and Self-Help Guide

By Ron Kaufman

When the habit interferes with the ability to grow, to learn new things, to lead an active life, then it does constitute a kind of dependence and should be taken seriously.

— Robert Kubey and Mihaly Csikszentmihalyi in the article "Television Addiction Is No Mere Metaphor," *Scientific American, February 2002*

Conquering an addiction is not easy. An addiction, by definition, is an uncontrollable compulsion to repeat a behavior regardless of its harmful consequences. Many types of addiction have been described, including alcohol, tobacco, drugs, gambling, food, sex, pornography, computers, and work. Adding television to that list should not be a stretch considering the ubiquitous presence of TV screens throughout our world. Additionally, the classic vacant stare of the TV watcher should also count as *prima facie* evidence of the medium's power.

In January 2004, Timothy Dumouchel of West Bend, Wis., threatened to sue the Charter Communications cable television provider for TV addiction. "I believe that the reason I smoke and drink every day and my wife is overweight is because we watched TV every day for the last four years," Dumouchel stated in a written complaint against the company. "But the reason I am suing Charter is they did not let me make a decision as to what was best for myself and my family and (they have been) keeping cable (coming) into my home for four years after I asked them to turn it off." Apparently, Dumouchel was never charged for his cable television.

In the end, Dumouchel decided not to go through with his lawsuit but commented that TV addiction is a real affliction. "I'm definitely addicted," he said. "When I'm home, it's on. I wanted to talk to my family. When you're watching TV, how much do you communicate with your family?" To those who scoffed at his accusations, Dumouchel commented, "I challenge anyone to keep your cable on and not turn (your TV) on for 30 days."

One could comment that if someone can be addicted to television, then people could be addicted to anything — and in a sense, this criticism is true. Any compulsive habit that causes the actor pain or negative repercussions would be defined as a type of addiction. Addictions are usually described as either physical dependence or psychological addiction and treatments vary between the two. Physical dependence, such as the one associated with nicotine or tobacco or hard drugs can be extremely strong and usually involves severe withdrawal symptoms. Dependence is serious business and usually will involve medical professionals to overcome.

For mental health professionals, television addiction is believed to exist as a type of behavioral addiction similar to pathological gambling. In 1990, a symposium at the convention of the American Psychological Association developed the definition of TV addiction as "heavy television watching that is subjectively experienced as being to some extent involuntary, displacing more productive activities, and difficult to stop or curtail." Though not considered an "official" mental disorder, there is a growing body of evidence that pieces together the framework of the TV addict.

This article will define and identify both the causes and symptoms of television addiction and then present a plan to help a person break free of compulsive TV watching.

Living in a Tele-Culture

A British psychology professor has proposed a theory that human brains are genetically predisposed to enjoy watching television. Geoffrey Beattie of Manchester University, the celebrity psychologist on the British reality-TV show Big Brother, has proposed many theories as to why humans like watching TV. One idea is "the fairytale factor," where people are interested in the lives of celebrities in much the same way stories such as Cinderella or Snow White are popular — maybe they too can go from rags to riches. Conversely, another Beattie theory is called "the Schadenfreude Effect," and this is described as taking pleasure in a celebrity's suffering. Both of these theories are considered natural and explain the allure of shows such as Entertainment Tonight or Hard Copy.

Beattie's main theory, however, is that the human brain will process audio and visual stimuli better than either text or images alone. "Television is such an effective medium because it provides a form of communication firmly embedded in our evolutionary past, the brain has after all clearly evolved to deal with speech in the context of the spontaneous images created by the human hand," writes Beattie.

His research confirmed that television is a superior method for advertising when compared to radio or newspaper. "We found that television is indeed a particularly effective communication medium for transmitting core information because it can split the message between speech and image, in the form of iconic gestures, and further that iconic gestures are an extremely effective mode of communication within television advertisements."

Hurray for television! "The brain simply likes telly," Beattie said in 2002. "Even I am surprised at how powerful television has been proved to be. No wonder it is the world's favorite medium. It's a perfect medium for advertising."

Even though Beattie is clearly a television industry cheerleader, he is describing a behavior that is already widely observed. Try having a conversation with somebody in the same room as a broadcasting television set and try not to look at the screen. The flashing colors, quick movements, and attractive people commonly portrayed on TV programs are irresistibly engaging.

Canadian media critic Marshall McLuhan said that "the medium is the message." What McLuhan saw in the 1950s and 1960s was how television was changing cultural perceptions of the world in profound and fundamental ways. "In the spiral of historic development, McLuhan says, we have returned . . . to a situation similar to that of tribal societies whose members could all congregate in the center of the village to listen to their leaders, priests, or shamans," explains Martin Esslin in the book *The Age of Television.*

"The age of civilization based on reading, on a written literature, is over," writes Esslin. "In our new era of oral communication, the linear, discursive mode of thought is going to be replaced, McLuhan maintains, by a primarily image-oriented type of perception and thinking."

If modern society is a tele-culture, then it should come as no surprise that video entertainment plays a huge role. A tele-culture, obviously, will give perennial approval for routine TV watching practices. No house is complete without a TV and today inexpensive LCD screens can literally place a TV set anywhere.

The U.S. Department of Labor reported in September 2004 that watching TV accounted for about half the leisure time on average for both American men and women. The Department's Time Use Survey showed that watching TV was third in total daily use of time behind working and sleeping.

Watching television is a culturally approved use of one's time. The average American will spend about three hours per day watching television, which adds up to 15 hours a week. If a person spends about nine hours sleeping, then at least one day's entire waking hours each week are spent watching TV.

The U.K. Office for National Statistics reported that around 85 percent of men and women watched television every day in 2002. The latest Social Trends survey shows that television tops the list of leisure activities for the United Kingdom.

Television's complete infusion into modern culture can be explained in a few ways. Esslin suggests that TV is a dramatic medium whose core nature is to portray the ordinary or mundane as exciting and compelling. Good television is dramatic and nothing interests people more than stories, both positive and negative, about others. "The ability of TV to transmit personality is, undoubtedly, the secret of its immense power. For human beings are insatiable in their interest about other human beings," writes Esslin. "This seems to me one of the basic human drives. Next to the satisfaction of the drives for food, shelter, and procreation, the satisfaction of the drive to gossip about the experiences of others must be one of the central concerns of all human existence . . . Television, with its unending stream of characters conveyed dramatically (whether fictional or 'real'), is the most perfect mechanized conveyor of that gossip."

Today's "water-cooler conversations" are often comprised of what appeared the previous day on television. Opinions are molded by television and the eyes delighted by the flashing colors and attractive TV personalities. Though the Internet can also bring information into the home, the Net lacks TV's drama and the ease of use. What could be easier than simply pressing the on button? Because people spend so much of their free time watching television, the medium has an enormous cultural effect.

"The identity of culture, the self-image of a nation, is formed by the concepts, myths, beliefs, and patterns of conduct that are instantly recognized by the members of that social entity as being particularly theirs," explains Esslin. "No other single factor of our present-day civilization — not the educational system or religion or science or the arts — is so all-pervasive, so influential, so totally accessible to and shared by all individuals in society as is the world presented by television."

Indeed, television's control over the cultural discourse makes it a seemingly indispensable resource in people's lives. There is a compelling cultural dogma that the "world presented by television" is the real and true world and one cannot possibly be a functioning member of society without a close familiarity with TV programming. In most cases, people cannot stand to live without their television set.

There is no doubt that television exerts a strong grip on the watcher. However, is a high amount of TV watching due to cultural norms combined with a genuine interest in what is broadcast or is the watcher simply powerless to turn it off? What are the factors that can mutate this devotion to television into a harmful addiction?

Sensory Confusion

Television's mighty grasp on the eyeballs of the viewer is partly due to the human body's inability to react to the transmitted programming. Images from the glowing, pulsing TV screen are stimulating; however the nature of the medium does not permit the body to respond appropriately. The body wants to react to the barrage of images, but cannot. This sensory disorientation — the TV watcher is visually and auditorily stimulated while remaining physically passive — confuses the mind. These conflicting messages and feelings succeed in creating an almost hypnotic trance in the viewer.

In his book *Four Arguments for the Elimination of Television*, Jerry Mander described how many avid TV watchers described the experience of sitting in front of the tube:

"I feel hypnotized when I watch television."
"Television sucks my energy."
"I feel like it's brainwashing me."
"I feel like a vegetable when I'm stuck there at the tube."
"Television spaces me out."
"Television is an addiction and I'm an addict."
"My kids look like zombies when they're watching."
"TV is destroying my mind."
"Television is turning my mind to mush."
"I feel mesmerized by it."

"If a television is on, I just can't keep my eyes off it."

Anyone who has spent time watching television is likely to agree with some, if not all, of these statements. Mander clarifies the comments by mentioning that not all the perceptions were negative. "Often the people who described themselves as 'spaced out' liked the experience. They said it helped them forget about their otherwise too busy lives," writes Mander. "Others found it 'relaxing,' saying that it helped them 'forget about the world.' Some who used terms like 'brainwashed' or 'addicted' nonetheless felt that television provided them with good information or entertainment, although there was no one who felt television lived up to its 'potential.'"

Mander's book was published in 1978, yet the experience of watching TV has not changed. Television is still a passive medium — one that requires the watcher to remain silent and still. Unlike any other leisure-time activity, watching TV is completely physically passive. (The only other comparison would be going to watch a movie; however, one must actually travel to the theater, and buy a ticket, popcorn, etc. Going to watch a movie is an actual experience or event, unlike watching TV, whose hours and hours of inactivity blend into each other.) The inactive nature of TV viewing creates an interesting psychological paradox: the more people watch, the worse they feel and, in turn, the more they watch.

The most complete study of TV habit and addiction comes from researchers Robert Kubey, a professor at Rutgers University and director of the Center for Media Studies, and Mihaly Csikszentmihalyi, professor of psychology at Claremont Graduate University. In the article "Television Addiction Is No Mere Metaphor," (Scientific American, Feb. 2002) Kubey and Csikszentmihalyi describe their experiment and results with a technique called the Experience Sampling Method:

"To track behavior and emotion in the normal course of life, as opposed to the artificial conditions of the lab, we have used the Experience Sampling Method (ESM). Participants carried a beeper, and we signaled them six to eight times a day, at random, over the period of a week; whenever they heard the beep, they wrote down what they were doing and how they were feeling using a standardized scorecard.

"As one might expect, people who were watching TV when we beeped them reported feeling relaxed and passive.

"What is more surprising is that the sense of relaxation ends when the set is turned off but the feelings of passivity and lowered alertness continue. Survey participants commonly reflect that television has somehow absorbed or sucked out their energy, leaving them depleted. They say they have more difficulty concentrating after viewing than before. In contrast, they rarely indicate such difficulty after reading. After playing sports or engaging in hobbies, people report improvements in mood. After watching TV, people's moods are about the same or worse than before.

"Thus, the irony of TV: people watch a great deal longer than they plan to, even though prolonged viewing is less rewarding. In our ESM studies the longer people sat in front of the set, the less satisfaction they said they derived from it. When signaled, heavy viewers (those who consistently watch more than four hours a day) tended to report on their ESM sheets that they enjoy TV less than light viewers did (less than two hours a day)."

In a paper entitled "Television Dependence, Diagnosis, and Prevention," Professor Kubey describes a cyclical effect of watching television. Heavy TV watchers tend to be people who feel anxious or lonely and watching TV provides a break from negative thoughts or ruminations. Providing a pseudo-social media experience, the television creates a virtual connection between the watcher and other people. However, this does nothing to help the real feelings of loneliness or boredom.

Kubey explains that "the possibility of a vicious circle, wherein the experience of negative moods and thoughts when alone and when unstructured, may interact with the ease with which people can quickly escape these feelings by viewing. As a result of many hours spent viewing television over many years, some people may become unpracticed in spending time alone, entertaining themselves, or even in directing their own attention."

Watching TV can never be a true substitute for real-life experiences. Kubey explains that his research shows that heavy viewers get trapped watching TV. "In short, a television viewing habit may be self-perpetuating," writes Kubey. "Viewing may lead to more viewing and may elicit what has been called 'attentional inertia,' i.e., 'the longer people look at television, the greater is the probability that they will continue to look.' Discomfort in non-committed, or solitary time, can lead to viewing, but after years of such behavior and a thousand hours or more of viewing each year, it seems quite possible that an ingrained television habit could cause some people to feel uncomfortable when left with 'nothing to do,' or alone, and not viewing."

Kubey's conclusion makes perfect logical sense. Television watching is not an "experience" but instead it replaces experiences. So TV watchers exchange the real world for the virtual one behind the screen. The cultural pressure and acceptance of heavy TV watching combined with the habitual nature of the medium can produce an unholy marriage between one's inactivity and boredom.

Breaking the Addiction

Is television addictive? Most psychological research suggests that TV can certainly become addictive and that heavy TV watchers display all the symptoms of a non-substance behavioral addiction. Breaking free of TV, and any addiction, is not an easy task. The difficulty in replacing television images with different (and more substantial) activities is the greatest obstacle breaking the addiction.

There is a basic theory in cognitive psychology called structuralism. Most closely associated with the work of Cornell psychology professor Edward Titchener, this theory contends that the mind breaks down life experiences into groups or concepts. Much like a chemist defines complex structures through its smaller parts and elements, the structural approach breaks down experiences and cultural identity into specific perceptions, notions and thoughts. Titchener believed that the complex world was made clear in the brain through an ordered thought process that included a vast array of individual parts.

Related to this is John Anderson's Adaptive Control of Thought (ACT) model. The ACT model breaks down elements of thought into nodes. These nodes contain a person's concepts and propositions and are put together in a person's head in order to make sense of the world. Anderson's model says that when people think of the past (long-term memory), they recall the essence of the experience and fill in the details with nodes of memory.

Breaking a television addiction involves replacing the virtual TV experience with real experiences. This is a choice. Choosing not to watch television and deciding to do something else with one's time and money is not life changing, only experience changing. Moderate and heavy TV watchers are creating nodes of experience in the mind filled with images and lifestyles proposed by the world of television. The addiction of watching TV is not physical, but behavioral. Moving away from the addiction requires the physical acts of turning off the tube and walking away from the set, but the choice is entirely cognitive.

[I've developed what I call] the "Kaufman Spectrum of Television Addiction" that is intended to assist those who wish to escape from the grasp of television. The spectrum shows four phases and by moving up or down the scale one can alter one's viewing habits:

The Phase 3 viewer is the addicted viewer. This is someone who rejects opportunities for interpersonal or active experiences and instead chooses to watch TV. In terms of one's cognitive development, this could be viewed as a harmful mode of activity. If we consider the ACT theory, one cannot truly make sense of the world without previous experiences (nodes of thought) with which the mind can call upon. If one's previous experiences are someone else's, such as the characters portrayed on the TV screen, then what is established as real life parallels life on the TV screen. Reality TV is not reality. Television only mimics reality and in most cases portrays the world in wild exaggerations.

The Kaufman Spectrum is used by changing behavior to move between phases. Moving from Phase 3 down to Phases 2 or 1 requires not only watching less TV, but also replacing virtual televised experiences with real ones. Moving between phases requires discipline and effort. Finding activities to replace television is not difficult; what is difficult is making the switch from inaction to action. One must choose to interact with other people and explore the unknown.

A moderate or heavy watcher will probably never move down to Phase 0 and totally remove himself or herself from the experience of television. After many years of TV viewing, going cold turkey is not realistic. However, it is possible to fill TV time with other activities and use the TV as a tool for relaxation rather than continue the subservience to habit.

Viewing Frequency	No TV Watching	Sporadic TV Watching (watch one or two particular shows each week)	Moderate TV Watching (watch at least one program per day)	Heavy TV Watching (more than 4 hours per day)
Television Habits	TV set remains off	Programs are watched in their entirety, then TV set is turned off.	Will research programs before watching. Balance between watching entire programs and channel surfing.	Watch TV out of habit, not interest. Heavy channel changing.
Social Habits	Involved with many non-TV activities. Have many hobbies and interests. Read a lot.	Watch TV out of interest and curiosity. Many non-TV interests and hobbies. Enjoy reading.	Watching TV high on list of favorite activities. Will plan social activities around TV schedule.	Frequent feelings of boredom. Will opt out of social events to watch television. Poor diet, exercise and reading habits.
	Phase 0	**Phase 1**	**Phase 2**	**Phase 3**

"I'd like to say I'd gone totally TV-free but it's not the case," explains Alan, a self-proclaimed TV addict in the U.K. who runs a Web log* describing his experience abandoning his TV-filled life. "But, then, saying that, I think I've found a comfortable middle ground where I am in charge and I don't need to be completely free of it. I know that sounds like an addict talking but I honestly think I've broken free of the chains of television, which is great.

"I no longer have it on just for noise and I watch only the odd couple of hours a week when my girlfriend is over . . . During the weekend we don't watch telly, as we go cycling and walking a lot. Plus, she has a horse to look after, which takes some time. . . I make a point of not watching the news in the morning, as I can listen to that on the car radio during the commute. When I get home I avoid sitting down on the sofa and instead I'll put on the radio, cook some dinner, then work on the computer or go out with friends. Towards the end of the evening I still avoid turning on the telly and go to bed to read a book. These aren't really conscious decisions anymore. . . . I just have no inclination to turn on the television."

"So, in a nutshell, I control the telly, not the other way around," says Alan. "If it does go on, because my girlfriend wants to watch something specific, then I turn it off again straight after... There's always something better to do. It doesn't tempt me anymore and it's no threat to my free time or sanity. I'm free!"

Clearly, Alan has found that having a rich and fulfilling life does not require spending hours and hours in front of the TV. Giving up television will sometimes require fighting a battle against boredom. Boredom is the mental state of suffering from lack of interesting stimuli. For moderate or heavy viewers, watching television is a popular activity because "there is nothing else to do." An extremely bored person can also acquire a general sense of dissatisfaction with life and then withdrawal from the world around them. Boredom also involves a lack of involvement with others and a dampening of interpersonal relationships.

"There are several things that lead us to the conclusion that entertainment television is lethal to social connection," explains Harvard professor Robert Putnam in a radio interview after the release of his book *Bowling Alone: The Collapse and Revival of American Community.*

> Part of it is the more entertainment television you watch, the less civically engaged you are. People watch *Friends* rather than having friends. And of course, you don't know which caused which, whether people decided to drop out and were left with television or they started watching television and then dropped out. The circumstantial evidence is pretty clear that television is actually the cause of this. There was a really fascinating study in a couple of towns in Canada were the sociologists got to the towns before television did and they were able to do before and after measurements of the effects of television — and as I would have expected, once television arrived in these towns, civic activity slumped substantially. — NPR, *All Things Considered,* May 31, 2000.

Breaking the television addiction requires making a choice. The famous Ellen Parr quote goes, "The cure for boredom is curiosity. There is no cure for curiosity." Watching TV fills the mind with the images and creativity of others; not watching TV fills the mind with freedom.

* Alan's blog is at *http://escapeyourtelevision.blogspot.com/.*

Bibliography

Beattie, Geoffrey Ph.D. and Dr. Heather Shovelton, "Making Thought Visible: The New Psychology of Body Language," Department of Psychology, University of Manchester, Manchester, U.K. 2003

Esslin, Martin, "The Age of Television," Transaction Publishers, 1982, 2002

Kubey, Robert, "Television Dependence, Diagnosis, and Prevention," Associate Professor, Department of Journalism and Media Studies, Rutgers University, New Brunswick, N.J., 1996

Kubey, Robert and Mihaly Csikszentmihalyi, "Television Addiction Is No Mere Metaphor," *Scientific American*, Feb. 2002

Mander, Jerry, "Four Arguments for the Elimination of Television," 1978

Reprinted with permission.

Source: *http://www.turnoffyourtv.com/healtheducation/addiction/addiction.html*

APPENDIX VI. BOOM CARS AND THE BOOM CAR CULTURE

The U.S. Department of Justice took an in-depth look at boom cars and the culture surrounding them as part of an effort to help police at the local level address the growing problem they posed. In developing its report, DOJ helped clarify the relationship between boom cars and the health of residents as well as between the boom car culture and the social health of the community. I reproduce a portion of the introductory section here because it provides a good framework for understanding the issue as both a health problem and a challenge to residents' rights.

Loud Car Stereos

Michael S. Scott

U.S. Department of Justice

Office of Community Oriented Policing Services

May 22, 2002

The problem of loud car stereos

The problem is attributable mainly to the use of special stereo equipment capable of producing extremely loud sound, rather than factory-installed stereo equipment. Most jurisdictions have some form of noise law that regulates loud car stereos. Police are concerned about loud car stereos for two main reasons: 1) they annoy some people, and 2) they inhibit drivers' ability to hear emergency signals on the road.

In some jurisdictions, drug dealers advertise by cruising neighborhoods with the car stereo turned up loud. In most jurisdictions, the problem of loud car stereos falls to the police to address, primarily because enforcement carries the risk of violent confrontation.

The problem of loud car stereos is more widespread than a simple tally of complaints would reveal. Perhaps only 5 to 10 percent of people bothered by any type of noise will file an official complaint, because other factors influence people. Many citizens are not aware of their legal right to quiet and do not know where they can register a complaint.

Consequently, the volume of official complaints about loud car stereos might indicate the existence of a problem, but not necessarily how intense or widespread it is.

Factors contributing to the problem of loud car stereos

Highly amplified car stereos emit a lot of low-frequency sounds through the systems' woofer speakers. Low-frequency noise is usually found to be more annoying than high-frequency noise at similar volume. The vibrations caused by the low-frequency sound waves can often be felt in addition to being heard. They cause glass and ceramics to rattle, compounding the annoyance.

Playing car stereos loudly can be an act of social defiance by some, or merely inconsiderate behavior by others. For yet others, it is a passionate hobby, an important part of their cultural identity and lifestyle. Judging by the sales marketing of car stereo manufacturers and dealers, the interest in car stereo competitions and the sums of money spent on car stereos, police are confronting a popular and lucrative phenomenon. It is not easy to change the behavior of those who see loud car stereos as an important part of their lifestyle.

Overexposure to noise is now understood to have a number of negative health and behavioral effects. Loud car stereos most obviously affect the car occupants' hearing. Noise from a variety of sources, including loud car stereos, can cause hearing loss, disturb sleep, increase stress, make people irritable, and make naturally aggressive people more aggressive. It can make people less likely to help others, and less likely to sit outdoors or participate in social activities. It can compel people to move out of neighborhoods they otherwise like, and thereby depress property values. Some people, such as schoolchildren, hospital patients, and the mentally ill, are especially harmed by exposure to loud noise (although loud car stereos may not be a major noise source for these subpopulations).

How annoyed people get about noise depends on a number of factors, including the following:

• The inherent unpleasantness of the sound. This varies widely among individuals and groups. What is music to one is noise to another.

• The persistence and recurrence of the noise. Most listeners can tolerate occasional loud noises more than persistent and recurrent loud noises.

• The meaning listeners attribute to the sound. The information content of the noise influences annoyance, so if listeners do not like the message of the music being played, they are more likely to be annoyed by loud car stereos. Some people perceive loud car stereos to be an expression of rudeness and selfishness, or even a form of aggression — a blatant defiance of social etiquette and norms. If listeners associate loud car stereos with people they think are dangerous, the noise problem seems even more serious.

• Whether the sound interferes with listeners' activities. For example, loud car stereos are more likely to annoy people during nighttime hours than during daytime hours because they disrupt sleep.

• Whether listeners feel they can control the noise. The less control one feels, the more likely the noise will be annoying.

• Whether listeners believe third parties, including police, can control the noise. If people believe a third party can control the noise but has failed to do so, they are more likely to be annoyed by the noise.

> Applying these factors to loud car stereos, you can see how the same sound can affect people quite differently: some will enjoy it, while others will hate it. People respond to noise in various ways. Some people complain to authorities, some take steps to insulate themselves, some adapt to the noise, and some move away from the noise. Those who complain greatly appreciate effective responses from authorities; no response or ineffective responses are often harshly criticized.

Source: *http://www.cops.usdoj.gov/pdf/e05021550.pdf.*

APPENDIX VII. CHECKOUT TV: WHERE'S THE 94 PERCENT WHO LIKE IT?

When the *Washington Post* ran a small, first-person piece on the reporter's first experience with TV in the checkout line at a grocery store, almost 30 readers sent in comments and every one of the comments expressed exasperation at the TV's introduction. Not one supported it. In the article, the reporter quotes a spokesperson for Premier Retail Networks, the media company that provides the programming, saying that 76 percent of customers surveyed watch the TVs and of that number, 94 percent say they're a good thing. Given the 100-percent negative response to the TVs in comments to the story, it's clear that the media company's survey failed to capture the high level of animosity many people feel toward being made captive to TV they didn't ask for. What's significant isn't that all of the letters are negative but that the level of animosity toward the TVs was so high. Here are excerpts from a handful of the letters that were submitted.

> "The minute I see my first TV at a checkout, I'll tell the manager, 'Watch me. I'm about to walk out of your store because I can't stand TV. You won't see me again until all the other stores in the area have the same damn thing....' " *Posted by Gene*

> "Where on earth do these marketing people get their information? Is there actually one normal person who enjoys these TVs?" *Posted by RB*

> "I'm either going to bring ear plugs to the grocery store or just shoot myself in the head when I see one of those TVs...." *Posted by Melissa*

> ". . . Online shopping and delivery are looking better all the time." *Posted by Fed Up Shopper*

"The supermarket TVs that I've seen are . . . a very unwelcome distraction. I do wonder how many times these [advertising] folks need to say that advertising is a "welcome distraction" before they actually believe it. It's not. *Posted by Shopper*

"Creative and voluntary advertisement presentation is fine, but like many of today's applied business behaviors undesired imposition is offensive and can only be changed by customer actions." Posted by *Pavlov's Antithesis*

"It's the adult version of BusRadio (the radio station they want to play on school buses). Talk about captive audiences. About five years ago I started using my waiting time in line as a time to meditate. This is seriously going to distract from being in the moment." *Posted by Momma Daria*

"I expect they use "did not complain" to mean "likes TVs" as the metric. I hate those things unless they have the sound off." *Posted by Michael*

"I think I'll write to my grocery stores around here and PRE-complain. I'm guessing the "zapper" remote control thingy [TV-B-Gone by Cornfield Electronics] that turns off TVs won't work." *Posted by Ughhh*

"This kind of over-the-top commercialism only happens because people let it. Folks, if you don't like this, as I don't, then get vocal about it. Pull the manager of the store over and let him or her know how you feel and that it makes you not want to patronize the store. If people speak with their wallets and enough hours of that manager's day get used up by people complaining about their marketing strategy I can guarantee you it will be short-lived.... *Posted by Jason*

"I switched HMO sites because of a loud TV, blaring soap operas in the waiting room. It was awful . . . Lord we will be a nation of illiterate zombies soon if this idiotic racket arrives at grocery stores. Thanks, posters, for showing I'm not alone in this view." *Posted by Jeannette*

"The only thing we poor consumers can do is stick to our guns, tell everybody who is in a position of power to do something about it, that we won't be taken in as a captive audience easily. We may never completely win, but we can keep the world sane by continuing to fight the good fight. I think we're soon going to add "going grocery" to our language. It will have the same meaning as "going postal." *Posted by Gene*

"I experienced checkout TV at Kroger's in Ann Arbor, Mich., about 1990. It was horrible. At the end of a busy day at work the last thing I wanted was to be assaulted in line at a grocery store where I was waiting to spend money. I complained and others must have also because it disappeared relatively quickly." *Posted by Ellen*

You can read the article and all 27 of the comments at the *Washington Post* at *http://voices.washingtonpost.com/thecheckout/2006/08/checkout_tv_super_marketing.html.*

Appendix VIII. Commercial TV and Radio in Schools

BusRadio and Channel One are two out-of-home media companies that have taken considerable heat over the years for their business models, which are based on the leveraging of children in a governmentally mandated captive-audience environment: public schools. At the core of concerns expressed by parenting, education, civic, health, and religious organizations is the appropriateness of commercial companies profiting from the requirement, enforceable by law, that all children attend public school if they're not otherwise enrolled in a recognized private- or home-school setting.

Included here is a selection of comments to a 2006 *Washington Post* article on BusRadio and a representative letter from a coalition of more than 40 organizations discouraging consumer products and services companies from buying ads on Channel One, the in-school TV network.

BusRadio

The number of comments generated in response to the *Washington Post* piece on commercial radio on school buses in 2006 was so large (more than 285) and so representative of different concerns people have over captive-audience media when it involves their children that it's valuable to reproduce a small sampling of the comments here.

Of course, not all of the comments were against the commercial radio service. As one person put it, having child-appropriate content piped into the bus is probably preferable to some of the music choices children make on their own:

"BusRadio needs a chance here. Music as a whole is very soothing, to adults as well as children. Out of a 44-minute broadcast, only eight minutes are being used for advertising. The broadcast [contains] age-appropriate [content]. I'd rather have that coming at my child than [music from] the next kid who has an iPod that has sexually explicit songs and thinks it's funny to hear swear words. If the program is regulated, it could be used as a great [education] tool. You can't automatically look at everything as being so bad; look at how [the programming] could be used for the good." *Posted by Stephanie*

But 90 percent of the comments were against the radio service, and for many of the people expressing their disapproval, the concern was less about the content than about the notion of captivity. Here are excerpts from a sample of the comments:

> "The whole idea of allowing anyone to pipe any messages into any audience where they do not have the right to leave and are forced to listen to the message is wrong!" *Posted by Donnie*

> "No, I do not want my children to be a captive audience to any kind of radio. One person wondered what all the fuss was about because children

can get a lot of advertising on TV and the average person watches four hours a day of TV. Not in our household." *Posted by Terri*

"Personally, as one who has taken a commuter bus to work, it sounds like my worst nightmare, being unable to think my own pleasant thoughts because of the constant intrusion upon the thoughts of controlled content radio." *Posted by Min*

"It seems to me that this is 1) a captive audience, and 2) someone's idea of how to make money off of children." *Posted by Mike*

"Advertisements to a captive audience composed of kids unable to handle being manipulated? Sounds like a serious invasion of privacy issue to me. See you in the courts, BusRadio and school systems!" *Posted by Gene*

"I realize that it's next to impossible to get children away from all of today's advertising in all of its many shapes and forms. What exacerbates this BusRadio situation is the fact that the children cannot escape it and the parents cannot control it. Therein lay the rub." *Posted by Tiphanie23*

"When did this even happen? This is a terrible idea. What on earth is wrong with leaving kids alone to think for themselves without constant input, be it electronic or otherwise? We're raising an army of kids who've been told how to think from so many sources for their whole lives." Posted by *Barnagirl*

"No, no, no, no, no. No ads (or any programming) on buses, no ads in schools, no fast food or junk food in cafeterias, no corporate sponsorship of school facilities. Schools: Don't undermine the hard work of parents trying to raising happy, healthy, aware and responsible children. Please." *Posted by Kirk*

"I find it utterly repulsive to think that those responsible for our children's public education would consider selling them out as captive audiences to advertising geniuses." *Posted by Deb*

"The media has done well to expand their abilities to "capture" the minds of children and others over the years. It has become very flashy, noisy, and can fill our minds with useless information. We are surrounded by TV, music, videos, and magazines. Media can become an addiction which is very difficult to break." *Posted by Ruby Maye*

"Not only am I against this because it is advertising to a captive audience, but also because I don't trust corporate America to determine what is appropriate music for our children. What's more, learning and development, especially social development, occurs when people interact with one another." *Posted by Pete*

"It is not right for a captive audience to have to listen to the bus radio. I'm annoyed when I get put on hold and have to listen to someone else's idea of music." *Posted by Patricia*

"I do not agree with holding my children as a captive audience for anyone!" *Posted by Rachel*

"Auggghhhhh!!! No! Is there no peace and quiet left in this world?!" *Posted by Andrew*

You can read all of the comments at *http://voices.washingtonpost.com/thecheckout/2006/08/post_9.html.*

Channel One

The in-school commercial TV network Channel One, which mixes ads targeted at children with news programming, launched in 1990 and has weathered unremitting criticism ever since. The company was sold in 2007 to a self-described "untraditional media company," Alloy, Inc., by media conglomerate Primedia, which cited falling revenue for the sale. Letters like the one excerpted below, which makes a moral appeal against supporting the company's business model, have most likely been a contributing factor to the company's falling revenue. The letter is signed by more than 70 individuals representing civic, education, health, religious, children, media, and parenting organizations who call it morally repugnant for companies to exploit for commercial purposes children subject to mandatory school attendance. The signatories are noteworthy because of their number, breadth, and caliber, so they're identified following the excerpt. This particular letter is to Alan Lafley, head of consumer products giant Proctor & Gamble. *Reprinted with permission of Commercial Alert.*

> Dear Mr. Lafley:
>
> We write to ask your company to stop advertising on Primedia's controversial in-school marketing program Channel One.
>
> As you know, Channel One shows about ten minutes of news, banter, music and filler, and two minutes of ads, to a captive audience of roughly eight million children as young as eleven years of age, in 12,000 schools each school day.
>
> Compelling impressionable children to view commercials during their limited school time is repugnant, and removing Channel One from our nation's schools is a high-priority education reform across the conventional political spectrum.
>
> Your company's advertising revenues are the lifeblood that keeps Channel One in business. Following are eight reasons not to advertise on Primedia's Channel One:
>
> 1. Channel One misuses the compulsory attendance laws to force children to watch ads. Joel Babbit, then-president of Channel One, explained in 1994 why advertisers like Channel One: "The biggest selling point to advertisers [is] . . . we are forcing kids to watch two minutes of commer-

cials." Last year, two Ohio children were sent to a juvenile detention facility for refusing to watch Channel One in school.

2. Channel One wastes school time. Each 30-second commercial on Channel One usurps over 66,000 hours of students' school time across the country. Channel One consumes the equivalent of one instructional week of students' school time each school year, including one full day watching ads.

3. Channel One promotes violent entertainment. It is irresponsible for Channel One to advertise violent movies, such as "Supernova," "The Mummy," and James Bond's "The World is Not Enough," when millions of parents are rightly worried about school shootings and violence.

4. Channel One wastes tax dollars spent on schools. A 1998 study by Max Sawicky and Alex Molnar, titled "The Hidden Costs of Channel One," concluded that Channel One's cost to taxpayers in lost class time is $1.8 billion per year. Every one of your company's Channel One ads is a theft of taxpayer money that should be spent on educating children.

5. Channel One promotes the wrong values to children. For example, Channel One advertised "Dude, Where's My Car?," a movie glorifying two potheads who got so stoned that they couldn't remember where they parked their car. In February, it advertised "Monkeybone," a crass movie about the battle between a cartoonist and his penis, symbolized by a monkey. Still worse, Channel One promotes the commercial culture in general, and teaches a curriculum of materialism, that buying is good, and will solve your problems, and that consumption and self-gratification are the goals and ends of life.

6. Channel One is bad for children's health. American children are suffering from an epidemic of obesity. Channel One likely makes this epidemic worse by aggressively promoting junk food and soda pop. Channel One often advertises Pepsi, despite a recent study in The Lancet that directly links the consumption of soda pop to childhood obesity. Given skyrocketing levels of childhood obesity and Type II diabetes, it is wrong for schools to teach children to eat high-calorie junk food.

7. Channel One corrupts the integrity of public education. In effect, Channel One appropriates the authority of schools and transfers it to the advertisers of these controversial products. By inviting Channel One's huckstering into the classroom, schools implicitly endorse what Channel One advertises, at high cost to the moral authority of teachers, administrators and schools.

8. Channel One promotes television instead of reading. The latest National Assessment of Educational Progress reading test showed that two-thirds of fourth-grade children could not even read at a proficient level. Children already watch too much TV, on average, about 19 hours and 40 minutes each week. Schools should encourage children to read, not to gaze at a TV set.

Channel One claims that it teaches current events and anti-drug messages effectively. Even if these arguments were true, there are other ways to teach children such lessons that do not involve compulsory watching of harmful ads in schools.

Many organizations oppose Channel One or its use of the schools for commercial advertising. The National Council of Teachers of English opposes "intrusions of commercial television, such as Channel One, in the classroom." The National PTA, National Association of State Boards of Education, Association for Supervision and Curriculum Development and other educational organizations oppose commercials in the classroom. In 1999, the Southern Baptist Convention, our nation's largest Protestant denomination, passed a resolution urging parents "to seek effective ways to protect their children" from Channel One's "advertising assault."

In its latest public relations effort, Primedia's Channel One professes to be a conservative, pro-family company. That claim is especially laughable since Primedia has merged with About.com, which distributes hard-core pornography on the Internet.

Even if you feel your company has the right to intrude on schoolchildren during their class time, we urge you to consider the public embarrassment and backlash your company may experience if you continue to misuse the school day, and continue your company's public association with Primedia's Channel One.

For the sake of our nation's children, we strongly recommend that you stop advertising on Primedia's Channel One, and issue a public statement encouraging other advertisers to do the same. We are grateful for your attention to this matter and look forward to hearing from you at your earliest convenience.

Sincerely,

Enola Aird, Director, The Motherhood Project, Institute for American Values

Joan Almon, Coordinator, Alliance for Childhood

Patricia Aufderheide, Professor, American University

David Bollier, author, policy strategist

David Bosworth, Associate Professor of English, University of Washington

Wally Bowen, Founder, Citizens for Media Literacy

Michael Brody, Chair, Television and Media Committee, American Academy of Child and Adolescent Psychiatry

Brita Butler-Wall, Executive Director, Citizens' Campaign for Commercial-Free Schools

Bettye M. Caldwell, Past President, National Association for the Education of Young Children

Nancy Carlsson-Paige, Professor of Education, Lesley University

Jason Catlett, President, Junkbusters Corp.

Ronnie Cummins, National Director, Organic Consumers Association

Matt Damon, actor

Gloria DeGaetano, CEO, The Parent Coaching Institute; author of *Television and the Lives of Our Children* and *Stop Teaching Our Kids to Kill*

Leon Eisenberg, Professor of Social Medicine and Professor of Psychiatry Emeritus, Harvard Medical School

David Elkind, Professor of Child Development, Tufts University; author, *The Hurried Child*

Amitai Etzioni, University Professor, George Washington University; author, *Next: The Road to the Good Society*

Michael Feinstein, Mayor, City of Santa Monica, California

Roy F. Fox, Assoc. Prof. of Literacy Education, U. of MO-Columbia; author, *Harvesting Minds* and *MediaSpeak*

Gilbert L. Fuld, former Member, Board of Directors, American Academy of Pediatrics

John Taylor Gatto, author, *The Underground History of American Education* and *Dumbing Us Down*

George Gerbner, President and Founder, Cultural Environment Movement; Dean Emeritus, Annenberg School of Communication

Rev. Tom Grey, Executive Director, National Coalition Against Gambling Expansion

Lt. Col. David Grossman, former Professor of Psychology, West Point; author, *On Killing* and *Stop Teaching our Kids to Kill*

Jaydee Hanson, Assistant General Secretary for Public Witness and Advocacy, General Board of Church and Society, United Methodist Church

Jane M. Healy, author, *Failure to Connect* and *Endangered Minds*

Mark Hickson, Professor and Chair of the Department of Communications Studies, University of Alabama at Birmingham

Carol Holst, Program Director, Seeds of Simplicity

Michael F. Jacobson, Executive Director, Center for Science in the Public Interest; co-author, Marketing Madness

Sut Jhally, Founder and Executive Director, The Media Education Foundation

Carden Johnston, Chair, Task Force on Commercialism in the Classroom, Alabama Chapter, American Academy of Pediatrics

Jean Kilbourne, author, *Can't Buy My Love: How Advertising Changes the Way We Think and Feel*

Rebecca T. Kirkland, Professor of Pediatrics, Chief of Academic General Pediatrics, Baylor College of Medicine

Naomi Klein, author, No Logo David C. Korten, author, *When Corporations Rule the World*

Velma LaPoint, Associate Professor of Human Development, Howard University

Diane Levin, Professor of Education, Wheelock College; author, *Remote Control Childhood*

Jane Levine, Founder, Kids Can Make A Difference

Susan Linn, Associate Director, Media Center of the Judge Baker Children's Center; Instructor in Psychiatry, Harvard Medical School

Dana Mack, Senior Fellow, Center for Education Studies: author, *The Assault on Parenthood*

Bob McCannon, Executive Director, New Mexico Media Literacy Project

Robert McChesney, Research Associate Professor, U. of Illinois at Urbana-Champaign; author, *Rich Media, Poor Democracy*

Ken McNatt, President, Students Against Commercialized Classrooms Organization (SACCO)

Robert A. Mendelson, Clinical Professor, Oregon Health Sciences University

Michael Mendizza, Co-founder, Touch The Future

Jim Metrock, President, Obligation, Inc.

Mark Crispin Miller, Professor of Media Ecology, New York University

Tom Minnery, Vice President of Public Policy, Focus on the Family

Alex Molnar, Professor of Education, University of Wisconsin-Milwaukee; Director, Center for the Analysis of Commercialism in Education

Kathryn C. Montgomery, President, Center for Media Education

Diane Morrison, Research Professor, School of Social Work, University of Washington

Ralph Nader

Mary O'Brien, author, *Making Better Environmental Decisions*

Peggy O'Mara, Editor and Publisher of *Mothering Magazine*

Gary Palmer, President, Alabama Policy Institute

Shelley Pasnik, children's media writer and researcher

Neil Postman, Chairman, Department of Culture and Communication, New York University; author, *Amusing Ourselves to Death*

Alvin F. Poussaint, Professor of Psychiatry, Harvard Medical School

Raffi, the children's troubadour, Founder and Chair, Troubadour Institute for Child-Honoring

Hugh Rank, Professor Emeritus, Governors State University; author, *Persuasion Analysis*

Lee Richardson, former President, Consumer Federation of America

Gary Ruskin, Executive Director, Commercial Alert

Phyllis Schlafly, President, Eagle Forum

Don Shifrin, past President, Washington Chapter, American Academy of Pediatrics

Tamara L. Sobel, Project Director, The Girls, Women and Media Project

John Stauber, founder, PR Watch; co-author, *Trust Us, We're Experts* and *Toxic Sludge is Good for You*

Inger Stole, Assistant Professor, Dept. of Advertising, University of Illinois at Urbana-Champaign

Victor Strasburger, Professor of Pediatrics, University of New Mexico School of Medicine

Sue Lockwood Summers, Director, Media Alert!

Frank Vespe, Executive Director, TV-Turnoff Network

Linda Wagener, Associate Dean, School of Psychology, Fuller Theological Seminary

David Walsh, President, National Institute on Media and the Family; author, *Selling Out America's Children*

Donald E. Wildmon, President, American Family Association, Inc.

Nancy Willard, Project Director, Responsible Netizen, Center for Advanced Technology in Education, University of Oregon

APPENDIX IX. TV IN COMMON SPACE: ACTIVISTS' GUIDE

Responsible-TV group White Dot has on occasion organized TV-turnoff events, sometimes in tandem with TV-Turnoff Week, an annual spring event championed in North America and parts of Europe by a coalition of organizations that includes the Center for SCREENTIME Awareness. To help individuals and groups mount their own TV-turnoff events, White Dot has made available on its Web site this light-hearted guide and downloadable handouts:

A Guide to Direct Action against TVs in Public Places

White Dot now has volunteers all over America and Britain taking part in protests against televisions in public places. Here is a guide to the kinds of things you can do.

Direct Action

When you hear the words "direct action" you may think of Greenpeace volunteers chaining themselves to whaling ships. If you want to chain yourself to the doors of a restaurant that has a TV then go for it! Tell us where to send the reporters. But you don't have to be confrontational. Here is what we aim to achieve:

1. Show customers they have a real say over how these places are run.

2. Show owners of restaurants and cafes that TV may be LOSING them customers.

3. Start a conversation about noise pollution, image pollution and public spaces.

4. Suggest to owners they use a TV-free atmosphere to attract customers.

5. Show that ordinary customers are wise to the way TV is being pushed at them.

6. Tell people about the new and growing industry in "captive audience television."

7. Show that ordinary customers HATE being a captive audience.

Places to Go

Televisions are now everywhere you go. Look for them in banks, supermarkets, filling stations, pubs, clubs, bars, restaurants, diners, cafes, barber shops, post offices, doctors' waiting rooms, hospitals, airports, train stations, cafeterias, airplanes, buses, subways, stationers, department stores, and even men's toilets.

Things You Can Do

The first thing to do is invite some friends. You'll feel less nervous as part of a gang, and remember: the large majority of people in pubs and cafes do not want the TV on. It's the TV's owner who should be feeling sheepish. Plan a route through town and turn it into a pub crawl.

1. Write down a few reasons why you don't like the TV sets on

2. Read some of the articles on WhiteDot.org

3. Have a look at www.aka.net ... and remind yourself why this is important

4. Download and print the materials on WhiteDot.org

5. You might wish to buy a TV-B-Gone universal remote. It turns off any TV set and White Dot makes some money

6. Talk the idea over with a friend and get used to answering questions

7. Remember: If you drink too much, coffee or alcohol, it could all get ugly

Once inside somewhere that is polluted by television, there are a number of ways to clean it up:

1) The Quiet Way

Walk into a cafe. Sneakily place the menu cards into all the menus. Turn off the TV. Leave. Repeat every day for a few days.

2) The Conversational Way

Walk into a cafe. Place menu cards in a few menus. Turn off the TV. See if anyone notices. Ask your fellow customers if they noticed. Ask if they like or do not like the TV on. Ask to speak to the owner. Point out that you turned off the TV and no one cared, or were happy it was off. Give him the signs advertising "We've turned off the TV," etc., and ask if he or she would like to offer their customers quiet times or days during the week.

3) Another Conversational Way

As above, but speak with customers first. Take a vote. If more people want it off than on, turn it off. Ask to speak to the owner and explain what you've done. Ask if he would like to put a questionnaire near the cash register, asking people if they like it or not.

4) The Campaigning Way

If a place has refused to talk to you or you've been thrown out, stand outside with a clipboard, asking people as they go in whether or not they want a TV on as they drink or eat. Be honest. Record all the "yes" answers and "no" answers. (The chances are very good that the "no" answers will outnumber the "yes" answers.) Gather lots of signatures. Call the press. Have them photograph you presenting the survey to the owner.

4) The Confrontational Way

Get together with five friends and arrange times of the day and week when you will go in and turn off the TV, leave menu cards etc. Keep doing it until you are thrown out. Call the media and invite them along. Have them film you being thrown out.

5) The Very Confrontational Way

Chain yourself to the railings.

The Press

Read through the "Ruined Diners" pages of our Web site [which features the downloadable signs below and accompanying explanatory text]. They will give you an idea of what we at White Dot are saying to the media

Call the local newspaper, etc., and send us an e-mail with a phone number so we can put you in touch with other reporters. If you speak to the press, just be yourself. Explain why you don't like TV in public places and that turning off the TV is just a way to show the people around you that they have a choice. Don't bother getting too serious or angry. On this issue, we are actually in the majority. Most people feel exactly the way you do. So don't speak too harshly. We win this argument just by having the conversation.

Important: If you have a TV-B-Gone and plan to use it in a news story, make sure the TV-B-Gone works on the TV in the place you are going! The TV-B-Gone turns off virtually any TV, but you want to be sure.

Afterwards

Most importantly, write to us and tell us how it went. What did people say? Who supported you and who got mad?

Ruined Diners Materials

Yes, you can turn off that TV when no one is looking. But that misses the point. Customers need to wake up and see what power they have. Restaurant owners need to see how "No TV" can equal "New Customers." Download and print these great tools:

"Today's Special" Menu Card

Hidden discretely in the menu of your favorite diner or coffee shop, this little beauty will jolt your fellow customers out of their distracted gaze.

"Valued Customers" Sign

Some people like some TV, others don't. Some days there is a big game on the box. Most days there isn't. Now the poor bar or restaurant owner has to deal with anti-TV campaigners! Show him or her you care by offering this polite notice to customers that if they like the TV, they watch it. And if they don't, they can turn it off. See? Everybody happy.

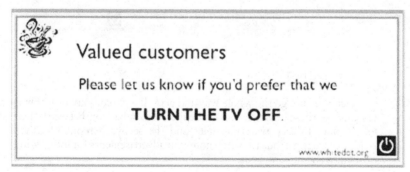

"We've Turned It Off" Sign

Owners of eating and drinking establishments should experiment. If they insist on having a TV in the corner (or in some cases on every wall you look) they should offer "TV-free Days" and use it to attract different kinds of customers on different days. Let the market decide!

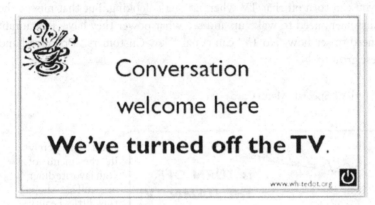

"We're TV Free" Sign

Oh, what does the market know? Someone has to play the bold vision-ary! Owners can put this sign on their front door and tell the world that they stand for good, old-fashioned eating and drinking, quiet reading, loud arguments, and laughter.

"Not Ruined by TV" Sign

In fact, why not go the whole way and get self-righteous about it? Own-ers can use these signs to draw a deliberate comparison between their wholesome, TV-free watering holes and the seedy, disreputable dives that force their patrons to watch non-stop advertisements for indigestion medicines and moving beds.

Conversation welcome here

This establishment *not*

RUINED BY TELEVISION.

www.whitedot.org

Customer Survey

Do you want these things on or not? Challenge the shop or restaurant owner to put this survey next to the cash register. Let customers say for themselves how much they like or hate TV sets interrupting their conversations.

Note: Direct action guide and card images reprinted with permission.

APPENDIX X. CAPTIVE-AUDIENCE MEDIA COMPANIES

The U.S.-based Out-of-Home Video Advertising Bureau and the Canadian Out-of-Home Digital Association have grown rapidly since their founding only a few years ago. Their strong growth comes at a time when traditional broadcast media is struggling with flat or declining ad revenue, reinforcing the migration of ad spending from traditional media, which consumers are turning off, to captive-audience platforms, which consumers can't turn off. The companies identified as members of the two organizations are listed here to show the scope and depth of growth in this new media sector.

Out-of-Home Video Advertising Bureau (Members as of early 2009)

Access 360 Media: *Retail, online, and mobile digital media*

Media network that reaches more than 170 million shoppers, ages 12 to 34, monthly, in an environment where they are "receptive to hearing your message via in-store, online, and mobile platforms." In-store screens and signage aim to extend brand relationship by "driving consumers to your Web site or to text in for offers, alerts, or content"

www.access360media.com

Adspace Mall Network: *Mall-based digital displays*

"Full motion" digital video and audio in a mall environment that aims to deliver "upscale consumers that are in a buying frame of mind"

www.adspacenetworks.com

AMI Meganet

Digital media in bars and taverns

Out-of-home market video medium with four networks of "no-repeat" content; "reinforce your message with spots running concurrently on TAP.tv"

www.amimeganet.com

Arbitron Out of Home: *Media and marketing research*

Local market consumer data, which advertisers can use to "show prospects that the types of people who are exposed to out-of-home media are the same types of people who patronize their businesses" and "analyze the time spent commuting versus the percentage of commuters who don't read newspapers"

www.arbitron.com

Arena Media Networks: *Out-of-home sports and entertainment network*

Programming and marketing platforms enable marketers to reach more than "90 million passionate fans" and "an elusive demographic currently available in professional sports stadiums and arenas"

www.arena-media.com

Billboard Planet, Inc.: *Billboard campaign platform*

Online exchange for leasing billboard space and "securing the best prices for large format printing" *www.billboardplanet.com*

BroadSign: *Digital signage management*
Software solutions to set up and manage digital signage networks and distribute and play back media files across locations, "transforming the fast-growing digital signage space into a new mass medium"
www.broadsign.com

Buzztime: *Digital media in restaurants and bars*
"Turn your location into an entertainment mecca where crowds gather and fun ensues"
www.buzztime.com

Captivate Network: *Elevator digital media network*
National network delivers more than 57.3 million monthly impressions to more than 2.6 million people. "We deliver your message to a captive audience in a focused, distraction-free environment," and "consistently generate strong, tangible results on behalf of our clients"
www.captivate.com

Care Media Holdings Corp.: *Health education media*
Advertiser-supported educational programming (under the *PetCare*, *KidCare*, and *HealthCare* brands) "within the captive audience environment of medical specialty offices"
www.caremediaholdings.com

CBS Outernet: *Out-of-home arm of the network giant*
Customized digital media networks and programming to grocery stores, pharmacies, medical waiting rooms, taxis, gas stations, and "other places where people shop, eat, travel and gather"
www.cbsouternet.com

Channel M: *In-store media*
"Effectively reach your target audience in an environment that is exclusive, tivo and clutter free...When people are in a store, they actually want to hear from you..."
www.channelm.com

ClubCom: *Digital media for the fitness industry*
"Powerful, unparalleled advertising platform reaching a captive audience consisting of the world's most qualified consumer groups"
www.clubcom.com

CNN Airport: *The news network of the broadcast giant*
"Available in 43 of the busiest U.S. airports and is seen in more than 2,000 gates and other viewing areas"
http://www.cnn.com/CNN/Programs/airport.network/

Danoo: *In-store programming*
Through contracts with "thousands of high traffic, high frequency, and high dwell time locations, Danoo delivers millions of uncluttered impressions to a highly sought-after audience in the top media markets"
www.danoo.com

EnQii: *Digital out-of-home provider*
"Networked digital out-of-home solutions for retailers, advertisers, and other media estate owners..." Digital View Media [one of three divisions] provides services to the "global screen media, captive audience networks industry"
www.enqii.com

Gas Station TV: *Digital network for gas stations*
"Reaches the consumer 'off the couch' and ready to take action"
www.gstv.com

Healthcare News Networks: *Healthcare provider TV network*
"Delivers both national health news and customized local content directly driven by patients' needs... ensures you reach the right people in the right place at the right time"
www.healthcarenewsnetwork.tv

Health Club Panel Network: *Digital network for health club facilities*
"Reaches approximately seven in every ten health club members working out in the top 20 [metro areas]"
www.healthclubpanel.com

IdeaCast: *Out-of-home advertising platforms*
Delivers digital, out-of-home TV advertising platforms that bring "compelling programming into consumers' daily out-of-home lives"
www.ideacast.net

IndoorDirect: *Restaurant digital media network*
"Restaurant customers are 'in action' when they eat out, usually on their way to another retail environment"
www.indoordirect.com

LevelVision: *Point-of-sale digital media provider*
"Brings advertising and informational messages to previously unreachable, highly desired commercial locations..." and helps businesses "sell more efficiently by engaging buyers in a uniquely direct way — in their natural line-of-sight, in their proxemic space, and at the point where most buying decisions are made"
www.levelvision.com

NBC Everywhere: *Out-of-home arm of the network giant*
"Reaches 1,000 gyms, 3,000 New York taxis, 8,000 schools, 1,005 grocery stores, 181 college campuses, as well as countless screens on commuter trains, arenas, and in Times Square; NBC Everywhere totals 3 billion impressions every year"
www.nbclocalmedia.com/platforms/

Nielsen Media Research: *Audience rating services applied to out-of-home platforms*
Tracks television and media-viewing habits
www.nielsenmedia.com

Office Media Network: *Office-based digital media platform*
"Broadcasts up-to-the-minute Wall Street Journal content throughout the day" to large-format, high-definition LCD flat-screens in "high-profile office buildings"
www.officemedia.net

OnSite Network: *Bars, sports-oriented restaurants digital network*
"Puts your brand in the thick of the action"
www.osn.net

Premier Retail Networks: *Digital media network for retail outlets*
Reaches more than "650 million shoppers every month; these shoppers spend $360 billion a year in more than 6,500 stores..." enables advertisers "to target consumers in the locations and markets that matter most. . . . When shoppers become buyers, PRN will make sure your brand is there."
www.prn.com

ProLink Network: *Digital media on golf courses*
Golf cart-mounted digital out-of-home marketing with a reach of "14 million golfers" providing on-screen advertising to a "captive and largely exclusive audience."
www.prolinknetwork.net

PumpTop TV: *Gas station media network*

Delivers news, entertainment and advertising to "millions of drivers as they fuel their vehicles at the gas pump; daylight-viewable LCD screens mounted at eye level on top of gasoline pumps at select, high-volume gas stations provide a broadcast television-like experience (video and audio) to a desirable, captive audience out of the home."

www.pumptoptv.com

Ripple TV: *Specialty retail media network*

Digital signage networks for "Borders, Jack-in-the-Box and Jiffy Lube"

www.rippletv.com

Samsung: *LCD and plasma displays*

"Video walls and out-of-the-box touch screen LCD solutions...can help you spread your message"

www.samsung.com

Screenvision: *Cinema advertising*

Delivers "national, regional and local movie theater advertising to promote your business at the movies"

www.screenvision.com

SeeSaw Networks: *Out-of-home media provider*

"Advertise where people work, play and socialize; intercept your audience in their daily routines"

www.seesawnetworks.com

Simon Media with OnSpot Digital: *Shopping mall digital media*

"Simon Brand Ventures, Simon's business-to-consumer arm, has pioneered the transformation of shopping malls into a medium where consumer brands can build one-on-one relationships with shoppers who make approximately 2.4 billion visits to Simon malls each year."

www.onspotdigital.com

Target: *Retail giant*

In-house digital network in "more than 1,500 stores"

www.target.com

Zoom Media: *Indoor advertising network*

"Targeted out-of-home solutions ... with more than 25,000 billboards in close to 5,000 locations" *www.zoommedia.com*

Canadian Out-of-Home Digital Association (Members as of early 2009)

Alchemy
Digital signage
"Adapting and re-purposing content elements such as video, graphics, text, photography, animation and audio to produce content suited to the unique capabilities of dynamic signage. . . ."
www.alchemyintrenational.com

Arsenal Media: *Digital signage networks and interactive kiosks*
Marketing and content solutions using multiple platforms, including "dynamic digital signage displays, interactive kiosks, wireless media and integrated online marketing systems"
www.arsenal-media.com

Barco: *Media products*
Visualization products, "purpose-built out-of-home media applications, for a variety of professional markets"
www.barco.com

Bell Canada: *Digital Media Solutions*
Digital signage, kiosks, and streaming media"
www.bell.ca

Broadsign International: *Digital signage software*
Provides "full campaign execution functionality, accountability, and scalability for digital signage networks"
www.broadside.com

Bunn Company: *Digital signage consulting*
Strategy, development, other consultation services to "investors, operators, suppliers, and users of digital signage in out-of-home environments"
www.lylebunn.com

Capital Networks Limited: *Digital signage software*
"Audience software platform" is used in digital signage projects for "creation, playback, and verification of content in applications ranging from large outdoor LED displays to in-store brand and product marketing"
www.capitalnetworks.com

Captivate Network: *Elevator digital media network*

National network delivers more than 57.3 million monthly impressions to more than 2.6 million people. "We deliver your message to a captive audience in a focused, distraction-free environment," and "consistently generate strong, tangible results on behalf of our clients"
www.captivate.com

Catalyst Media Group: *Media network for healthcare facilities*
"Single source for media, verified audience metrics, and access to millions of health conscious Canadians"
www.catalystmediagroup.ca

Coxcom Inc.: *Digital signage networks installation, maintenance, and service*
Supports network build with project management
www.coxcominc.com

Daktronics: *Outdoor visual displays*
Large digital visual displays "usually fabricated from LEDs"
www.daktronics.com

Fourth Wall Media: *Digital and interactive kiosk networks*
"Production services for "out-of-home digital networks in retail, transit, hospitality, events, and conferences"
www.fourthwallmedia.com

Gel Communications: *Point-of-purchase digital signage*
"Effective digital signage programs combine proven in-store merchandising techniques with the impact and reach of digital technology, to get results. We translate your product's features into exciting, relevant and compelling consumer benefits. And then we deliver them clearly to your target audience, right at the point of purchase."
www.gelcommunications.com

Harris Corporation: *Digital signage programming, distribution*
"High-definition presentations, scheduling for targeted programming, and advertising by time, event, region, zone, venue, and monitor."
www.broadcast.harris.com
iTechnology Digital Advertising Solutions: *Digital signage provider*
Specializing in "interactive digital screens, animated and interactive advertisements, promotions, coupons, contests, way-finding, recruiting; traditional digital LCD and Plasma screens are also supported"
www.itechdas.com

LG Electronics: *Commercial electronics*
Digital signage for lodging and hospitality, business-to-business, healthcare, and channel markets"
www.lg.ca / www.lgcommercial.com

NEWAD Media Inc.: *Digital media company*
"eBoards are unique in their ability to combine high-definition visual and sound to capture the attention of consumers all the while giving you the advantage of being the only advertiser per board. The motion activated video plays on a 15-inch LCD screen in a loop and is complimented with a poster in the same frame; 2,400 advertising locations ... in restaurants, bars, fitness centers, and colleges"
www.newad.com

ONESTOP Media Group: *Digital network operator*
"Turnkey" out-of-home digital network operator, focusing on the hospitality, transit, and retail industries"
www.onestopmediagroup.com

OnSite Media Network: *Digital network for sports stadiums and office towers*
Reach more than 10 million consumers through "targeted day-parting, customized length of messaging, full screen and split screen options, national, regional and local opportunities, product placement, interactivity and integration"
www.onsitemedianetwork.com

Outdoor Broadcast Network Inc.: *Out-of-home marketing solutions*
National network of "full-motion LED video boards" through which advertisers can "engage their consumers in a creative and powerful way"
www.obn.ca

PHSN: *Digital media for healthcare waiting rooms*
"Enhances the waiting room experience for health care facility visitors ... by providing entertaining and informative programming and literature, customized to the environment"
www.phsn.ca
POPMedia: *Digital signage provider*
Content management, hosting, and maintenance
www.popmedia.net

Rogers Media: *Digital network solutions*

Narrowcast network platform using Rogers Media content
www.rogers.com

Sharp Electronics: *Commercial electronics*
LCD technology
www.thesharpexperience.com

Shopcast: *Digital media for national retail outlets*
"Non-traditional media buying opportunity... vendors target their communication through the purchase of advertising space specific to their product or category in retail stores"
www.ek3.com

Sign Association of Canada: *Trade association*
Represents companies in the Canadian sign industry
www.sac-ace.ca

Smart One Media Inc.: *Integrated digital media and technology*
With partner, operates indoor digital ad network with more than "700 high-definition LCD panels; offers turnkey digital solutions, network development and management, maintenance, creative production, logistics, and engineering"
www.smartonemedia.com

VenueVisions Media Systems: *Digital information delivery*
Advertising and real-time information delivery systems with which businesses "deliver high impact advertising and time-sensitive information to locations anywhere in the world from a central location"
www.venuevision.com

Zoom Media: *Indoor advertising network*
"Targeted out-of-home solutions ... with more than 25,000 billboards in close to 5,000 locations"
www.zoommedia.com

APPENDIX XI. RESPONSIBLE-MEDIA ORGANIZATIONS

There are many organizations in the U.S., Canada, and Europe whose mission is all or in part advocacy for a common-sense approach to the use of media. It's neither possible nor particularly useful to list them all here, but a partial list can be a good starting point for identifying groups whose mission concerns the role of media in our society. Here is a handful whose resources I've relied on for this book along with some information about them.

Action Coalition for Media Education
Albuquerque, N.M.

Founded: 2002

Mission Statement: "We live in the most heavily mediated society in world history. Powerful media tools — print, radio, television, the Internet — can bring a rich diversity of information into every home and school. Yet just a few multi-national corporations (Big Media) own much of the media that shape our 21st century culture. Independently-funded media literacy education plays a crucial role in challenging Big Media's monopoly over our culture, helping to move the world to a more just, democratic and sustainable future. Free of any funding from Big Media, ACME is an emerging global coalition run by and for media educators, a network that champions a three-part mission: 1. Teaching media education knowledge and skills — through keynotes, workshops, trainings, and institutes — to children and adults so that they can become more critical media consumers and more active participants in our democracy; 2. Supporting media reform — No matter what one's cause, media reform is crucial for the success of that cause, and since only those who are media-educated support media reform, media education must be a top priority for all citizens and activists; 3. Democratizing our media system through education and activism."

Web site: *www.acmecoalition.org*

Campaign for a Commercial-free Childhood
Boston

Founded: 2000

Mission: CCFC's mission is to reclaim childhood from corporate marketers. A marketing-driven media culture sells children on behaviors and values driven by the need to promote profit rather than the public good. The commercialization of childhood is the link between many of the most serious problems facing children, and society, today. Childhood obesity, eating disorders, youth violence, sexualization, family stress, underage alcohol and tobacco use, rampant materialism, and the erosion of children's creative play, are all exacerbated by advertising and marketing. When children adopt the values that dominate commercial culture — dependence on the things we buy for life satisfaction, a "me first" attitude, conformity, impulse buying, and unthinking brand loyalty — the health of democracy and sustainability of our planet are threatened. CCFC works for the rights of children to grow up — and the freedom for parents to raise them — without being undermined by commercial interests.

Web site: *www.commercialfreechildhood.org*

Commercial Alert
Washington, D.C.

Founded: 1989

Mission: Commercial Alert's mission is to keep the commercial culture within its proper sphere, and to prevent it from exploiting children and subverting the higher values of family, community, environmental integrity and democracy. Commercial Alert's mission is to keep the commercial culture within its proper sphere, and to prevent it from exploiting children and subverting the higher values of family, community, environmental integrity and democracy.

Web site: *www.commecialalert.org*

Center for SCREEN-TIME Awareness (formerly TV-Turnoff Network)
Washington, D.C.
Founded: 1994

Mission: Center for Screen-Time Awareness provides information so people can live healthier lives in functional families in vibrant communities by taking control of the electronic media in their lives, not allowing it to control them.

Web site: *www.tvturnoff.org*

Center for Successful Parenting
Indianapolis, Ind.
Founded: 1998

Mission: The Center for Successful Parenting, a 501(c)(3) organization, is committed to make the nation aware of the negative effects violent media has on children and to move the nation to action. America's culture used to protect our children. Today they live in a society that glorifies violence. If they don't become conditioned to commit violence themselves, they live in fear of violent acts by others. Our vision is to move parents, leaders in health, business, education, public safety and other disciplines to action in changing our culture to protect children from media violence in all formats. The Center for Successful Parenting research has empirically linked the following consequences to children viewing violence: impaired brain function, violent behavior, distorted perceptions of reality, and toleration of real-life aggressive behavior.

Media violence triggers aggressive behavior in those with aggressive tendencies.

Web site: *www.sosparents.org*

National Institute on Media and the Family
Minneapolis, Minn.
Founded: 1996

Mission: Our children are in trouble. Kids from preschool through high school are laying building blocks for success in school and life. They include self-discipline, the ability to delay gratification, perseverance, imagination, and respect.

Study after study shows that poor media habits undermine every single one of these building blocks. Instead of being given the tools and experiences they need to succeed, more and more kids are shaped by a media culture that promotes more, easy, fast, fun, violence and disrespect.

Web site: *www.mediafamily.org*

Noise Free America
Madison, Wis.
Founded: 2002
Mission: Noise Free America is dedicated to fighting noise pollution, especially from boom cars, car alarms, leaf blowers, and motorcycles. Take a look at our *legislative agenda* to reduce noise in our communities.

Web site: *www.noisefree.org*

Noise Pollution Clearinghouse
Montpelier, Vt.
Founded: 2001
Mission: The mission of the Noise Pollution Clearinghouse is to create more civil cities and more natural rural and wilderness areas by reducing noise pollution at the source. We have organized to raise awareness of noise pollution and help communities take back the commons from those acting like bullies. Our efforts include building a library of resources and tools concerning noise pollution, establishing links to other groups that have similar collections, establishing networks among local noise activists, assisting communities and activists who are working to reduce noise pollution, and monitoring and advocating for stronger noise controls.

Web site: *www.nonoise.org*

Right to Quiet Society
Vancouver, B.C.
Founded: 2002
Mission: The Right to Quiet Society's Objectives are to promote awareness of noise pollution and the dangers of noise to our physical, emotional, and spiritual well-being; to work for noise reduction through better regulation and enforcement; to encourage responsible behavior regarding noise; to foster recognition of the right to quiet as a basic human right. We do not seek to create an absolutely quiet world. However, we want to see a world where quiet is a normal part of life and where it is possible to listen to the sounds of nature without the constant intrusion of machine noise and artificial stimuli. We want our homes to be havens from unwanted noise, and we ask that the soundscape of our public spaces, like the air we breathe, be respected. We insist on our right to listen — or not listen

— to music and other programmed audio, or canned music, according to our own tastes and moods, without having other people's choices forced on us wherever we go. And we want to be able to attend movies, listen to speeches, or go dancing without unreasonably loud amplification of noise. The Right to Quiet Society for Soundscape Awareness and Protection is a non-profit organization registered in 1982 under the British Columbia Society Act.

Web site: *www.quiet.org*

White Dot
Chicago and London
Founded: 1996

Mission: We're against all TV. Why not? It's not the good or bad programs you watch White Dot is campaigning against, but the activity of viewing — the hours you spend in front of the TV set, the things you will never do as a result, and a lifestyle that is as lifeless as it is heavily promoted. Television is an industry.... Right now the average viewing time in America and Britain is four hours a day — half the time you are not sleeping or working. That is a huge commitment of time, and a great deal of money depends on your continued loyalty. When your TV set is not telling you what to buy or what to think or how to feel, it is shouting at you: Stay tuned! Don't touch that dial! Don't miss this episode! In fact, White Dot and the television industry have this in common: we couldn't care less what you see on TV. We talk about what happens on the screen, only because we know it is the battleground, but the prize is your supposedly "hum drum" real life and what you do there.

Web site: *www.whitedot.org*

Supporting material and references are organized under the same headings that appear in the text.

Chapter 1. Silence at 99¢ a Pop

I use Kim Jong-il in my example because in North Korea all radios, unless they're clandestinely owned, are modified to receive broadcasts only from the country's three government networks (*http://news.bbc.co.uk/1/hi/world/asia-pacific/ country_profiles/1131421.stm*). Talk about a captive-audience platform.

I've been a journalist for almost 25 years and, like many of my peers, I've spent the last decade trying to find novel ways to get content in front of audience groups in the face of people's changing media consumption habits. Push e-mail newsletters, mailings, print marketing, DVDs, blog posts, Web videos. The drive to capture people's attention is never-ending, but you wonder if at some point a line must be drawn so that you're not actually force-feeding someone something they haven't asked for. What the efforts that I've used all have in common is in the point of control. In all of these cases the point of control is with the user, not the producer. With audience-captivity, the point of control is with the producer.

Although many taxi riders are too preoccupied to notice what's playing on the backseat TV (and indeed, they might be watching their own TV show on their PDA), the number of complaints over taxi TV far outnumber the number of positive comments, at least in the comments I read during my research. And these comments were not on anti-TV Web sites, where you'd expect to see them, but in forums of mainstream consumer publications and, even more tellingly, TV trade publications. Here are just a few examples. The first two are from the *New York Times* (*http://cityroom.blogs.nytimes.com/2008/06/26/taxi-tvs-now-with-more-con-*

tent/), and the second two are from trade publication *TV.Com* (*http://www.tv.com/story/7876.html*).

• Ugh! So an ongoing nuisance gets more annoying. The first thing I do in a taxi with one of these [TVs] is to wait for it to reset and then push the off button. *Posted by cityjane*

• I turn it off immediately. I hope they include 'off' switches when they start installing TVs in every restaurant, public bathroom and other areas. *Posted by TG*

• Are they crazy? Is our nation so addicted to media that we need this now? Can't they find a better way to spend money? *Posted by Carolee99*

• Is this a joke? People watch the meter, not an LCD TV. Posted by *redthor*

The question of how successful we can be at tuning out an intensive visual media like TV is made complicated by our biology. There's no shortage of evidence suggesting TV is particularly hard for us to ignore because of the way we're visually programmed to capture rapid movement. Researchers typically relate our predilection for TV viewing to an "orienting response" that we exhibit whenever we're confronted with novel or sudden visual stimuli, something TV is especially well-suited to provide, particularly today's programming, which, after 60 years of evolution is characterized by quick cuts and zooms to hold viewers' attention. You can get a good backgrounder on this in a *Scientific American* article, "Television addiction is no mere metaphor," that ran a few years ago and is available online at *http://www.sciam.com/article.cfm?id=television-addiction-is-n-2002-02*.

Schweitzer's quote is from a *Broadcasting and Cable* piece that Commercial Alert makes available on its Web site at *http://www.commercialalert.org/issues/culture/television/television-everywhere*. A listing on Spokle.com has Schweitzer as CBS marketing chief starting in 2004 and still in that position as of 2008.

I interviewed Jean Lotus in late 2005. She also talks extensively about captive–audience environments on the Web site for White Dot at *http://www.whitedot.org/issue/iss_story.asp?slug=TVsForCaptiveAudiences*.

The Allison Romano quote is reprinted on the Web site of Commercial Alert, the public interest group focused on curbing the spread of commercial messaging in non-commercial space. The article was written for a TV trade publication, *Broadcasting & Cable*, and the publication deserves credit for at least including in the article an honest discussion about how much people want to be confronted with unwanted media. Romano writes, "Indeed, one concern is whether people want to be entertained all the time. Some customers complain that in-store networks are annoying, and commuters lament the droning that interrupts their quiet ride home." You can find the article on Commercial Alert's site at *http://www.commercialalert.org/news/Archive/2006/07/television-everywhere*.

You can read the dissent by Associate Justice William O. Douglas in *Public Utilities Commission of the District of Columbia et al. v. Pollak et al*, as well as the case in its entirety, online at *http://caselaw.lp.findlaw.com/scripts/getcase. pl?court=us&vol=343&invol=451*. The legal citation for the case is 343 U.S. 451 (1952).

The Jack Powers quote is from the Web site of the Pervasive.TV Project at http://in3.org/tv/about.htm. The Pervasive.TV Project is neither a critic nor a supporter of the emergence of TV outside the home; it's what you might call a truth-teller because it sees its role as describing rather than evaluating, changes in the digital communications environment.

When Enough is Enough

It's beyond my resources to identify all of the organizations whose mission is in whole or in part to curb the unwanted intrusion of electronic media, but here are a dozen that have been created since at least 2002:

- Action Coalition for Media Education
- Campaign for a Commercial-free Childhood
- Commercial Alert, Washington, D.C.
- Center for Screen Time awareness
- Center for Successful Parenting
- National Institute on Media and the Family
- Noise Free America, Madison, Wisconsin
- Noise Pollution Clearinghouse, Montpelier, Vt.
- Parents Television Council
- Right to Quiet Society, Vancouver, B.C.
- Sound Rights, Seattle, Wash.
- White Dot
- World Forum for Acoustic Ecology

You'll find a little more information on 10 of these in Appendix IX.

A good example of commuters organizing to oppose TV on their light rail line is in Toronto, where just a few years ago the city's public transit authority entered into a deal with a subsidiary of media giant Viacom to install TVs in the city's subway stations and trains. An initial effort by residents in opposition to the TVs failed when the transit board voted in favor of the plan, "even though public opinion was heavily opposed," according to local interest group Toronto Public Space Committee. However, after an additional eight months of opposition and "hundreds and hundreds of e-mails," the board held a second vote and the proposal was reshaped: TVs would be allowed in the stations but kept out of the cars. In Atlanta, opposition was given voice by a local newspaper columnist, who used his print media platform on behalf of riders who felt their rights as individuals were being infringed upon by TVs in the stations, although the

TVs were not removed as a result. In Washington, which as of late 2008 had not yet installed its TVs, the opposition has been persistent since the regional transportation authority announced its plans about five years ago to add TVs as part of an effort to ramp up its advertising revenue; riders sent in letters to both the transportation authority and the *Washington Post* after a transit board meeting that discussed the media plan, and you can usually find online comments in opposition to the plan whenever it's talked about in the *Post*.

The American Public Health Association has a dozen reports, position papers, fact sheets, and other communications in its online database on the negative health effects of television on children as well as adults. Among its concerns: TV is linked to increased attention deficit disorders in children, and children with a TV in their bedroom are less likely to engage in healthy activities such as walking and exercising. You can find out more on its Web site at *http://www.apha.org/APHA/ CMS_Templates/SearchResults.aspx?NRMODE=Published&NRNODEGUID=%7bF7157 E3E-1E92-49A2-A816-9279564B7052%7d&NRORIGINALURL=%2fsearchresults%2ehtm %3fquery%3dtelevision&NRCACHEHINT=NoModifyGuest&query=television.* Mohammad Akhter, APHA's executive director in the late 1990s, told Commercial Alert members in a letter that a more enlightened approach to TV would be one of the most important healthcare actions people could take to improve health in their households. "Few single steps would do as much for the nation's health — physically and in other ways...then to simply turn off our television sets...." Commercial Alert archived the letter on its Web site at *http://lists.essential.org/commercial-alert/ msg00009.html*.

TV-B-Gone sales should be a wake-up call to media companies banking on the rise of captive-audience platforms to reach audiences. The company sold 11,000 units in the first month after the launch of its online ordering system. That was in 2004. In the three years to 2007 the company posted $1.5 million in sales, according to *The Wall Street Journal* (*http://64.233.169.104/search?q=cache:S9_svl3h1RUJ:www. paulos.net/press/Revenge%2520by%2520Gadget%2520-%2520WSJ.com.pdf+lawmakers+res pond+to+loud+TVs&hl=en&ct=clnk&cd=4&gl=us*). You can read about the company's success with its universal remote on its Web site, *www.tvbgone.com*, or you can read some of the hundreds of articles on it. A good one is by the *New York Times*, which Altman's company posted on the media page of its Web site at *http://www. nytimes.com/2004/12/12/magazine/12TELE.html?_r=1&oref=slogin*.

The Wall Street Journal ran an informative article on the number of "annoyancetech" applications submitted to the U.S. Patent Bureau in 2006. It said the number of patent applications for these devices almost doubled in the 10 years to 2006. "These devices are ... a way for people to bridge the gap between the birth of a new form of annoyance ... and the point at which lawmakers finally organize a response," the article says. You can read it at *http://64.233.169.104/search?q=cache:S9_svl3h1RUJ:www.paulos.net/press/Revenge%2520by%2520Gadget%2520-%2520WSJ.com.pdf+lawmakers+respond+to+loud+TVs&hl=en&ct=clnk&cd=4&gl=us.*

Noise Free America on its Web site links to about a dozen model anti-noise ordinances that specifically target boom cars among other types of noise violations. A Tuscaloosa, Ala., provision in its noise ordinance is fairly typical: "Loud or raucous sounds or noises. It shall be unlawful for any person to willfully make, cause, or continue any noise which disturbs the peace or quiet of any residential district and which exceeds eighty (80) db(A) during the hours of 6:00 a.m. until 9:00 p.m. or which exceeds seventy-five (75) db(A) from 9:00 p.m. until 6:00 a.m. at any property line within a residential district or upon any public street or right-of-way within, or bordering upon, any residential district within the corporate limits of the city." Another typical provision is in the noise ordinance of Buffalo, N.Y.: "The use and operation of any sound-reproduction device in a vehicle which would constitute a threat to the safety of pedestrians or vehicle operators or would deprive the public of the right to the safe, comfortable, convenient, and peaceful enjoyment of a public street, park or place for public purpose and would constitute a threat to the safety and welfare of the public." You can read these ordinances at *http://www.noisefree.org/cityord.php.*

The fuller John Cage quote about his silent composition is, "I have nothing to say/and I am saying it/that is poetry/as I needed it." (*http://interglacial.com/~sburke/stuff/cage_433.html*) But if cage is the originator of the silent song, he has plenty of imitators. There are at least nine silent pieces on iTunes, according to a *New York Times* piece on the subject at *http://query.nytimes.com/gst/fullpage.html?res=9505E3DF17 3AF93AA35751C0A9629C8B63.*

There are many articles on people using white noise machines at work to help block out distracting sounds, a problem on the rise today as office workers increase their use of speaker phones and desktop audio and video conferencing. One article says, "Many people secretly suffer at work because of their lack of ability to concentrate in the workplace, feeling that they should be able to just ignore the constant distraction. Lack of concentration is a very real issue for people who are more sensitive to noises....

A white noise machine dissipates the sound...." The article has an agenda, because the writer represents natural-sound products, but it captures a very real problem. You can read the article at *http://www.articlesbase.com/non-fiction-articles/increase-productivity-with-a-white-noise-machine-37384.html.*

Louise Story talks about audience captivity leading to more showdowns in "Anywhere the eye can see it's likely to see an ad," which ran in the *New York Times* in early 2007. You can access it at *http://www.nytimes.com/2007/01/15/business/media/15everywhere.html?_r=1&pagewanted=print*. In opening that piece, she says, "add this to the endangered species list: blank spaces."

There are experts on both sides of the grade inflation issue but the vast bulk of the analyses conclude that grade inflation is real. If you want a more complete bibliography on grade inflation research and articles than you can get on Wikipedia, the University of Lethbridge, in Alberta, has a good one at *http://people.uleth.ca/~runte/inflation/biblio.htm*.

A good article that encapsulates the view that worries over TV when it comes to children are inflated is "Watch out for studies about TV harming kids" published by the American Press Institute. It can be found at *http://www.american-pressinstitute.org/pages/resources/2006/05/watch_out_for_studies_about_tv/*.

A summary of the study by Center on Media and Child Health is available at *http://www.cmch.tv/RESEARCH/fullrecord.asp?id=1679*. The study, called "When the television is always on: Heavy television exposure and young children's development," appeared in the journal *American Behavioral Scientist* in 2005. Here's an excerpt from an abstract of it:

> *Objective:* To examine the prevalence and influence of heavy television exposure among infants, toddlers, and preschoolers in the U.S.
>
> *Design:* Survey study of parents of young children...
>
> *Subjects and setting:* 1,065 parents of children, ages 6 months to 6 years. Parents were contacted via telephone, using random-digit-dialing, with 10 attempts at each number. Response rate was 40 percent . . . .
>
> *Outcome Measures:* Child's membership in a heavy-TV household (TV always or almost always on). Child's reading ability, behavior imitative of TV programming.
>
> *Results:* 35.8 percent of children lived in heavy-TV households. Among children 0-2 years, heavy-TV exposure was significantly related to the parental belief that educational TV is important and use of TV as a babysitter.... Among children 3–4 years and 5–6 years, heavy-TV exposure was significantly related to TV availability . . . . Children from heavy-TV households in the two older groups were significantly more likely to be non-readers, controlling for parental education . . . .
>
> *Conclusion:* Parental attitudes towards TV viewing and household TV availability were common determinates of heavy-TV exposure among

young children; children in heavy-TV households spent less time reading and were more likely to be unable to read.

Chapter 2. The New World of Captivity

You can read about the controversy over Western Development Corp.'s three big screens in Washington, D.C.'s Chinatown at *http://www.washingtonpost.com/wp-dyn/content/article/2008/02/02/AR2008020201138.html*. That coverage includes residents' complaints and Miller's response.

Some blogs that covered the issue Chinatown-screen issue closely cite estimates of the number of people who see the TV ads each day at *http://goodspeedup-date.com/2007/2168* and *http://pqliving.com/?p=971*.

Judith Shulevitz's quote on TV being like air conditioning is at *http://www.slate.com/id/2136372/*.

Like Polar Ice Caps, But Faster Melting

All network TV ad revenue trends are from TNS Media Intelligence in New York City. You can get actual figures, by year, at the following URLs (from which the data used for the chart on declining ad spending were culled:

2003:

> *http://advertisingprinciples.com/docs/USadvertisinggrowth.pdf*

2004:

> *http://www.tns-mi.com/news/03082005.htm*

2005:

> *http://www.businesswire.com/portal/site/google/?ndmViewId=news_view&newsId=200 60227005902&newsLang=en*

2006:

> *http://www.rtoonline.com/Content/Article/Mar07/2006AdvertisingExpenditures031407.asp*

2007:

> *http://www.tns-mi.com/news/03252008.htm*

There are other sources covering the decline in network TV advertising. Among them: *http://www.wikinvest.com/concept/Decline_in_Television_Advertising* and *http://www.wikinvest.com/concept/Impact_of_Internet_Advertising*.

There's a wealth of data measuring the shrinking audience base of network TV. Here are a few places to go to get that information:

> *http://www.boingboing.net/2005/04/12/in-decline-tv-radio-.html, http://www.technology-corner.net/2007/tv-loosing-more-and-more-ground-to-online-media.html, http://www.ebusi-nessforum.com/index.asp?layout=rich_story&doc_id=2227&categoryid=&channelid=5&searc*

h=audience, http://8.12.42.31/2003/nov/25/business/fi-nielsen25, http://www.businessweek.com/ magazine/content/05_30/b3944030.htm.

Data for the chart on the decline in network primetime audiences are from http://tvbythenumbers.com/2008/12/03/updated-where-did-the-primetime-broadcast-audience-go/9079.

You can read about online ad viewing doubling, at the expense of network TV, at http://www.straight.com/article-162465/more-choose-their-tv-online.

Data on the doubling of online streaming video viewing is from http://www.pod-castingnews.com/2008/09/26/online-video-audience-has-doubled-in-one-year/.

Betsy Schiffman's *Wired* piece is at http://blog.wired.com/business/2008/10/yet-an-other-rea.html.

The Mark Mitchell quote is at http://www.mediapost.com/publications/index. cfm?fuseaction=Articles.showArticleHomePage&art_aid=45095. Maureen Ryan, a media critic in Chicago, talks about the migration out of network TV too at http://www. msnbc.msn.com/id/24458848/page/2/.

The share of place-based TV compared to other outdoor advertising is report-ed at http://www.tvweek.com/news/2008/05/tuning_in_to_promo_entertainme.php.

Data for the two charts on the annual growth of ad spending on place-based digital media platforms are from PQ Media at http://www.pqmedia.com/about-press-20080827-dooh2008.html.

The Patrick Quinn quote is at http://www.pqmedia.com/about-press-20070430-aooh.html.

Beaubien's quote is at http://www.tabonline.com/pdf/Jack%20Myers%20artical%20 Nov%2014%2005.pdf.

The Pervasive.TV Project forecast is at http://in3.org/tv/about.htm. The quote from Jack Powers, who heads up the group, is at http://in3.org/tv/outdoor/index.htm.

You can access Lyle Bunn's 2004 white paper at http://www.soundandcommunica-tions.com/video/2004_09_video.htm.

Elevator TV

Captivate Network's share of elevator TV penetration is at http://captivatenet-work.biz/about-us/about-us.asp .

The move by the Wall Street Journal Office Network into elevator TV was reported in a July 23, 2007, *MediaPost* piece by Erik Sass that you can access at *http://www.mediapost.com/publications/index.cfm?fuseaction=Articles.showArticleHomePage&art_aid=64385*. Prior to the expansion, the company focused its out-of-home TV network on screens located in offices and office lobbies.

Coverage of captivate Network's patent infringement lawsuit against the Wall Street Journal Office Network is in *Mass High-Tech*. According to the piece, Captivate says Office Media Network infringes upon four of its patents on the distribution and display of short messages in elevator cabs. Each of the patents describes a method for providing information to the display units. Captivate calls the infringement "willful" and is seeking damages, attorney fees, and an injunction. The lawsuit was filed in U.S. District Court in Delaware. The piece can be accessed at *http://www.masshightech.com/stories/2008/02/11/daily60-Captivate-Network-files-patent-suit-against-Chicago-competitor-OMN.html*.

DiFranzia's remark about the dysfunctional character of elevator behavior is in many articles and news releases. I take his quote from the book *Mass Affluence*, the relevant portion of which can be accessed online at *http://books.google.com/books?id=LLmU8dWCem4C&pg=PA196&lpg=PA196&dq=Michael+DiFranza+AND+eye-contact&source=web&ots=u4v5eO4W9F&sig=xvtveWxdTeM5_Eldc436lvnQMcMe&hl=en&sa=X&oi=book_result&resnum=4&ct=result#PPA197,M1*.

DiFranzia mentions the 90-percent approval rating of his elevator TV field test in a press release at *http://www.captivate.com/pr-article.asp?ID=41*.

The question about whether elevator TV is an example of someone's "insufferable video pollution," and the response by the place-based TV executive, is in the online publication *Live Science* at *http://www.livescience.com/technology/071130-unavoidable-screen.html*.

The quote from Sally Kalson, a Pittsburgh *Post Gazette* columnist, is at *http://www.post-gazette.com/pg/04259/379496-149.stm*. The quote from Les Blomberg is in her piece.

Taxi TV

All 13,000 taxis overseen by the New York Taxi and Limousine Commission were slated to have TVs by early 2008. In mid-2007 about half did, according to this piece in the *New York Times* at *http://www.nytimes.com/2007/12/15/arts/television/15watc.html?_r=1&oref=slogin*.

The NY10 Taxi Entertainment Network quote is at *http://ny10taxi.com/*.

The comment that taxi TV is a "grotesque intrusion" is from a commenter with the handle *Meursault* and appears on the Web site of *New York* magazine. You can find it and other comments at *http://nymag.com/daily/intel/2008/04/ taxi_tv_turn_it_up_or_turn_it.html.*

John Del Signore's quote on the *Gothamist* is at *http://gothamist.com/2008/07/24/ some_taxi_tvs_always_on.php.*

The Brian Morrissey quote is at *http://adweek.blogs.com/adfreak/2007/09/taxi-tv-is-ok-i.html.*

The anti-taxi-TV comments by Jerry Stiller and other celebrities are at *http:// nymag.com/daily/intel/2008/04/taxi_tv_the_celebrities_weigh.html.*

The celebrity comments on New York taxi TV are at *http://nymag.com/daily/ intel/2008/04/taxi_tv_the_celebrities_weigh.html.*

The long, highly irate taxi commuter quote is from Gregory Moore, a big band leader in New York City. The quote is in John Del Signore's post on the *Gothamist* is at http://www.yellowcabnyc.com/nyc-taxi/malfunctioning-taxi-tv-screens.

Point-of-sale TV

You can read about the rocky start of place-based TV in a *New York Times* piece at *http://query.nytimes.com/gst/fullpage.html?res=990CE6D91F38F937A25754C0A9639582 60&sec=&spon=&pagewanted=all.*

The 700 million in place-based viewership is quoted in a *MediaPost* piece at *http://www.mediapost.com/publications/index.cfm?fuseaction=Articles.showArticleHome Page &art_aid=45095.*

The Nigel Hollis comment on the reach of Wal-Mart TV and the Frost & Sullivan estimate of TV penetration in stores were noted in a piece by *Digital Signage News* at *http://digitalsignagenews.blogspot.com/2007_09_01_archive.html.*

The two quotes from Wal-Mart customers are at *http://digitalsignagenews.blogspot.com/2007/03/wal-mart-tv-lets-advertisers-surprise.html.* The first quote, about the TVs being "creepy," is in the article and refers to a quote on a *USA Today* story. The second quote is from a commenter who uses the handle *Ib* and is in response to the Digital Signage News piece.

Nielsen discusses its launch of its out-of-home audience measuring division in a September 2008 press release at *http://www.nielsen.com/media/2008/pr_080918.html.*

The quote by Ceril Shagrin is at *http://query.nytimes.com/gst/fullpage.html?res=990C E6D91F38F937A25754C0A963958260.*

Premier Retail Networks makes its sales pitch to prospective advertisers on its Web site, at *http://www.prn.com/aboutus.html.*

All 27 of the comments to the *Washington Post* article on checkout TV are at *http://voices.washingtonpost.com/thecheckout/2006/08/checkout_tv_super_marketing.html*.

Gas Station TV

Information on ABC PumpTop TV Network is at *http://www.reuters.com/article/pressRelease/idUS113859+07-Jan-2008+PRN20080107*.

Information on Gas Station TV, including data on its market penetration, is at *http://www.gstv.com/press/gas-station-tv-surpasses-the-1000-station-mark.php*.

The quote from Roy Reeves on PumpTop TV successfully engaging consumers is in a Reuters dispatch, at *http://www.reuters.com/article/pressRelease/idUS113859+07-Jan-2008+PRN20080107*.

The series of quotes on the annoyance of gas-pump TVs were in response to a story announcing a relationship between Westinghouse Digital Electronics and PumpTop TV. Westinghouse is the country's fourth largest LCD screen manufacturer in the U.S., according to the report. The writer wasn't familiar with gas station TVs and asked if any of his readers were. They were, and, as the quotes make clear, they weren't happy about it. You can read the story at *http://digitalsignagenews.blogspot.com/2007/04/westinghouse-and-adtek-to-supposedly.html*.
Here are the quotes and the handles of the people who left them.
"I avoid using Esso stations ..." *Posted by King Gong*
"I find those things so annoying I will not go to stations that have them...." *Posted by Annonymous*
"Here's the question: will the screens turn off enough users?...People don't need nor want to be assaulted by noise and advertisements every moment of the day...." *Posted by Bill Gerba*

Restroom TV
The annual restroom advertising sales figures are from 2004 and are quoted in coverage by *Advertising Age* at *http://www.getindoors.com/adage_article.cfm*. The IBAA doesn't make current figures available on its Web site.

The luxury public restrooms sponsored by Charmin have made their appearance in more cities than just New York City but the latter restrooms represent a multi-year commitment. You can read about the publicity stunt in many places. Here's where I first learned about them: *http://wcbstv.com/watercooler/new.york.city.2.872229.html*.
The Kansas City *Star* interview with Michael Ouijas of In Ad TV is on the advertising company's Web site at *http://www.inadinc.com/press_5.html*.

An item on Lifetips.com says there are about 50 TVs in the restrooms at Kennedy International Airport: *http://publicrestrooms.lifetips.com/cat/64412/public-restroom-advertising/.*

IBAA's Turner makes his remarks in the same Advertising Age piece in which the annual bathroom TV ad spending is quoted, at *http://www.getindoors.com/adage_article.cfm.*

Burdick's quote is in the same piece as Turner's, above.

The quote from the "Magic Mirror" marketing representative is at *http://www.ecplaza.net/tradeleads/seller/5087000/magic_mirror_innovative.html.*

I enjoyed reading Brian Fuller's essay on restroom TV going one step too far in the rush to put TV everywhere. In my excerpt of it, I moved some sentences around to make it flow better with my text, but I believe I kept his work faithful to his original meaning. You can read his essay at *http://www.eetimes.com/op/show-Article.jhtml?articleID=196602743.* Of course, he's not the only one who doesn't like restroom TV. There's another good piece on the disturbing nature of the advertising push, specifically relating to the "magic mirror," in a piece on the online tech publication *Dvice* at *http://www.eetimes.com/op/showArticle.jhtml?articleID=196602743.* It's interesting how some of the most forceful critics of the invasive use of TV are techies. These two comments critical of restroom TV are representative of many such comments I came across in reference to all types of captive-audience media.

Doctor's Office TV
You can find some statistics on Healthy Advice's growth at the company's Web site at *http://www.healthyadvicenetworks.com/etp/about-healthy-advice.html.*

Healthy Advice Network's contention that new prescriptions will go up 8-12 percent if they're included in its TV programming is on its Web site at *http://www.healthyadvicenetworks.com/etp/waiting-room.html.*

You can find the definition of NRx as "new prescriptions" at *http://acronyms.thefreedictionary.com/NRX.*

Adriane Fugh-Berman's essay in the Bioethics Forum on the problem with waiting-room TV in doctors' offices is at *http://www.thehastingscenter.org/Bioethicsforum/Post.aspx?id=294&terms=Adriane+Fugh-Berman+and+%23filename+*.html.*

You can learn more about Fugh-Berman at *www.fugh-breman.com.*

Lawrence Wittner's essay on the difficulty of trying to recover from surgery while having to listen to TV you can't control is at *http://hnn.us/articles/44904.html*.

The BBC coverage of the Kafkaesque situation with the TVs that wouldn't shut off in the U.K. would actually be kind of funny if it weren't so traumatic for the people involved. The piece, which ran in 2004, is at *http://news.bbc.co.uk/1/hi/health/3607531.stm*.

Street-Furniture TV

Remarks from Jean Luc Decaux on the installation of TVs in "street furniture like bus stops is in the *Jack Myers Business Report* at *http://www.tabonline.com/pdf/Jack%20Myers%20artical%20Nov%2014%2005.pdf*. The news about Cemusa installing TVs in bus stops throughout New York City is in the same report.

You can read about the Nokia street-furniture demonstration in *Advertising Age* among other places. The *Ad Age* piece, by David Polinchock, is at *http://blog.futurelab.net/2006/10/advertising_age_mediaworks_str.html*. You can see it on YouTube, too, at *http://www.youtube.com/watch?v=5-bNZRAypgQ*.

Jack Powers' quote on Times Square getting the street-furniture TV trend rolling is at *http://in3.org/tv/outdoor/index.htm*.

Gym TV

The Hallet piece on the habit of TV in gyms was written for the *Washington Post* but I picked it up from the *Denver Post*, at *http://www.denverpost.com/headlines/ci_10993740*.

The comment from the first online forum on gym etiquette, hosted by Johnstone Fitness, is at *http://forums.johnstonefitness.com/archive/index.php/t-1301.html*. It was posted by *Busy Child*. The comment from the second online forum on gym etiquette is at *http://parvita.wordpress.com/2008/02/02/the-gym-the-inconsiderate-annoying-bsob/*. It was posted by *Mia*.

The IdeaCAST figures were at *http://www.ideacast.net/* in early 2009.

The comment from the gym member who relies on the gym to watch TV shows she otherwise wouldn't watch is at *http://mr-t-in-dc.livejournal.com/223685.html*. It was posted by *HipchickinDC*.

"Cardio Cinema" as well as the health concerns of watching TV while working out are both in the Hallet piece, at *http://www.denverpost.com/headlines/ci_10993740*.

The YMCA manager who talks about the problem with ACSM workout guidelines makes his comments at *http://www.fitness.com/articles/127/annoying_problems_in_gyms.php. It was posted by John Izzo.*

The gym patron who kicked her habit during an episode of "MTV Cribs" posted her comment at *http://www.crankyfitness.com/2008/04/five-good-reasons-to-quit-gym.html.* It was posted by Crabby McSlacker.

Place-Based TV in General
The quote by Diorio is at http://publishing2.com/2006/09/12/everything-is-media-the-real-world-edition/.

Michael Spindler's quote is from his blog, *The Branded Pantry,* at *http://brandedpantry.com/2008/06/05/big-bets-on-the-fourth-screen/#more-32.*

The statistics on the number of video screens and the sale dollars they generate are in a piece by out-of-home video consultant Lyle Bunn in an October 2008 *Digital Signage Today* piece called "Top 10: Digital out-of-home is an advertiser's most powerful tool." He quotes data provided by Suzanne Alecia, the president of the Out-of-Home Video Advertising Bureau. The piece can be accessed at *http://digitalsignagetoday.com/article_printable.php?id=20904&page=166.*

Mark French's quote about his company's intention to make people watch the screen is at *http://www.reuters.com/article/PBLSHG/idUSN1665277220080116.*

The data on NBC Everywhere's performance is at *http://www.tvweek.com/news/2008/01/nbcu_expands_outofhome_digital.php* .

Schweitzer's quote is from a *Broadcasting and Cable* piece that Commercial Alert makes available on its Web site at *http://www.commercialalert.org/issues/culture/television/television-everywhere.*

Market ambitions of CBS Outernet are detailed in a *Broadcasting and Cable* piece at *http://www.broadcastingcable.com/article/CA6523999.html.*

As an example of how deep in-store TVs will penetrate, in 2008, TVs were in thousands of grocery stores across the country. Just one company, SignStorey, owned by CBS, had TVs in 1,400 stores. "We are now able to provide our advertisers with 25 percent to 40 percent market coverage," Tom Green, the company's senior vice president of sales, said in 2007 after his company had acquired a rival. The Tom Green quote on expansion of grocery store TV is at *http://www.signstorey.com/news/Captive%20Audience%20Final%20Release%204-26-07.pdf.*

The Arbitron estimate of out-of-home TV viewers is at *http://www.medialifemagazine.com/artman/publish/printer_11276.asp*.

You can learn more about the growth of the Canadian Out-of-Home Digital Association at its Web site *at http://www.the-cdsa.org/place_based.html*.

Life-Pattern Marketing

I interviewed Jean Lotus in 2005. Her comments on captive-audience environments at *http://www.whitedot.org/issue/iss_story.asp?slug=TVsForCaptiveAudiences*.

Wittner makes his comment in his History News Network essay at *http://hnn.us/articles/44904.html*.

The quote from Monte Zweben is at the Web site of SeeSaw Networks at *http://www.seesawnetworks.com/services/whitepapers/*. And the elucidation of life-pattern marketing is on the same site at *http://www.seesawnetworks.com/about/*.

White Dot's database of complaints about TVs in restaurants is at *http://www.whitedot.org/campaigns/ruineddiner.asp*. The commenters aren't identified at the site. Instead, they're asked to fill out a form at White Dot and their comments are compiled in a table.

Chapter 3. TV in Public Spaces

The comment on PBS commentator Mark Glaser's anti-captive audience essay is at *http://www.pbs.org/mediashift/2006/03/cnn-everywheredo-we-need-tv-in-public-spaces079.html*. It was posted by *Spring Suptic*. About a dozen comments in all were posted. One of the other comments was, "The person who referred to television as 'an open sewer in one's living room' was insulting open sewers," posted by *Eve*.

The letter from Gary Ruskin of Commercial Alert on the introduction of TVs on subways and other modes of public transit is at *http://www.commercialalert.org/issues/culture/television/commercial-alert-asks-bush-to-defend-reading-on-the-bus-and-train-from-noisy-tvs*.

Aaron Patrick's coverage of Terminal 5 in London's Heathrow is at *http://inel.wordpress.com/2008/02/14/t5-heathrow-where-your-heart-beats-faster-not-only-on-valentines-day/*. Jonathan Goldsmid-Whyte's quote is included in that piece.

The comments on PBS commentator Mark Glaser's anti-captive audience essay are at *http://www.pbs.org/mediashift/2006/03/cnn_everywheredo_we_need_tv_in.html*. The first comment, which calls TV in public places "a public nuisance," was posted by Joseph. The second comment, that calls TV "swill," was posted by *Eve* and can be accessed at *http://www.pbs.org/mediashift/2006/03/cnn-everywheredo-we-need-tv-in-public-spaces079.html.*

Profits v. Rights

The Blomberg quote is from his article "Noise, Sovereignty and Civility" in the Journal for the League for the Hard of Hearing. That article is reprinted in its entirety in Appendix III.

You can access portions of Anna McCarthy's book, *Ambient Television*, online at *http://books.google.com/books?id=qxj3t835slEC&pg=PA275&lpg=PA275&dq=CNN+A ND+place-based+media&source=web&ots=QoeEFAfvIT&sig=6l_BP9U6YvIYoODGC4Jt-AwiMuU&hl=en&sa=X&oi=book_result&resnum=2&ct=result#PPA147,M1.* The discussion of Colin Campbell is at page 109.

Read about the effort to keep TVs off Toronto's subway at *http://www.publicspace.ca/ttcvideo.htm.*

The editorial praising defeat of the Toronto subway TV initiative is at *http://illegalsigns.ca/2008/01/21/why-the-ttc-rejected-video-ads-in-subway-cars/.*

The patent application for the subway TV system is at *http://www.freepatentsonline.com/6700602.html.* The applicant defines his system this way: "A television system for subway cars [that] includes a plurality of TV monitors mounted at intervals along the cars, at the junction of the sidewall and the ceiling, and a central video signal source unit such as a video tape player, video disk player, computer-based digital video recorder or television receiver, connected to the video monitors. Programs of short duration, e.g. 5-15 minutes, matching the average length of a subway ride, and comprising advertising messages, news bytes and the like are played and displayed in the monitors repeatedly during the subway ride."

It's worth looking at the patent applicant's rationale for a subway TV platform in some detail:

> "Entertainment of passengers on subway cars has until now generally been ignored, since the average journey taken by a passenger on a mass transit subway system is usually short, lasting perhaps fifteen minutes. Nevertheless, subway transit riders offer an attractive audience for visual advertising messages, as evidenced by the proliferation of advertising signs which commonly adorn a subway car. In addition, mass transit systems such as subways are in need of extra sources of revenue, to keep passenger fare structures at an affordable level as operating costs rise, and to avoid decreased ridership as a result.

> "It is an object of the present invention to provide a public service message display system, entertainment system and advertising system for mass transit subway cars.

"It is a further object to provide a novel source of extra revenue for a mass transit subway system.

"The present invention provides a television public service message display, entertainment and advertising system for subway cars, in which television monitors are provided at spaced intervals in subway cars, to display short duration televisual entertainment and advertising features to subway riders. The system is designed so that advertising spots on it can be sold by the transit system to potential advertisers and sponsors, for extra revenues for the transit system. It takes advantage of the fact that subway riders are, for the most part, occupying a subway car under relatively crowded conditions but for only a relatively brief duration. They are looking for something on which to focus their attention during their brief ride, whilst at the same time often finding it inconvenient to open newspapers, magazines or the like under crowded circumstances and becoming bored by static advertising or other displays around them. The present invention provides properly positioned television monitors displaying moving images of news items, advertising material and the like, viewable by substantially all riders in the car, and filling their need for visual entertainment during the brief duration of their subway ride." *Source: http://www. freepatentsonline.com/6700602.html.*

Eric Martin's comments about TVs coming to Washington, D.C.'s Metro subway system are at *http://www.badads.org/november03.shtml.*

The quote from Carlton Sickles defending Metro's decision to add TVs as part of its future ad mix I took from Martin's column in which he discusses the ads, at *http://www.badads.org/november03.shtml.* In his column, Martin takes issue with Sickles' contention that the influx of new ad platforms is necessary to keep the subway system operating effectively. Martin puts it this way:

"Stop right there, Mr. Sickles. You and the rest of the Metro board have to do no such thing. To meet a previous shortfall, you raised fares and cut costs. In the current situation, however, you plan to overturn more than a quarter-century of asceticism and calm environments and plaster intrusive advertisements on nearly every available surface, all to raise a mere $15 million with a $45 million still outstanding. You will still have to raise fares and cut costs, but in the meantime you will have permanently destroyed the transit experience of more than a million riders each day. Blanketing the atmosphere with intrusive, unwanted advertising is no long-term solution to budget difficulties, only a long-term blight on your city, your lifestyle, and your tenure on the board."

The *Washington Post* reported Sickle's remarks, too, at *http://www.spodek.net/press/ washingtonpost_031114.pdf.*

The comment critical of the introduction of TVs on Washington, D.C.'s Metro subway system is at *http://www.washingtonpost.com/wpdyn/content/article/2008/04/05/ AR2008040502122.html.*

A *USA Today* piece that lists subway systems that have TV systems in the works is available on the Web site of Commercial Alert, at *http://www.commercialalert.org/issues/culture/public-spaces/subways-tune-in-to-new-revenue*.

Carrie Trousel's essay can be read at *http://www.riverwestcurrents.org/2004/January/001277.html*.

The anti-bus TV comments are on a blog called the "laist," and can be read at *http://laist.com/2005/06/23/bus_ride_boredom_buster.php*. Not all of the comments are negative. Out of five comments, three were against the TVs, one was neutral, and one favored the TVs: "I saw one of these screens about a year ago on the subway twice, and then it vanished, and I was wondering what had happened. They were kind of cool, but the problem was where it was located; only a few people could see it at any one time." The comment calling bus TV "splendid" was posted by *JH* and the one asking who thought bus riding is boring was posted by *fette*.

The growth of the company Transit TV is covered at *http://biz.yahoo.com/prnews/080707/clm095.html?.v=71*

And you can read about the company at *http://www.transitv.com/*.

Comments on the L.A. bus TVs, including the one in which they're described as a torture device, is at *http://hereinvannuys.blogspot.com/2006/11/transittv-new-metro-torture-device.html*. It was posted by *abh1wordpress*. It can also be found at *http://hereinvannuys.wordpress.com/2006/11/*.

Captive Children

Commercial Alert's letter to the Florida school board urging defeat of a proposal to put commercial radio on school buses is at *http://www.commercialalert.org/news/news-releases/2007/10/commercial-alert-letter-to-seminole-county-school-board-regarding-bus-radio*.

Sen. Dorgan's quote criticizing Bus Radio is at *http://www.commercialexploitation.org/actions/busradio.htm*.

The *Washington Post* coverage of BusRadio and the more than 285 comments are at *http://voices.washingtonpost.com/thecheckout/2006/08/post_9.html*. For the selection of comments I include in the text, the commenters these are the names or the handles of the people who posted them, in order: *NoVa, Phyllis W. Mosteller, Kevin Helmold, Mae Kamin, Bryan,* and *Janie Patterson*. I reproduce a small selection of the comments in Appendix VII.

Bus Radio market penetration is touted at *http://www.busradio.com/about*.

Organizations belonging to the coalition seeking to ban commercial radio on school buses and its letter to consumer products companies that would advertise on the radio service are both at *http://www.obligation.org/busradioarticle.php?recordID=742*.

For criticism of Channel One News you can start with the discussion on Wikipedia at *http://en.wikipedia.org/wiki/Channel_One_News*.

Ralph Nadar's criticism of Channel One was summarized in an *Education Week* article at *http://www.unesco.org/courier/2000_04/uk/apprend.htm*.

Channel One's defense of its in-school news is at *http://www.channelone.com/static/about/*.

The coalition letter to advertisers on Channel One asking them to stop providing financial support to the network is on Commercial Alert's Web site at *http://www.commercialalert.org/issues/education/channel-one/commercial-alert-coalition-launches-campaign-against-primedias-channel-one*.

News that Primedia considered shutting down Channel One in 2006 because of revenue appeared among other places in *Folio:* magazine, which covers media companies. It described Primedia's concerns over Channel One's financial viability this way: "Primedia says it will classify its education segment, home to the struggling Channel One Network, as a 'discontinued operation' in the fourth quarter while it explores strategic options for the assets of the segment. The company did not say what the strategic options would entail, but speculation is that it is looking to sell the segment." You can access the brief at *http://www.foliomag.com/2006/look-back-2006-month-month-highlights-years-biggest-stories*.

Chapter 4. Outdoor Rooms: When Memory Goes Missing

You can read about the Atlanta wind turbine controversy on the CNN Web site, at *http://www.cnn.com/2007/TECH/science/10/09/pip.wind.energy/index.html*.

Hume's full quote, from *A Theory of Human Nature*, is, "It is not contrary to reason to prefer the destruction of the whole world to the scratching of my finger." Hume is advancing a moral relativism. The quote is in chapter two, part III, section 3.

The Bend, Ore., clothesline controversy was the subject of a lengthy *Wall Street Journal* piece, which is available online at *http://online.wsj.com/public/article/SB119007893529930697.html*.

I say iPods and other personal electronic devices ideally, but not always in reality, limit their audio to the individual user because people's use of headphones or ear-buds is no guarantee that the audio won't leak out for everyone else to hear. Indeed, anyone riding a crowded subway or bus knows through experience that the audio from people's music or hand-held TV device can get quite loud, especially when you're surrounded by several people with the devices. As one person says in a comment to a taxi TV article in *New York* magazine, "If I could mute the iPods on the subway or the people who sing along with them (off key) because they think they're the next American Idol, I would. Scientists, stop working on those jetpacks and work on a selective muting device." The comment is at *http://nymag.com/daily/intel/2008/04/taxi_tv_turn_it_up_or_turn_it.html*.

There's an exchange about the Canadian house-ramming incident in an online discussion forum at *http://www.extremeskins.com/archive/index.php/t-98229.html*. An article on the Hong Kong ear-biting incident is at *http://www.nonoise.org/news/1997/aug24.htm#Argument%20Over%20Noise%20Leads%20to%20Arson%20and%20Assault* and the Birmingham suicide is at *http://www.nonoise.org/news/1998/mar29.htm#Noisy%20Neighbors%20Helped%20Drive%20English%20Man%20to%20Suicide%20Coroner%20Finds*.

You can read about sociologist Jack Levin's notion of "homicides over argument" online at *http://www.projo.com/news/content/neighborhood_disputes_05-21-08_ONA791O_v42.38e9f5c.html*.

The Staudacher quote is at *http://www.consciouschoice.com/1999/cc1206/note1206.html*.

The Pinkowish and Sauter quote is on the *Alternet* Web site, at *http://www.alternet.org/story/91463/*.

Among the coverage of outdoor rooms by HGTV is this segment: *http://www.hgtv.com/hgtv/pac_ctnt_988/text/0,2496,HGTV_22056_60026,00.html*.

The quote from Deidra Darsa of the Health, Patio and Barbeque Association, is at *http://www.bobvila.com/HowTo_Library/Outdoor_Rooms-Exterior_Features_and_Spaces-A3300.html*.

The Hometoys.com quote by Joe Pantel on the weatherization of his outdoor TVs can be found at *http://www.hometoys.com/ezine/08.06/pantel/interview.htm*.

Anti-glare glass on outdoor TVs is discussed, among other places, at *http://www.cepro.com/article/focusing_on_outdoor_tv_runco_shows_new_high_bright_model/*

One example of TV sizes can be found at *http://www.electronichouse.com/article/pantel_announces_new_outdoor_tv_sizes/*.

Statistics on the growth of outdoor living rooms, which draws on data from the American Home Furnishing Alliance, can be found at *http://onlineathens.com/stories/062907/living_20070629004.shtml*.

Everyone Deserves to Enjoy My Lifestyle

You can access "Home sweet apartment: a text analysis of dissatisfaction with apartment homes" online at *http://64.233.169.104/search?q=cache:3Qk-WFfPPcwJ:www.ugapropertymanagement.com/working_papers/TextAnalysis.pdf+noise+satisfaction+research&hl=en&ct=clnk&cd=129&gl=us*.

An abstract of the article in the *Journal of Performance of Constructed Facilities* is at *http://cat.inist.fr/?aModele=afficheN&cpsidt=19874507*.

The full report by the U.K. researcher, Diana Weinhold, on noise can be found at http://mpra.ub.uni-muenchen.de/9885/1/MPRA_paper_9885.pdf.

The Netherlands study can be found at *http://www.xs4all.nl/~rigolett/ENGELS/neighbours/gwsumry.htm*.

The *Rental Property Reporter* piece in which noise is identified as the most common tenant complain from the Apartment ratings Web site is at *http://216.147.103.80/*

i-column/mar02.htm. The quotes taken from the Apartment ratings Web site are all from Reno, Nev., apartments at *http://www.apartmentratings.com/*.

The renter complaint, on the online community forum, which I reproduced only in part and edited for clarity, is in the online forum at *http://ths.gardenweb.com/forums/load/apt/msg0419490930002.html*.

The Minneapolis "sound conditioned" apartment was being advertised online at *http://storefront.dexonline.com/ginkel-properties*.

The U.K. study finding an especially large jump in suburban noise complaints can be found at *http://www.timesonline.co.uk/tol/news/politics/article2310654.ece*.

The quote by Karen Orr on the invasion of TVs and radios to the suburbs is at *http://www2.tbo.com/content/2008/jul/25/na-noise-pollution-drives-urban-sprawl/*.

The Blomberg quote is at *http://www.focustamworth.org/CSM_03_10_05.htm*.

Golden Rays Shining on Me at My Leisure

The Gregg Kilday quote is from his *Hollywood Reporter* blog at *http://www.risky-businessblog.com/2007/04/new_ways_to_ann.html*.

You can read the *Naples Daily News* piece on the amplified sound law at *http://www.naplesnews.com/news/2008/Jul/04/having-party-you-better-have-permit-bonita/*.

A summary of the Pasco County residential noise restrictions is at *http://www.grandoaksfl.com/Documents/Noise%20Ord.pdf*.

It's interesting that prior to the 1960s, noise exposure was not widely considered appropriate for regulation. It took passage of the National Environmental Protection Act in 1969 and the Noise Pollution and Abatement Act in 1972 to put noise exposure on regulators' radar screen. Following passage of these two acts, in addition to actions by the federal government to curb noise in federally funded transportation projects (like highway development), cities and states began writing their own rules. Now, of course, thousands of cities have their own noise ordinances. You can access a selection of local noise ordinances online at the Noise Pollution Clearinghouse database online, *http://www.nonoise.org/lawlib/cities/cities.htm*, although the information at that source is limited because it hasn't been updated in at least four years, but it makes a good starting point for research. You can learn a little about the history of noise regulation in the Wikipedia entry on the topic, at *http://en.wikipedia.org/wiki/Noise_regulation*.

The Pantel marketing copy extolling the virtues of catching the big game in your backyard while enjoying a barbeque was on the company's home page in fall 2008 at *http://www.panteltv.com/*.

Coverage of the controversy over George Mason University's outdoor sign can be found at *http://www.washingtonpost.com/wp-dyn/content/article/2006/09/13/AR2006091300819.html* and also at *http://www.washingtonpost.com/wp-dyn/content/article/2007/01/05/AR2007010502488.html*.

The Los Angeles sign controversy is covered by the *Los Angeles Times* at *http://articles.latimes.com/2007/aug/20/business/fi-digital20*.

TV and the "Orienting Response"

The *Scientific American* article on TV addiction by Robert Kubey and Mihaly Csikszentmihalyi is at *http://www.tri-vision.ca/documents/TV_Addiction.pdf*

Judith Warner's write-up of the lecture by the neuropsychologist William Stixrud on the "orienting response' and our TV fixation is at *http://warner.blogs.nytimes.com/tag/television/*.

Kubey's research on the self-reinforcing feedback loop TV proves people who are trying to escape negative thoughts is discussed in a little detail by Ron Kaufman in his article on TV addiction, which is reprinted in Appendix IV.

Chapter 5. Boom Cars: as Funny as a Heart Attack

There's so much research on the health effects of noise exposure that it's a matter of picking and choosing which sources to reference. You probably can't go wrong starting with a World Health Organization report that sums up key research, at least as of a decade ago, as part of a community noise guide it developed. You can find that at *http://www.who.int/docstore/peh/noise/Comnoise-1.pdf*.

Data for the chart on decibel levels and physiological effects are culled from two Web sites, at *http://www.noiseoff.org/level.1.php* and *http://www.ehponline.org/members/2005/113-1/focus.html*.

The quote by Deepak Prasher can be seen in the *Guardian* at *http://www.guardian.co.uk/science/2007/aug/23/sciencenews.uknews*.

For the simplest summary of the use of rock music by the U.S. military to oust Manuel Noriega go to the Wikipedia entry at *http://en.wikipedia.org/wiki/Manuel_Noriega*.

You can read about the sonic weapon that works just on kids, and the human rights issue it raises, at *http://www.theregister.co.uk/2008/02/12/buzz_off_mosquito/*.

The Lin quote is on the Web site of a Canadian research publication called *Global Research* and can be accessed at *http://www.globalresearch.ca/index.php?context=va&aid=9554*.

How loud do "boom cars" get? One audio specialist looks into it at *http://www.digital-recordings.com/publ/pubnoise.html*.

The Loudest Urban Environment on Earth

The *New York Times* piece on Cairo noise is a great article. It can be read at *http://www.nytimes.com/2008/04/14/world/middleeast/14cairo.html?_r=1&emc&ex=1208318400&en=0459aad6a6249cbd&ei=5087%0A&oref=slogin*.

You can access information on recent municipal noise ordinances at Noise Free America, at *http://www.noisefree.org/modelord.php*, and the law library at the Noise Pollution Clearinghouse, *http://www.nonoise.org/lawlib.htm*.

New York City's ambitious effort to get noise under control is reported in the *New York Times* at *http://query.nytimes.com/gst/fullpage.html?res=9A01EFDC1F31F93BA35755C0A9629C8B63&n=Top/Reference/Times%20Topics/Subjects/I/Ice%20Cream*.

Let Me Tell You What I Think of You

You can read the U.S. Department of Justice report on boom cars in full online at *http://www.cops.usdoj.gov/pdf/e05021550.pdf*.

Stories like this Cincinnati shooting have been compiled by an organization called Lower the Boom, at *http://www.lowertheboom.org/trice/crime.htm*.

The Boss ad is at *http://www.noisefree.org/boomcarads/docu0025.JPG*.

The JBL "Hate your neighbors" ad is at *http://www.noisefree.org/boomcarads/docu0006.JPG*.

The Audiovox ad about putting the under 40 set in cardiac arrest is at *http://www.noisefree.org/boomcarads/docu0042.JPG*.

You can see Noise Free America's collection of malicious boom car ads at *http://www.noisefree.org/boomcars/boomcarads.php*.

The Mobile Enhancement Retailers Association's statement on promotions can be found at *http://www.merausa.org/Resources/Industry_Best_Practices/promotions.asp*.

The Mobile Enhancement Retailers Association's statement on the proposed St. Louis noise ordinance is at *http://www.merausa.org/Whats_New/Press_Releases/press33.asp*.

The car stereo industry has been trying to make the installation of aftermarket products (which would include the customized car stereos of boomers) easier to install and repair. The way that car manufacturers have computerized car components has made aftermarket stereos more expensive to install. You can read about these issues at *http://www.mobileelectronics.com.au/forums/lofiversion/index.php/t55611.html* and *http://www.righttorepair.org/*. These and other pressures on the car stereo industry are looked at in a variety of articles, including "What's killing the car stereo industry?" at *http://jalopnik.com/361916/whats-killing-the-car-stereo-industry* and "Car stereos hit a distressing low note," at *http://www.usatoday.com/money/autos/2008-07-28-car-stereos_N.htm*.

The Orlando Sentinel piece with the boom car aficionado who doesn't mind the cost of a ticket is at *http://www.noisefree.org/newsroom/nfa-display.php?id=118*. The Ted Rueter quote on the insufficiency of a $70 fine as a boom car deterrent is in the same article.

Undercurrent of Anger

The letters to Michael Wright are on his Web site at three locations: *http://members.aol.com/mpwright9/uk.html*, *http://members.aol.com/mpwright9/noise11.html*, *http://members.aol.com/mpwright9/hatemail.html#1*

You can get a summary of Kantian ethics at a Stanford University site, *http://plato.stanford.edu/entries/kant-moral/*.

Chapter 6. You Hear Me, Therefore I Am

I took "insufferable" in the section head from a piece about workplace rudeness on ThompsonNet by David Butcher. In the piece he refers to a Randstad survey of workplaces annoyances and, although they weren't at the top of the survey, the use of speaker phones and other noisy devices like cell phones were cited. Read the piece at *http://news.thomasnet.com/IMT/archives/2007/11/making_the_work_insufferable_irritants_rudeness_incivility.html.*

The study on office environments, in which the term acoustical privacy is used, was commissioned by an office furniture manufacturer, Steelcase, which clearly has an interest in making competitive work stations. But since that interest isn't at odds with the idea that office workers like quiet, I include it here. You can read the report at *http://www.steelcase.com/na/files/7cb9c62afdc4497e96fcac714b5b3 fc2/Workplace%20Privacy.pdf.*

The Emory white paper, called "Do cubicles help productivity or hurt it?" is at *http://knowledge.emory.edu/article.cfm?articleid=962.* The question about productivity isn't academic since 70 percent of office works today work in cubicles, according to the Emory paper. What's interesting is that Robert Propst, the designer who's credited with launching the cubicle concept in 1968 as a way to bring down barriers in the workplace, has since repudiated them.

The Wikipedia entry on white collar workers puts their percentage in the workforce at close to 60 percent based on 1990 U.S. Census figures: *http:// en.wikipedia.org/wiki/White-collar_worker.*

The study by the American Society of Interior Designers (ASID) was done in partnership with Steelcase, above.

You can read office etiquette commentary on Yelp.com at *http://www.yelp.com/ topic/san-jose-office-etiquette---speakerphones-and-nail-clipping.* It was posted by *Helen A.* I edited the commenter's remarks slightly to remove some repetitions. One of the responses to the commentator's complaint is quite a gem: "I used to sit between two people (all in cubes) and when they wanted to talk, instead of taking a twelve step stroll, one would call the other, who would then talk to the caller on speakerphone." It was posted by *elaine "slightly older" I.*

Peter Post's comment on the proper etiquette for speaker phone use is at *http:// www.boston.com/business/articles/2004/10/10/whats_the_proper_use_of_a_speaker_phone/.*

As a fun aside, it's worth noting that *Wired* magazine has listed speaker phones as one of five annoying gadgets that should be banned. As the editors say, "A speaker phone's advantages are far outweighed by the fact that it can be used to play music. Specifically (and you might detect the voice of experience here), really bad rap music on the train to the beach. Back in the eighties, there was a penalty involved in portable tunes, and it came in the form of a backbreaking boom box equipped with around fifty D-Cell batteries. Now there is no barrier, and anyone can pollute public spaces with what they obviously believe to be music loved by everyone there. Worse, the speakers are terrible. Bass becomes buzz, drums become tinny taps, and vocals distort. At least the old 1970s boom boxes packed a decent punch."

The other four gadgets that should be banned (and note that most involve noise) are Bluetooth headsets, custom ringtones, e-books, and GPS units. The list of gadgets generated more than 100 comments, most in agreeing that speaker phones belong at the top of the list. As one person says, "Don't get me started on speaker phones!" Those who disagreed that noisy gadgets like speaker phones should be in the list didn't disagree with their annoyance per se but in how we should respond to them. Rather than complain about them, we should either ask them not to share their noise with us or tune them out with a gadget of our own: "If you are not sophisticated enough to carry your own personal society-blocking devices such as headphones, earpieces, and hand-held distraction device, than you deserve to be emotionally upended by the chaos that is modern civilization," one person says. That's true enough, but who wants to live in a world in which people tune one another out? The whole point of rules of etiquette is that they enable people to live together in a positive, not a negative, manner. You can read the comments at *http://blog.wired.com/gadgets/2008/09/five-antisocial.html.*

Among the studies correlating a reduction in work performance with open-office environments and distracting noise are "Stress and open office noise," based on a 1997 experiment involving 40 women conducted by Cornell researchers. You can read an abstract of the findings at *http://www.ncbi.nlm.nih.gov/pubmed/11055149.* Another one was conducted in Denmark in 2004 and can be found at *http://www. ncbi.nlm.nih.gov/pubmed/15663458?ordinalpos=1&itool=EntrezSystem2.PEntrez.Pubmed. Pubmed_ResultsPanel.Pubmed_DiscoveryPanel.Pubmed_Discovery_RA&linkpos=1&log$=re latedarticles&logdbfrom=pubmed.*

Gary Evans interview on WebMD can be accessed at *http://www.webmd.com/ news/20020226/open-office-noise-increases-stress.*

Cortisol as the "stress hormone" is talked about in Wikipedia at *http:// en.wikipedia.org/wiki/Cortisol.*

There's another study that makes a slightly different case about office noise, and that's that it's a bigger problem for introverts than extraverts. Indeed, extraverts seek out noise at regular intervals, apparently because they prefer noise to extended periods of quiet concentration. Introverts, on the other hand, have trouble concentrating in noisy conditions:

"In numerous experiments introverts have showed higher sensitivity to noise during mental performance compared to extroverts, while extroverts often cope with a boring task even by requesting short periods of noise during performance. Correlation analyses have regularly revealed a highly significant negative relation between extroversion and noise annoyance during mental processing. Numerous studies have shown that people with high noise sensitivity may be prevented from achieving the same work results as other people in noisy environment, thus leading to psychosomatic, neurotic or other difficulties. Positive relation between noise annoyance and subjective noise sensitivity might be very strong.

Our results have shown, after matching with the results of other relevant studies, that more stable personality, with extroversive tendencies and with a relatively lower subjective noise sensitivity measured with standard questionnaires, may be expected to better adapt to noise during mental performance, compared to people with opposite personality traits."

There's a summary of this study at *http://www.ncbi.nlm.nih.gov/pubmed/14965455? ordinalpos=1&itool=EntrezSystem2.PEntrez.Pubmed.Pubmed_ResultsPanel.Pubmed_Discov-eryPanel.Pubmed_Discovery_RA&linkpos=4&log$=relatedreviews&logdbfrom=pubmed.*

Here are a few other studies looking at office noise and worker productivity:

"The cognitive psychology of auditory distraction: 1997 Broadbent Lecture," (1999), *British Journal of Psychology*, D. Jones.

"Disruption of office-related tasks by speech and office noise," (1998), *British Journal of Psychology*, S. Banbury and D. Berry

"Habituation and dishabituation to office noise," (1997), *Journal of Experimental Psychology: Applied*, S. Banbury and D. Berry

"A case study of office speech noise distraction and work productivity," (1997) Summary of a six-month longitudinal field study at a customer site, Armstrong, Inc.

The group of universities that established the videoconferencing guidelines is called the South West London Academic Network, and the rules can be ac-cessed at *http://74.125.95.104/search?q=cache:drwL_TabGS4J:www.swlacademicnetwork. ac.uk/documents/LiveClassroomforStaffMeetings14_02_08.doc+desktop+video+conferencing+ without+headphones&hl=en&ct=clnk&cd=1&gl=us.*

The *Wall Street Journal* piece on the rise of TV viewing online during office hours is at *http://blogs.wsj.com/biztech/2008/02/14/network-tv-the-new-workplace-distraction/.*

Cell Phones: Mine is Indispensable; Yours is Insufferable

Al Neuharth's essay on cell phone courtesy is at *http://www.usatoday.com/news/ opinion/2002/07/19/neuharth-cellphones.htm.*

The Joe Howry essay is at *http://www.venturacountystar.com/news/2007/sep/30/rude-cell-phone-manners/.*

Here's an excerpt from the summary of the U.K. cell phone study, which you can access at *http://www.informaworld.com/smpp/content-content=a713819773-db=all.*

> Sixty four members of the public were exposed to the same staged con-versation either while waiting in a bus station or travelling on a train. Half of the conversations were by mobile phone, so that only one end of the conversation was heard, and half were co present face-to-face conversa-tions. The volume of the conversations was controlled at one of two levels: the actors' usual speech level and exaggeratedly loud. Following exposure to the conversation participants were approached and asked to give ver-bal ratings on six scales. Analysis of variance showed that mobile phone conversations were significantly more noticeable and annoying than face-to-face conversations at the same volume when the content of the conver-sation is controlled. Indeed this effect of medium was as large as the effect

of loudness. Various explanations of this effect are explored, with their practical implications.

Chapter 7. Creating a New World of Stress

The National Academies Institute of Medicine's 2005 report, *Preventing Child-hood Obesity: Health in the Balance*, is at *http://findarticles.com/p/articles/mi_m0CYP/is_/ai_n15736927*.

You can read Jane Healy's commentary on TV and ADHD on the White Dot Web site at *http://www.whitedot.org/issue/iss_story.asp?slug=ADHD%20Toddlers*.

The *Pediatrics* article on TV light and sleep disorders is at *http://pediatrics.aap-publications.org/cgi/content/full/116/4/851*. The remarks in a summary of the study, called "The association between television viewing and irregular sleep sched-ules among children less than three years of age," are insightful and an excerpt is worth sharing:

> Children in the United States watch more than 19 hours of television per week. Notably, this viewing begins very early in life and may be in-creasing, given recent attempts to market television to younger viewers. Recent studies have shown that significant proportions of infants and toddlers exceed the American Academy of Pediatrics recommendations that children under two years of age should not watch any television and those over two years of age should be limited to under hours per day.
>
> Many adverse effects of television viewing on children and adolescents have been documented. These effects include obesity, aggressive behavior, decreased physical activity, attention problems, and sleep disorders. Con-siderably less research, however, has focused on the impact of television viewing on infants and toddlers, despite the fact that they spend large and potentially increasing proportions of time with media.
>
> Healthy sleep habits are an important part of ensuring high-quality sleep. Television viewing, among school-aged children and adolescents, has been shown to be associated with poor sleep habits and disordered sleep. Cross-sectional studies found that television/videotape viewing was associated with late bedtimes and sleep disturbances among school-aged children and adolescents. One longitudinal study demonstrated that high levels of television viewing during adolescence might lead to the development of sleep problems in early adulthood. Whether televi-sion viewing has an impact on the sleep patterns of infants and toddlers is unknown, although good sleep hygiene is no less important for this group of children.
>
> Several theories have been proposed as potential mechanisms to explain the association between television viewing and sleep disturbances. One theory is that television may have an actual physiologic impact on its viewers. It may be that the bright light of the television before sleep af-fects the sleep/wake cycle through suppression of the release of melatonin. A second theory is that television may have a psychologic impact on its

viewers. Children may watch programs that are developmentally inappropriate for their ages or have violent content. Violent programming has been shown to have a negative impact on children's behavior and may also inhibit the relaxation necessary for sleep induction, although this has not been demonstrated. A third potential mechanism explaining the relationship between television viewing and sleep disturbances is parental priorities. Parents of children who watch significant amounts of television may be poor limit-setters in general and not enforce rules with regard to both television viewing and regular sleep times.

Sleep problems are very common among children, ranging in prevalence from 25 percent to 69 percent. Because of this fact, as well as the lack of information on the impact of television viewing on the sleep of infants and toddlers, we conducted a retrospective cohort study to test the hypothesis that television viewing by infants and toddlers would be associated with irregular naptime and bedtime schedules."

Michael Breus talks about TV light and sleep in his blog, "The Insomnia Blog," at *http://www.theinsomniablog.com/the_insomnia_blog/2007/02/strategies_for_.html*. It's worth noting that some of the research Breus references doesn't find TV reducing viewers' sleep but rather the viewers' *perception* of how much sleep they get. As he says, "Internet and TV use prior to bed may have less to do with how long you sleep at night and more to do with how much sleep you really need and the quality of that sleep."

The research by L.K. Friedrich and A.H. Stein is summarized at *http://www.iptv. org/kids/grownups/resources/researchitem6.cfm*.

TV Doesn't Make You Not Dumb
The pro-TV study, "Does Television Rot Your Brain?" by Matthew Gentzkow and Jesse Shapiro can be read in its entirety at *http://www.dcmp.org/caai/nadh174.pdf*.

Mass Communication Theory can be accessed in part at *http://books.google.com/ books?id=W-R5bJCHer4C&pg=PA163&lpg=PA163&dq=Schramm,+Lyle+and+Parker&sour ce=web&ots=8V23MKGEIb&sig=xWNr6lhw61SVkJegqYAFF7YBhFc&hl=en&sa=X&oi=bo ok_result&resnum=2&ct=result#PPA162,M1*.
The White Dot *Action guide against TV in public places* is at *http://www.whitedot.org/ issue/iss_story.asp?slug=ruinedDinersActionGuide*.

The Wrong Way to Fight
The effusive TV-B-Gone testimonials are at *http://www.tvbgone.com/cfe_tvbg_re spons.php?PHPSESSID=87a65f3e2d802c5c79ba6ee96566f895*.

The comment from the critic of TV-B-Gone, who says it's wrong to turn off someone's TV without their permission, is on the Web site Habeas Corruptus at *http://www.christopherketcham.com/index.php?paged=2.* Notwithstanding the writer's edgy language, the argument is right on target, in my view, because it understands turning off someone's TV stealthily, without their consent, as a form of vandalism, although he doesn't use that word.

The *Wall Street Journal* article on "annoyancetech" applications is at *http://64.233.169.104/search?q=cache:S9_svl3h1RUJ:www.paulos.net/press/Revenge%2520by%2520Gadget%2520-%2520WSJ.com.pdf+lawmakers+respond+to+loud+TVs&hl=en&ct=clnk&cd=4&gl=us.*

Chapter 8. What It All Boils Down to: Users v. Stewards

The Louv interview can be read online at *http://www.grist.org/news/maindish/2006/03/30/louv/.*

The *Washington Post* piece on conflict over national parkland use is at *http://www.washingtonpost.com/wp-dyn/content/article/2008/08/11/AR2008081102040.html.*

An example of a government report on conflicting uses of public parkland can be seen on the U.S. Forest Service Web site at *http://www.fs.fed.us/recreation/programs/ohv/.*

The quote by William Jeakle is at *http://www.pbs.org/mediashift/2006/03/insiders_takewhy_public_tvs_wo.html.*

The Usurpation of Autonomy

You can look at excerpts of "The Murderer," in *The Golden Apples of the Sun* (Bantam: 1964) on Amazon. After you bring up the book, search inside the book using the term "Brock."

Signing the Ultimate Pact

Jeffrey Stein's quote, from an article called "How dumping TV allowed me to quit my job, create an online business, and fund my retirement account," is at *http://www.savingadvice.com/blog/2007/07/17/101625_how-dumping-tv-allowed-me-to-quit-my-job-create-an-online-business-and-fund-my-retirement-account.html.*

Piccione hosts his own blog, where he talked about going TV-free, at *http://davidpiccione.com/blog/i-stopped-watching-tv-and-here-is-what-i-think/.*

Mark French's quote about his company's intention to make people watch the screen is at *http://www.reuters.com/article/PBLSHG/idUSN1665277220080116.*

Schweitzer's quote is from a *Broadcasting and Cable* piece that Commercial Alert makes available on its Web site at *http://www.commercialalert.org/issues/culture/ television/television-everywhere.*

The quote by Stephen Freitas is at *http://www.sideroad.com/consultants/Marketing-Consultant-Stephen-Freitas.html.*

Lyle Bunn says you "cannot not look" at digital content in *Digital Signage Today* at *http://digitalsignagetoday.com/article_printable.php?id=20904&page=166.*

The quote by Fred Margolin was made specifically in reference to eating establishments with place-based TV, but his point is applicable to all types of commercial environments. It can be found at *http://www.tvweek.com/news/2008/05/ tuning_in_to_promo_entertainme.php.*

The quote by William Jeakle is at *http://www.pbs.org/mediashift/2006/03/ insiders_takewhy_public_tvs_wo.html.*

The online-forum quote by the *Wired* reader is in response to the magazine's column on five anti-social gadgets. You can access it at *http://blog.wired.com/gad-gets/2008/09/five-antisocial.html.*

Commercial Alert gives kudos to George W. Bush for encouraging families to turn off their TV at *http://www.commercialalert.org/issues/culture/television/groups-praise-bushs-statement-about-tv-the-best-weapon-is-the-off-on-button.* And, of course, Barack Obama, when he was running for president in 2008, always made news when he admonished families to turn off the TV so the kids can do their homework without distraction. As he put it, "The truth is, government can't do it all. As parents we need to turn off the TV, read to our kids, give them that thirst to learn." That quote is at *http://www.nationaljournal.com/njonline/as_20080424_9901.php.*

Chapter 9. What does a responsible-media environment look like?

The New World of Consensual Captivity
The Central Wisconsin Airport case study of the use of directional audio is at *http://www.panphonics.com/downloads.html*

Privacy Filters
3M's description of its privacy filters is at *http://solutions.3m.com/wps/portal/3M/ en_US/ComputerFilter/Home/*
The Tony Smith quote is at *http://www.reghardware.co.uk/2006/05/26/review_3m_ laptop_privacy_filter/page2.html*

The use of the "microlouver" technology to different types of screens is at the 3M site at *http://solutions.3m.com/wps/portal/3M/en_US/ComputerFilter/Home/*

Dual-View Screens

The Tech Japan piece on Sharp's dual-view screen is at *http://solutions.3m.com/wps/portal/3M/en_US/ComputerFilter/Home/*

Directional audio

A good introduction to directional audio is in a publication of the University of Southern California called Illumin. You can read the piece by Philip Hirz at *http://illumin.usc.edu/article.php?articleID=80*

Active Sound Cancellation

Panphonics describes its active noise cancellation process in a white paper at *http://www.panphonics.com/anc.html*

On the history of anti-noise to fight noise, see for instance an article in Time magazine at *http://www.time.com/time/magazine/article/0,9171,959165,00.html*

Applying Rules to Seed Solutions

Arbitron Out-of-Home is t *http://www.arbitron.com/outdoor_companies/home.htm*
Information on Nielsen Out-of-Home is at, for example, *http://www.mediapost.com/publications/?fa=Articles.showArticle&art_aid=103825*
Both the commuter train and the sound truck cases decided by the Supreme Court are in the appendices.
I didn't know about the movements to regulate the wearing of perfume and the bottling of drinking water until I caught references to them in an Economist article, which you can access at *http://www.economist.com/books/displaystory.cfm?story_id=13813444*
A good starting point for state secondhand smoke laws is from the American Lung Association at *http://slati.lungusa.org/reports/SecondhandSmokeLawsFactSheet6-09.pdf*
The Web site for Christopher Snowdon's book on the anti-smoking movement, *Velvet Hand, Iron Fist*, is at *http://velvetgloveironfist.com/*

Public Space: Where My Tax Dollars Are at Work

A typical example of a "lack of empathy" article is this ChicagonTribune article at *http://blogs.chicagotribune.com/news_columnists_ezorn/2007/04/remembering_tha.html*
The statement by the Mobile Enhancement Retailers Association on the need to tone down inflammatory audio ads is at *http://www.merausa.org/Resources/Industry_Best_Practices/promotions.asp*

There are so many articles on how operators of restaurants and other gathering places are trying to curb rude cell phone conversations that one wouldn't even know where to begin to list them. I like this one in the Los Angeles Times, at *http://articles.latimes.com/1999/jul/15/news/mn-56218*, because it's an early one. It shows that rudeness became a problem early on.

People are already starting to complain about outdoor rooms, but unlike with other annoying conditions, like rude cell phone use, the trend is too new for people to be talking to one another about it. Thus, the effect is as if there's no opposition to it. That's why I say this will change over time; once people start talking to one another about it, some type of organized opposition will appear.

Afterword

You can view *The Black Swan* on Amazon at *http://www.amazon.com/gp/reader/1400063515/ref=sib_dp_pt#reader-link*.

Acknowledgements

My appreciation to Ted Rueter, founder of Noise Free America, Jean Lotus, co-founder of White Dot, Ron Kaufman, founder of Turn off Your TV (www. turnoffyourtv.com), and Carla Moore, who's battled the boom car subculture. Appreciation also to Gary Ruskin, former director of Commercial Alert, for our e-mail exchanges on the Washington Metro and Bus Radio issues. Any mistakes, mischaracterizations, or inaccuracies in the text are my own.